GHOST TOWNS
OF **MUSKOKA**

GHOST TOWNS
OF MUSKOKA

Andrew Hind & Maria Da Silva

NATURAL HERITAGE BOOKS
A MEMBER OF THE DUNDURN GROUP
TORONTO

Published by Natural Heritage Books
A Member of The Dundurn Group
3 Church Street, Suite 500
Toronto, Ontario, M5E 1M2, Canada
www.dundurn.com

Library and Archives Canada Cataloguing in Publication
Hind, Andrew
      Ghost towns of Muskoka / Andrew Hind & Maria Da Silva.

ISBN 978-1-55002-796-9

      1. Muskoka (Ont.)--History. I. Da Silva, Maria II. Title.

FC3095.M88Z58 2008   971.3'16   C2008-900233-4

1   2   3   4   5   12   11   10   09   08

Cover and text design by Erin Mallory
Copy-edited by Jennifer Gallant and proofread by Ellen Ewart
Printed and bound in Canada by Transcontinental

Cover photos: Top left: Workers at the Falkenburg sawmill (also on p. 51), courtesy of Muskoka Heritage Place Collection, Huntsville, Ont.; Top right: The former Swords general store (also on p. 21), courtesy of Andrew Hind and Maria Da Silva; Bottom: Unidentified building, possibly the train station in Falkenburg Station, courtesy of Patricia Evans.

Except where otherwise noted, present-day photos are provided by Andrew Hind and Maria Da Silva.

Care has been taken to trace the ownership of copyright material used in this book. The author and the publisher welcome any information enabling them to rectify any references or credits in subsequent editions.

                                                            J. Kirk Howard, President

      Conseil des Arts   Canada Council   Canada      ONTARIO ARTS COUNCIL
                         du Canada   for the Arts   CONSEIL DES ARTS DE L'ONTARIO

We acknowledge the support of the **Canada Council for the Arts** and the **Ontario Arts Council** for our publishing program. We also acknowledge the financial support of the **Government of Canada** through the **Book Publishing Industry Development Program** and **The Association for the Export of Canadian Books** and the **Government of Ontario** through the **Ontario Book Publishers Tax Credit Program** and the **Ontario Media Development Corporation.**

This book is intended as a tribute to the early settlers of Muskoka, who endured unimaginable hardships in order to lay the foundations for the land we know and love today.

CONTENTS

8   *Acknowledgements*

10   *Introduction*

16   Chapter 1: Swords

33   Chapter 2: Rosseau Falls

49   Chapter 3: Falkenburg Junction

72   Chapter 4: Dee Bank

87   Chapter 5: Germania

111 Chapter 6: Ashdown Corners

134 Chapter 7: Millar Hill

151 Chapter 8: Cooper's Falls

175 Chapter 9: Lewisham

189 Chapter 10: Monsell

204 Chapter 11: Uffington

229 Chapter 12: Seldom Seen and Other Ghost Towns

241 *Notes*

265 *Bibliography*

267 *Index*

272 *About the Authors*

ACKNOWLEDGEMENTS

We would like to express our thanks and appreciation to the following individuals, groups, and organizations for the assistance provided us in writing this book: Roberta Green of the Huntsville Public Library, Ruth Holtz and the staff at the Bracebridge Public Library, Jack Sword, Diane Rotz, Barbara Paterson, Shirley Jordan of the Christie Historical Committee, Patricia Evans, Aubrey Bogart, Carol Fraser, Jim Taverner, William Allen, Robert Constable, Ben Boivin, Larry Matthews, William Cooper, Frank Cooper, Paul Simek, Kelly Collard and the Rosseau Historical Society, Mary Beley, Velda Gilbert, Doreen Nowak, the staff at the Rosseau Public Library, Lyle Crawford, Mary Fitzmaurice, Evelyn Weis Lawrie, and Krista Havenaar at Inn at the Falls for her hospitality.

Andrew's Personal Acknowledgements

Writing this book would not have been possible without the patience and sacrifice of our families, who accepted our preoccupation with Muskoka's history for more than two years. Likewise, it would not have been possible if not for the descendants of pioneer families who warmly embraced our project and shared their memories with us.

While researching the various ghost towns, we trekked through woods and drove down rutted roads that were often little more than trails, always eagerly anticipating what we would find. In the end, what I found surprised me more than any derelict building or haunting ruin. What I found was a new respect for my co-writer and friend, who endured countless hours in libraries and many more in the forests of Muskoka with never-failing enthusiasm. Thank you, Maria, for writing this book with me and making a long-held dream become reality.

Maria's Personal Acknowledgements

I would like to thank my family for their understanding and patience while Andrew and I researched this book. I would also like to thank Andrew for sharing history with me in a way that allowed me to truly connect with the past. I never got tired of looking for remnants of ghost towns or meeting descendants of the early settlers who were brave enough to conquer the wilds of Muskoka.

In writing this book, we hope to encourage future generations to embrace history and treasure any relic they might find. And to all the wonderful people we met in our journeys, thank you for your memories.

INTRODUCTION

As late as the middle of the nineteenth century, Muskoka remained a remote wilderness, unsettled, barely explored, and foreboding in its darkness and silence. The Ojibway migrated seasonally through the region, and the occasional trapper endured months of solitude to earn a meagre living, but there was little incentive for homesteaders to press into the region. To Europeans, Muskoka's impenetrable forests, ever-present rock, and countless swamps would have seemed imposing and intimidating.

But while Muskoka would have been unappealing to homesteaders, it held vast appeal to industrialists.

The richness of its pine stands was a temptation that was becoming increasingly difficult to ignore. Spurred on by a building boom on the American east coast and the needs of Britain's shipbuilding industry, lumber companies became increasingly anxious to harvest the valuable timber.

There was an impediment to their plans, however. The lack of permanent inhabitants and infrastructure meant it was impossible to exploit the region's resources. Settlers meant roads, a ready pool of labour to draw upon, horses to haul logs through the woods, and provisions for the camps that only nearby farms could provide. Without these necessities, it would be impossible for lumber companies to cull the trees economically, and the resources of Muskoka would forever remain untapped.

Consequently, starting in the 1850s, the lumber interests began to pressure the provincial government to open up the area for settlement. The result was the "Colonization Road Scheme," whereby the government surveyed and built various roads leading into the wilderness from the settled south, opening up these hinterlands to settlement. The Free Grants and Homestead Act provided up to two hundred acres of land free to anyone eighteen years or older, subject to certain conditions being met: the settler had to clear and cultivate fifteen acres and build a dwelling for habitation, reside on the lot six months a year, and clear at least two acres per annum over a period of five years to obtain a deed for the land.

Essentially, for those willing to take the giant leap of faith needed to invest their futures in the bounty of an untamed terrain, land along these colonization roads was free for the taking.

Among the first of these colonization roads was the Muskoka Road. Beginning at Washago, at the northern end of Lake Couchiching, the crude trail twisted northward into the heart of the wilderness. From it, three branch roads led deeper into the dark forest: the Parry Sound Road, which led westerly from Bracebridge to Georgian Bay; the Peterson Road, which led east from Bracebridge; and the Nipissing Road, which led north from the Parry Sound Road near Rosseau to Lake Nipissing. From these main arteries, other roads would eventually branch off to serve the anticipated influx of settlers.

It so happened that the interests of the lumber companies coincided with the needs of land-starved immigrants, because by the middle of the nineteenth century Ontario had exhausted its supply of available land in the south and settlers were looking northward for land to call their own.

Lured by the offer of free land, their courage fortified by dreams of new opportunities and new lives, thousands of settlers packed up their worldly goods and trudged along these primitive roads to take up bush farms. As the colonization roads crept northward, settlement followed apace. Inevitably, hamlets and villages appeared at convenient crossroads locations, around the inns that dotted these colonization roads, or along rivers that presented sufficient power to operate vital mills.

There were far more recognizable villages in Muskoka a century ago than there are today. Before the era of the automobile, back when roads were often impassable and the distance a wagon could travel in one day was roughly nineteen kilometres, settlers had to have everything close at hand. Stores, mills, craftsmen, taverns, post offices, schools, and churches — all could be found in the countless small hamlets that dotted the rugged landscape. Most had a population of less than one hundred, but all had a tangible sense of community and all residents looked upon their hometowns, small and obscure though they may be, with real pride. And rightfully so. After all, they had a hand in building and shaping them.

Some of these communities are still with us today and, thanks to modern tourism and the appeal of cottage living, are as vibrant as ever. Others, sadly, eventually fell by the wayside and became ghost towns, victimized by the ebbs and flows of history. More than a few communities died after the forests had been depleted of harvestable lumber, depriving the villages of their reason for being and their inhabitants of their livelihood. Others failed when farmers were defeated by the shallow and rocky soil typical of the region, a soil that is almost utterly useless for farming. Most, however, died slow deaths that were brought about by a culmination of mortal ailments.

This book tells the stories of eleven of Muskoka's numerous ghost towns. But *Ghost Towns of Muskoka* isn't intended as a eulogy for these dead villages. Rather, it's a celebration of their life. Instead of looking upon ghost towns as communities that have died, we prefer to look at them as villages that *lived*, if only for a short time.

What This Book Does

Many historians have noted that all history is local history. That state-ment is particularly true in this case, as this book focuses its attention on a handful of small, obscure, and largely forgotten Muskoka com-munities. At their respective peaks, even the largest of these settlements was home to no more than one hundred people, so the stories related within these pages are by definition personal and intimate. They are the life experiences — tragedy and triumph, loss and levity — of a small group of people, a narrow cross-section of Muskoka's vast and varied tapestry of humanity.

But at the same time, their stories are universally Muskokan in nature. The hardships these people endured, the rhythm of their lives, and their day-to-day experiences were mirrored by those of countless people in villages across the breadth and width of Muskoka. To read this book is to understand the development of Muskoka through the years and to gain insight into its unique character. In that light, *Ghost Towns of Muskoka* isn't local history at all, but rather regional history.

In any event, and semantics aside, this book is intended as resource for preserving the legacy of eleven once vibrant communities.

We believe that the best way to foster a genuine respect and passion for history is to encourage people to experience it up close. Therein lies the second stated goal of this book: to serve as inspiration and guide for people wishing to explore Muskoka's ghost town heritage. The mission statement played a defining role in how the book was designed. We wanted the information to be easily accessible, quick to locate, and rapidly digestible so as to be of immediate use while visiting a site. At the same time, we aimed to include information unsurpassed in both depth and accuracy by any other available printed source.

To achieve that aim, we divided the book into eleven chapters, each one devoted to a specific ghost town. Within each chapter, you'll find a general overview of the community and its history, including the remains that can be seen today, as well as entries on prominent people and landmarks. Scattered throughout the text are dozens of photos and maps, both modern and contemporary, intended to bring the villages alive in the mind's eye and to serve as points of reference for those wishing to explore them in person. We've also included a chapter detailing, in capsule form, the story of a half-dozen more ghost towns that will appear in the intended sequel to this volume.

Finally, it should be acknowledged that two of the communities — Swords and Ashdown Corners — technically do not exist in Muskoka, lying on the wrong side of a boundary line drawn by surveyors. They are very much a part of the Muskoka story, however, being bound to the region by proximity, transportation links, interpersonal relationships, economics, and a host of other socio-political factors. This is our justification for including them in the book; we trust readers will accept the explanation and the reasoning behind it.

Visiting Ghost Towns

There's no doubt that visiting a ghost town can be a fun and rewarding experience. However, there are some hints, garnered in many cases from our own travels and travails, that we'd like to pass along to ensure things go smoothly for you.

In general the most ideal times to visit a ghost town are early spring and late fall, when there is no foliage to obscure hidden remains. Trust us when we assure you how difficult it can be to explore ghost towns in the height of summer. When visiting Swords, we nearly walked past a two-storey home, located not more than one hundred feet off the road, because of the dense brush of the regrown forest. And that's forgetting for a moment the clouds of mosquitoes that you often have to endure.

In early spring or late autumn, the paths of old roads can be clearly seen, foundations located, old buildings enjoyed and photographed. They are also much more atmospheric times; the leafless, colourless landscape adds a touch of the macabre that seems to enhance the ghost-town-hunting experience.

There is often much to see. Frame buildings are the rarest find. Many were victimized by wood salvagers, and they tend not to stand up well to the elements at any rate. Oftentimes, such buildings will have been reduced to rotting and sagging shells, their original purposes ill-defined. In all cases, proceed with care around these ancient structures. All uninhabited buildings should be considered unsound.

Much more common than finding entire buildings is locating relics of former habitation. Foundation holes will provide telltale evidence of buildings long past, fence posts will often denote farmers' fields, and vague trails leading off into regenerated forests will speak of abandoned roadways and railway lines. Watch for lilac bushes; these hardy shrubs are not native to Canada and were brought over by settlers to beautify their properties. The presence of a lilac shrub will almost always betray former human presence.

Some relics may be located on private property. While we've found most land owners to be hospitable and willing to grant permission to explore, it's important always to respect private property. Do not trespass.

It reflects badly on all of us who enjoy the experience of exploring Ontario's past through her ghost towns.

Remember that most ghost towns are located in the wilds. Dress accordingly. Wear sturdy hiking books, as well as both pants and a long-sleeved shirt to protect against mosquitoes and poison ivy.

1
SWORDS

As you take a drive on Swords Road you might come across a little bit of history. Look closely to find a century-old church and, not too far away, a pioneer-era general store. This, you might think, is all there is to see, but hidden behind the overgrown brush and tall trees lie forgotten relics for curious eyes to find.

Buildings from long ago stand where they can't be disrupted by constant passersby. And when you walk the area, you become amazed at how well the buildings have held up to the passage of time. There are even flowers thriving in former gardens with very little sunlight to sustain their growth, and for a moment you might begin to think someone — a shade from the past, perhaps — is tending these grounds.

The former hamlet of Swords is indeed draped in a ghostly shroud. But for those who are willing to peer beneath it, a fascinating story emerges.

Swords can trace its origins back to the mid-1870s, when several settlers staked claim to land alongside the Nipissing Colonization Road. Amongst them were members of the Sword clan: David, John, and Thomas. But to say there was anything resembling a community here at the time would be misleading. Instead, all that existed was a collection of crude log homesteads spread out over kilometres of dense woods.

Things likely would have remained that way if not for the vision and stubborn determination of one man: John Rudolphus Booth. Booth was a lumber and railway magnate whose holdings included the Canada Atlantic Railway, which stretched from Ottawa to the Maritimes. In the 1880s he added extensive timber rights in Algonquin Park to his empire.[1]

At this point, Booth's thoughts turned to a railway line that would stretch across the central Ontario highlands to serve his vast new timber limits. At the same time, by finishing the railway at the shores of Georgian

Bay he hoped to share in the lucrative grain traffic by offering a shortcut to the ports in the west.

In July 1891, the Ottawa, Arnprior and Parry Sound Railway (OA&PSR) was formed. Four years later, the line was complete, running from Ottawa in the east to Parry Sound in the west, and just happening to pass through Swords. That twist of fate, a surveyor's whim, assured Swords of a bright — if brief — future.

Except, of course, the hamlet wasn't called Swords then. When the OA&PSR built a shack-sized flag stop and a siding there, they named it Maple Lake Station after the nearby body of water. The community took the name as its own, and it would remain Maple Lake Station for more than a generation.

Booth's railway transformed the lives of the area's settlers seemingly overnight, providing prosperity heretofore unimagined.

The railway allowed the Maple Lake area to be opened to lumber interests, and in 1894 the Ludgate Lumber Company (in which the Sword family owned interests) bought significant tracts of land and began felling trees. To facilitate their efforts, the company built a general store and three homes for workers just south of the tracks at Maple Lake Station.

Within a few years, a real village had emerged. There were a dozen or so homes, a church, a schoolhouse, and a blacksmith. John and Annie Sword opened the Maple Lake Hotel, a rambling two-storey structure that, though it shrank in comparison to Muskoka's luxury resorts, was easily the grandest building for many miles. Initially the hotel was frequented almost solely by loggers intent on drinking away their paycheques. Later, the Maple Lake Hotel became popular among American tourists who wanted to experience adventure in the "Canadian wilderness."

In 1900, the Ludgate Lumber Company sold its buildings in the village, though it continued to log in the area for several more years. The three workers' homes became private residences, while the general store was purchased by Thomas Sword, who later received the lucrative post office contract and ran it out of his mercantile.

The 1910s to the early 1920s was sort of a gilded era in the brief history of Maple Lake Station, and everyone seemed to recognize that much of this success was owed to the Sword family and their diverse holdings. As a result, when it came to light in 1925 that the community would have to change its name because of confusion with another Maple Lake Station, the residents unanimously voted to adopt the name Swords.

Ironically, by the time the village's name was officially changed, a slow decline in its fortunes had already begun. Timber in the highlands of central Ontario was largely played out by 1930, and so train traffic began to slow appreciably. Shortly beforehand, the Maple Lake Hotel had closed due to lack of business.

With the hamlet deprived of its two main sources of income, the community stagnated and people began to move away. The railway station was abandoned in 1946, and trains stopped running along the line entirely a decade later. As for the general store, it lasted longer than the rest, continuing to serve the small local populace until it too closed in 1967.

As the decades pass, the former village merges further into the mists of time. Thankfully, some relics of the past yet remain.

The general store, for example, remains in surprisingly good shape and still displays old signage in its windows. To the south of the store, obscured by the dense foliage that laps up against the side of the road, are the two former lumber company homes and several more dilapidated outbuildings. About a kilometre to the south is an attractive schoolhouse dating back to 1904 that remains in use as a community centre. On the grounds you'll note a hand-powered pump from which schoolchildren would have drawn their drinking water.

For its part, the old OA&PSR remains very much in evidence. Though the track has long since been lifted, the roadbed — bisecting Swords Road and disappearing into the bush on either side — remains in excellent shape and is used frequently by hikers and snowmobilers.

Though the remnants of Swords are becoming harder to find as the forest encroaches upon it, when you emerge into the sunlight and leave the weathered buildings behind, you realize it's all for the best. It's the forest's canopy, after all, that hides the buildings from vandals and protects them from the elements, either of which might destroy this wonderful piece of the past.

Swords Schoolhouse

Though it's not hidden by the overgrown forest — in fact its grounds are well tended — the best preserved of Swords's surviving buildings is the century-old schoolhouse. It's amazing how well this little building has withstood Mother Nature all these years.

In the early years of the twentieth century, Maple Lake Station had grown large enough that a clear need for a schoolhouse to educate local children had emerged. To address this concern, James Smith donated a parcel of land on the east side of Swords Road about a kilometre south of the village proper.[2] Money for the school's construction was loaned by Mrs. Margaret (Sword) Waugh. The first teacher was Mrs. William Stoneman.

The one-room school (SS #1) was built in 1904 by Mr. Holton and his sons from the neighbouring hamlet of Edgington. One notable

Courtesy Christie Historical Committee.

Class photo from SS #1 Swords taken in October 1913 when the community was at its peak. Back row (l-r): Vera Clifford, Gordon Helmkay, Alec Lawson, and Fred Mullen; middle row: Maggie Bathen, another Clifford child, Marion Morrison, Blanche Morrison, Bertha Smith, and Madeline McCauley; front row: Archie Mullen, Margaret Morrison, Ruth Lawson, Edna McCauley, Eva Bathen, and Angus Mullen.

feature that sets it apart from other schoolhouses of its era is the single front entrance. Most of its contemporaries had two entrances: one for boys, and the other for girls. Inside, one would have found a wood stove located in the centre of the room in a vain attempt to adequately warm the entire building. Shelves containing library books covered the lower half of the south wall, above which hung maps and charts. The school proudly boasted a piano, which would have been a real luxury for this period. Behind the school stand the original outhouses, requisite porcupine damage and all.[3]

As the school was also intended to serve as a community centre for Swords and the surrounding farms, and nearly everyone who attended would be arriving by wagon or sleigh, a driving shed was erected at the time of construction. This building, which was large enough to easily accommodate more than half a dozen horses, stood in the southeast corner of the lot. The driving shed has long since been demolished.

Because there was no dedicated church in Swords, from the very beginning the schoolhouse found itself playing host to religious services. A Methodist minister from Orrville would tend to the spiritual needs of the community every weekend during the summer months, a practice that was only discontinued in 1967, when Swords was no longer considered a separate parish from Orrville. For a number of years after 1914, the Methodists were joined by Pentecostal services and Sunday school classes, though both ceased by the 1940s.

In December 1936, the school was closed due to low attendance and pupils were transported by wagon or sleigh to SS #2 in Edgington. By 1941, however, attendance had risen sufficiently for the Swords school to be reopened. The little building was challenged for space when the Turtle Lake schoolhouse (SS #5) was closed in 1948 and its students transferred to Swords.

The Swords schoolhouse remained in use until 1958, when students began busing to the new Christie Central School. After it closed, the township agreed to sell the building to the Maple Lake Club for one dollar. Thereafter, it has seen continuous use as a community centre.

As a tangible link to Swords's past, the old schoolhouse remains central to the community's identity. As such, it is lovingly tended and remains in good repair. Money for its upkeep is raised through fund-raisers, such as an annual bake sale held at the schoolhouse in July.

Swords General Store

Another building that has withstood the ravages of time is the weathered old general store. Though it's silent now, just imagine all the stories it could tell.

The general store was the social centre for the community, where people gathered to share news, tell tall tales, and create the tight bonds for which small towns are known. Saturday night was the traditional time to "go to the store." In the winter, people would huddle around the big pot-bellied stove, while in the summer they lounged in the shade of the long verandah. Regardless of the season, this was a place to take a welcome reprieve from a physically demanding life to relax with good neighbours, and for children it was often the only opportunity to play

The general store was the heart of the community for more than half a century. Though derelict it still stands today, a haunting reminder of the ghost town of Swords.

with others beyond their own family.

Swords owed the existence of its store to the Ludgate Lumber Company. When it began lumbering operations around Maple Lake in 1894, the lumber company built a store on the southwest corner of the railway crossing to cater to the needs of their workers. The men's wages were paid partly in tokens that could be redeemed for goods at the mercantile. On June 1, 1897, a post office opened in the store, as was common in those days. Both the mercantile and the post office were operated by managers employed by the Ludgate Lumber Company.[4]

In 1900, the store was sold to Thomas Sword, who operated it successfully for more than twenty years and oversaw its period of greatest prosperity. The store sold everything from groceries to clothing, farm implements to candy, and everything in between. It was equivalent to a Wal-Mart of the era, stocking everything a villager could reasonably desire.

After Thomas died in 1921, the business was assumed by his widow, Lyde. She was assisted by her brother, Walter Cornish, but Lyde Sword proved to be a capable businesswoman in her own right, managing both the store and the post office.

Lyde Sword was a woman of principle, and decided she would no longer sell tobacco in her store. The village men, predictably, were quite upset at the inconvenience. No one wanted to ride to Orrville, some three miles distant, just to purchase tobacco. Soon enough, a local gentleman by the name of Jim McRoberts filled the void by selling this commodity, as well as canned goods, out of his home. While she may have had strong morals, Lyde Sword was a businesswoman first and foremost. It wasn't long before she bought out her competition and, realizing the error of her ways, began stocking tobacco once more.[5]

In 1928 she petitioned the town council to allow her to erect a gas pump at the front of her store, a request that was granted assuming she accepted all responsibility for it. That same year the lonely widow married George Walton.

Together they ran the business for a few years, but in 1930 they sold the store and transferred the postal contract to John Lawson and his son Wilson. It was the younger Lawson and his wife, Harriet, who served as proprietors. They would be the last owners, running the store despite an increasingly reduced clientele as the village withered away.

The end came on January 31, 1967, when the post office was closed upon the introduction of rural mail delivery in the area. This loss dealt the Swords general store a fatal blow, and within the year it was closed. However, the Lawsons' three daughters continued to use it as a seasonal home for many years thereafter.

Almost forty years on the store remains in remarkable condition. Old signs can still be seen in the windows and on the exterior walls, and if you pause on the verandah, you can almost hear the gossip and friendly conversation of the villagers who gathered here all those years ago to enjoy one another's company.

Swords Rail Station

The Ottawa, Arnprior and Parry Sound Railway was the longest railway ever built and owned by one man anywhere in the world. Running more than four hundred kilometres over the rugged hills and dense forests of central Ontario, simply building it was an epic undertaking. Everything about the railway — its size and scope, the gruelling toil required to build it, the stature and ambition of owner J.R. Booth, and the wealth it generated — was big and impressive. And then there was the station at Swords.

Constructed in 1896 and originally known as Maple Lake Station, it was only ever a flag station, meaning trains stopped only when it was signalled that passengers or cargo awaited pickup. The wood-frame building was modest in size and appearance, measuring about 12 feet by 24 feet with little in the way of adornments. Inside, there was a stove to provide warmth, benches along the ways for awaiting passengers, and little else.

Small though it might have been, the prospects of the community it served passed through its doors. The lumber it shipped out and the tourists it brought in provided the reason for Swords's founding and created the wealth that allowed the village to prosper for several decades. Simply put, without the railway and its station, there would have been no Swords.

The station was located directly opposite the general store and beside the hotel, on the southeast side of the railway crossing. A siding was built to facilitate the transfer of lumber cut at the nearby mill onto awaiting flatbeds. There was also a small freight shed, where train crews would leave any parcels or mail destined for the village and the surrounding area. The postmaster at Maple Lake Station had access to the building and was responsible for distributing the mail.

The OA&PSR was an extremely busy line. Loaded with wheat from the Prairies and lumber or logs from the forests of Ontario's north, more than twenty-five trains rattled through Swords on a daily basis. With this amount of traffic, accidents were bound to occur. Derailments, in particular, were a hazard that train crews were all too familiar with. One such accident occurred in Swords during the early 1920s, when an east-bound train burdened with grain jumped the tracks just past the station. The locomotive and several cars came to rest in a tangled mass of steel in a field alongside the tracks. Luck smiled down on Swords that day.

Courtesy Jack Sword.

A train derailed near Swords Bridge on October 4, 1902. There were no casualties in the accident. Note the spilled grain; much of the goods transported by the Ottawa, Arnprior and Parry Sound Railway was wheat from the Prairies.

There were no fatalities, either among the train crew or the villagers. A mechanical malfunction was apparently at fault.[6]

In 1925, the Canadian National Railway (which had bought out Booth's railway) decided to rename the station to avoid confusion with another Maple Lake Station along its lines. Thereafter, both the railway facility and the village itself were known as Swords. By this time, train traffic along the line was slowing appreciably. From a peak of more than twenty per day a decade before, the number was by then reduced to perhaps ten trains. And it only continued to plummet. In 1946, citing a lack of use, CN made the decision to close the Swords station. The entire line was closed a decade later.

The villagers never had an opportunity to preserve the station for posterity, even if they had wanted to. Shortly after it was closed, a railway employee purchased the little building, dismantled it in a hurry, and hauled it away. No one knows to where, or its ultimate fate. Residents of Swords were extremely upset; no one had even known the station had been for sale, and the secretive manner in which the whole affair took place seemed to be a slap in their collective faces.[7]

Until recently, a tree along the tracks had borne the old station sign announcing Swords, but it too was stolen. All that remains is the former rail line, now a well-groomed recreational pathway known as the Seguin Trail. Just a mile or so along the trail to the east are the impressive concrete remains of a railway bridge spanning a marshy creek; these are the best reminders of Swords's bygone rail days.

The tiny station at Swords stood apart from the general grandeur of the OA&PSR. But modest though it may have been, the station dictated the fate of an entire community, and its closing marked the symbolic death of Swords.

Maple Lake Hotel

Prior to 1894, John Sword and his wife were homesteaders struggling to make a modest living on their farm south of what would be the village of Swords.[8] A few short years later, they were prospering and considered the most genteel people in town. This stunning reversal of fortune was owed to the success of the Maple Lake Hotel, the inn they built and operated.

When officials of the OA&PSR announced the approximate route of their tracks, John Sword recognized that it would have to pass south of Maple Lake on its way from Orrville to Parry Sound. He also recognized that the railway would bring economic opportunities. Eager to take advantage of his foresight, he purchased a piece of land that he was sure would lie astride the tracks where it crossed Swords Road.[9]

John Sword guessed right. After the OA&PSR laid its tracks, trains passed within a stone's throw of his property. He then made the most of his good fortune by building a two-storey frame hotel catering to railway passengers, which he named the Maple Lake Hotel. It had a wide, shaded verandah, half a dozen modestly furnished guest rooms, and a large bar. Maple Lake Hotel was hardly luxuriant, especially in comparison to the grand resorts lining the larger Muskoka Lakes, but it was the height of hospitality in Christie Township.[10]

At first, however, its main business came from serving up drinks to the men working the logging camps in the area. As a popular watering hole, the bar could become boisterous at times, but the strong-willed Annie Sword kept the booze-soaked men in line. Anyone who didn't meet her standards of behaviour was promptly ushered to the door.

One story, related in *Meanderings and Memories*, a publication of the Christie Historical Committee, serves to highlight Annie's forceful character. It seems she used to sit on the verandah and, ever obsessed with protecting her hardwood floors, inspect the boots of the patrons to ensure they didn't have caulks on their soles. If someone did have caulked boots and refused to remove them, she would provide a shingle for him to stomp on. The shingle would stick to the caulks and then the gentleman would be free to go on in for a drink. Those who still refused were kindly, but firmly, asked to leave the premises. With no other option for drink and companionship in the area, there were very few individuals who tested Annie.[11]

By the late 1890s, Maple Lake Hotel had become known as a favourite Canadian wilderness destination, especially among a group of colourful and wealthy Americans who, eager to sample a taste of the "true northern wilds," every year endured the long and monotonous journey aboard a chartered train called the *Buffalo Flyer*. Such was their loyalty to the resort that, even when the *Flyer* was discontinued in 1905, they continued to make the trip by touring car, an expedition that would take the better part of three days. The tourists were a sort of surrogate family to the townsfolk, who came to eagerly anticipate their annual visits. Many eventually bought cottages on Maple Lake.[12]

In addition to the hotel, John Sword also owned the Tally-Ho Coach Line, which ran stages from the steamer docks at Rosseau and Port Cockburn to his resort. To facilitate this business, he had a private phone line run from the Maple Lake Hotel to these ports, which enabled him to keep abreast of the comings and goings of the steamships. This was actually the first phone line in Christie Township, predating public telephone lines by more than a decade.

When John and Annie decided to retire from the hospitality industry around 1914, the hotel was sold to their nephew, Percy Sword, and his new wife, Katherine. Unlike their predecessors, however, Percy

Courtesy Christie Historical Committee.

Percy Sword and his wife, Katherine, on the porch of the Maple Lake Hotel posing with fish caught by guests. The couple ran the hotel during its final years of operation. Note the general store in the background.

and Katherine catered their entire business to seasonal tourists and ran Maple Lake Hotel during summer months only. The First World War put a dent in their business, especially after the Americans entered the conflict in 1917, and it never really recovered. As a result, the Maple Lake Hotel closed around 1925.

A wing was torn off the building shortly thereafter, and it became a private residence to several generations of Swords. But after being in the family for almost a century, the aging building was sold in the early 1970s and torn down to be replaced by a modern home. The once fine hotel vanished, just as did the community it served.

Today, a white bungalow stands where the Maple Lake Hotel once welcomed wealthy American guests and quenched the thirst of rugged lumbermen.

Ludgate Lumber Company

The area around Maple Lake is heavily forested with hardwood trees, a mixed blessing to the early settlers. The dense forest made attempts at clearing the land for cultivation backbreaking and time consuming, but it also represented a potentially rich resource. Unfortunately, for the first few decades, this potential could not be realized simply because in the absence of railways there was no means of getting logs to distant markets.

That all changed when the OA&PSR passed through.

Recognizing an opportunity to harvest this previously untapped forest around Maple Lake, the Ludgate Lumber Company — of which David Sword was a partner — purchased significant tracts of land at the south end of the lake in 1894 and quickly raised a large sawmill on its shores.[13] As there was no fall of water to harness for powering the saws, a steam boiler and engine had to be imported and laboriously dragged to the mill site. Soon the woods were ringing with the sound of dozens of axes cutting into trees, and the constant buzz of the sawmill echoed across the lake's placid surface.

From the start, the mill at Maple Lake was a large enterprise that operated year-round. To cater to the mill hands and their families who would have to live in this isolated setting, the Ludgate Lumber Company built a general store and several cabins around the railway tracks. Thus was born the village of Swords.

The area economy was heavily dependant upon lumbering. In the poor soil, local farmers were hard pressed to grow more than their families needed to survive, and therefore had little surplus to sell. Most of their income came from winter lumbering, either in the employ of the Ludgate Lumber Company or in their own woodlots felling trees that they then sold to the company. The smooth surface of the frozen lake provided the easiest route for hauling logs to the mill, far easier than over the rolling terrain and through the thick woods. On a good day one could see up to thirty teams of horses hauling logs across Maple Lake, some coming from as far as thirty kilometres away.

While local farmers worked in lumber camps or in their own woodlots only during the winter months, the lumber company itself continued to cut trees year-round. During the summer months, logs were towed across Maple Lake to the awaiting mill by a device known as a horse crib. Horse cribs were huge rafts of squared timbers with a spool three or four feet in diameter in the centre. Eight-foot-long arms extended from the spool, to which a horse was hitched. Behind the crib was a block of logs corralled together by an encircling fence of timbers.

The process was simple but tedious. Men in a rowboat would go a quarter-mile ahead of the crib and drop a four-hundred-pound anchor into the lake. A sturdy rope ran from the anchor to the crib, and when the horse walked around the spool it slowly wound this rope in, thereby towing the crib and the attached logs across the lake. When the crib finally reached the anchor, the men in the rowboat would then lift it off the lake bed, carry it another quarter-mile, and repeat the process. Maple Lake is a mile across, so it would take half the night to complete the crossing. It was worth it, though, because a typical crib could pull about two thousand medium-sized logs at one time.

It was vital that cribs could transport so many logs, because the mill on Maple Lake had an insatiable appetite. Up to five thousand board feet of lumber could be cut on a productive day, and tens of thousands of logs would be consumed in a single year. Finished lumber was transported

Courtesy Christie Historical Committee.

A typical logging crew. The teamster holding the reigns is Guy Smith, a legendary lumberman who married into the Sword family. Also standing atop are Tom Kingshott, Embert Miesenhiemer, and Wildred Smith. Standing on the ground is David Sword.

from the lakeshore to the railway siding a mile distant by horses pulling wagon-sized railcars over a narrow gauge railway that had been built upon a plank boardwalk. From the siding, the trains of the OA&PSR would ship the lumber to points farther east, in particular the ports of New England.

Sometime between 1900 and 1910, the Ludgate Lumber Company sold its mill and accompanying land at Maple Lake to the Sheppard Lumber Company. The mill remained in operation for another decade or so, but by the early 1920s the saws had fallen silent. The timber was largely played out, and that which remained wasn't sufficient to keep the mill profitable.

The loss of the sawmill was a profound blow to Swords. Lumbering had kept the farms in the area viable considerably longer than would otherwise have been the case, and when this source of supplemental income was lost most local farmers simply could not survive and were forced to move away.

The Sword Family

Even a community as small as Swords was would have been home to many families, most of whom quietly went about their existence with little fanfare. But in every village there are those families who tend to leave their mark behind, and it is through their lives that we can learn about the history of their communities.

The story of Swords is intertwined with that of the family after which it was named. True, many others had contributed to the community's development and to the tapestry of everyday life within the quiet rural hamlet, but none had their fingers in as many pies as did the Swords: they were farmers, lumbermen, postmasters, proprietors of the general store, owners of Maple Lake Hotel, stagecoach operators, and more. Their personal successes were reflected in that of the community as a whole.

The Sword clan originally hailed from Scotland but in the 1850s immigrated to Glengarry Township, Ontario, a region heavily populated by their kinsmen. The steady migration of French settlers from Quebec into the township over the next few decades caused many Scottish settlers to uproot themselves once more, and the Swords were no different. Their new destination was Parry Sound District.

Thomas Sword was already a middle-aged man when he arrived in Christie Township with his wife and children — David, John, and Margaret — in 1870 and established a homestead on Lot 19, Concession 2. Unlike many early settlers, he wasn't dismayed by the dense forests and thin soil that made agricultural pursuits so difficult in Muskoka. It was never his intention to make his livelihood from farming. Rather, he earned his living from the trees themselves. Thomas Sword was a logging foreman, one of the best. His services were in demand by large logging companies all across the Muskoka–Parry Sound region and beyond. In fact, his reputation spread as far south as Michigan and as far west as British Columbia.

David Sword, Thomas's eldest son, inherited much of his father's expertise and followed him into the lumber camps. He spent his whole life in the bush and was still working in the industry alongside his son-in-law, Guy Smith, well into his seventies during the 1920s. David also inherited his father's farmstead, and built an impressive two-storey brick home called Riverdale upon the property. It was probably the finest home in the area, but unfortunately it burned down in 1918. After that, David built the brick home and barn that today stand on the northeast corner of the railway–Swords Road crossing.

Thomas's other son, John, as we've learned earlier in this chapter, built and operated the Maple Lake Hotel and ran the Tally-Ho Coach Line.

The Maple Lake Hotel later passed into the hands of his nephew, David's son, Percy Sword. Even after it ceased functioning as a hotel, Percy and his wife, Katherine, remained and raised their family in the building. Percy also handled the local milk run, gathering milk from area farms to deliver to the Georgian Bay Creamery in Parry Sound.

Percy's brother, Thomas, was the long-time owner of the Swords general store and was known as one of the most considerate and kind individuals in town. You'd be hard pressed to find anyone who would have an ill thing to say about Thomas Sword.

Their sister, Ella, wed Guy Smith, one of the most accomplished lumbermen in the Muskoka–Parry Sound region. His mother worked at the Maple Lake Hotel, eking out an existence after her husband had died young. At the age of ten, Guy rolled a stout fence post into a pond and, in his own words, "got to manage that cedar post so that when I started to drive the big pine, I could walk over it just the same as you walk on the road." He joined his first lumber camp at the tender age of fourteen, after convincing a neighbour to take him along when he left to join the Seguin drive. The youngster never looked back.[14]

By the time siblings Percy, Thomas, and Ella were having families of their own, the village of Swords was already into a steep and unrecoverable decline. Many of their children eventually moved away in search of work, while those who remained lacked the opportunity to leave a mark as definitive as those left by their pioneering parents.

Nevertheless, three generations of Swords had played prominent roles, perhaps the defining roles, in the development of their community. It's revealing that their friends and neighbours should decide to name the village in their honour.

2

ROSSEAU FALLS

Hidden away in a small cove on Lake Rosseau's idyllic northern shores, far beyond the reach of Muskoka's early roads, lay the remote hamlet of Rosseau Falls. It was a company town in the truest sense, a community that existed on the fragile foundations of a single industry: logging. For decades it prospered from the harvesting of old growth trees, but when the timber along the Rosseau River watershed inevitably played out, the hamlet found itself without purpose and was soon abandoned. Today, little tangible evidence remains of the community's brief existence, and even memories are faded and fleeting.

The Rosseau River, now as then, runs serenely for eighteen kilometres from Long Lake before finally pouring into Lake Rosseau through a tempestuous chute. In 1877, forty-year-old Peter Mutchenbacker received a land grant for one hundred acres adjacent to the falls and, in partnership with the Snider Furniture Company of Waterloo (which already operated mills at Bala and Gravenhurst),[1] built a large sawmill and shingle mill at the location. Each spring thereafter logs that had been cut in the heavily forested interior over the preceding winter were sent barrelling down the river to gather in the lake below. After the spring drive, both Mutchenbacker Bay and the adjacent Cardwell, or Four Mile Point, Bay were packed so tightly with logs that one could quite literally walk from one shore to the next without getting wet feet.

When the mill was switched from water power to steam power it prospered as never before, shipping out its lumber at a rate unequalled by any other mill along Lake Rosseau's northern shores. In a good year, upwards of 1.5 million board feet of lumber were cut, with the wood shingle mill operating alongside. The mills, lumberyards, wharves, tramways, and boilers alone covered an area nearly half a square

Courtesy Diane Rotz.

A slightly idealized but fundamentally accurate painting of Rosseau Falls circa 1890.

kilometre. It was during this period of prosperity and frenzied activity that village of Rosseau Falls began to take shape.

In the shadow of the mills stood several cabins housing the families of the mill hands, which at any one time might number fifteen to twenty men (in later years, when the mills began operating in reduced capacity, some homes were only seasonally occupied). Mr. Mutchenbacker's original log home was replaced by a fine board-and-batten structure, which was reputed to be one of the first private residences built in this manner locally. A general store operated out of an addition at the rear of this home and was joined on December 1, 1880, by a post office. The post office was designated Rosseau Falls, so the name was extended to the community it served. At the time, Rosseau Falls was home to about forty people.

Despite being less than five kilometres from the village of Rosseau, the little mill community had no road access and was largely isolated from the trappings of civilization, such as they were in nineteenth-century Muskoka. The only regular means of communication or resupply were the mail ship that thrice weekly made a round trip of Lake Rosseau and the Snider Company's steam tug, appropriately named the SS *Rosseau*.

This little vessel laboured hard for the company. Not only did she resupply the village, but she also towed barges overloaded with cut lumber and shingles to the railheads at Gravenhurst and, when the company's demand for logs exceeded the Rosseau River's capacity, began towing logs that had been harvested from the Shadow River watershed (just west of Rosseau) to the awaiting mills.

By the 1890s the lumber industry had begun to pass Muskoka, and so the Snider Lumber Company slowly shed its assets. In 1896, the mills at Rosseau Falls were sold back to their original owner and carried on under the name Mutchenbacker Brothers, for Peter's sons Asa and Herman, who increasingly ran the operation for their aging father. With the SS *Rosseau* no longer serving the village, Peter Mutchenbacker's personal yacht *Theresa* (named for his wife) was pressed into service.

Despite new ownership, the mills and the village itself carried on uninterrupted. Asa, it seems, took control of the mills' daily operation, while Herman ran the store and post office.

Ten years later, however, the mill was sold again. The new owner was the Kaufman Furniture Company of Kitchener. Eventually, the Kaufman company placed the mill under the stewardship of long-time mill hand John Fry, who in turn was succeeded in 1924 by his son, Albert Fry. By this time the signs were already apparent to anyone who cared to look that Rosseau Falls didn't have long to live. The forests along the Rosseau River were rapidly being cleared of harvestable lumber, and once gone the mills and the village that depended upon it for their existence would rapidly disappear.

Rosseau Falls slowly eroded over the ensuing years. First, the mills began operating at reduced capacity for much of the year, and therefore several of the workers' cabins were occupied only seasonally. Then, on November 19, 1928, the post office was closed, and the store ceased operation soon after. By this time, the shingle mill was no longer functioning

While the sawmill continued to operate seasonally for another decade or so, employing only a few hands and producing lumber on a limited scale for local consumption only, the hamlet of Rosseau Falls was no more.

In the half-century that followed Rosseau Falls's demise, the entire site was intruded upon by modern cottages that erased most of the more striking remains. The mills, the workers' cabins, and the extensive wharves are all gone.

The remnants of Rosseau Falls are huddled around the river's mouth and unfortunately are on private property. A lone piling from the dock protrudes forlornly from the water, and the crumbling shell of the power-house lies partially obscured by foliage along the shore. Clearly visible in the shallows are aging timbers and a veritable hoard of rusting metal relics — spikes, hooks, and other sundry items. The only remaining building is the old foreman's home, which is occupied seasonally as a cottage.

Mutchenbacker Bay and the Rosseau River chute are located south of Highway 141 on Rosseau Road 3. For an intimate view of the rocky chute and Mutchenbacker Bay below, stop at the bridge and walk along the river's banks. While the water slows to a trickle during dry summers, each spring the Rosseau River thunders into Lake Rosseau in an angry maelstrom of churning water that is impressive in its sheer, unbridled

We climbed down the rocky chute that is Rosseau Falls to its base as it empties into beautiful Lake Rosseau. The sawmill would have been at left and the steam boiler at right (the concrete foundations of which still remain). Lying submerged in the shallows were numerous rough-hewn planks that would have been cut at least seventy-five years earlier.

power. If you look carefully enough you'll see holes drilled into the rock, some of which still have metal bars protruding from them. These represented the right side of the old mill chute, a wooden causeway that prevented logs from lodging in the elbows and pools that are on this side of the river.

Rosseau Road 3 ends at Four Mile Point Beach. Today its sandy beach and shallow, warm waters make it ideal for swimming, but a century ago it would have been thick with sawdust and milling detritus.

Rosseau Falls Store/Post Office/Foreman's Home

The sole survivor of Rosseau Falls's fleeting existence is a quaint board-and-batten building. It was once the centre of this thriving mill hamlet, serving not only as home to successive foremen but also as general store and post office for the small population. Now, instead of selling wares and posting letters, the structure offers only seasonal respite as a summer guest cottage.

After the mill was up and running, one of Peter Mutchenbacker's first acts was to build a house suitable to a man of his station. Prior to that, he and his family had lived in a rather modest log home, but after a few years, with his five children growing older, the little cabin must have seemed full to overflowing. Clearly, the family needed a new home. In addition, there were appearances to be upheld. It simply wouldn't do for the foreman of such a large mill to be living in a rough-hewn log cabin.

The home subsequently built was quite impressive considering the frontier atmosphere that still prevailed along most of Lake Rosseau's northern shores. It was a large, two-storey structure and was noted for being one of very few board-and-batten homes in the vicinity at that time. Large windows and a wraparound porch overlooked the water. From them residents could, and presumably still do, enjoy the glorious view of Mutchenbacker Bay and Lake Rosseau.

Within a few years of the mill's founding, the demand for lumber had grown so voracious that it was operating year-round. Workers who previously were employed only seasonally now took up permanent residence at Rosseau Falls. As a real hamlet emerged, and with the nearest store in Rosseau five miles away by boat, it was recognized that an on-site mercantile was required to cater to the needs of the community. Consequently, an addition was built onto the rear of the Mutchenbacker home to house a small general store, with the mill foreman himself, or a member of his family, serving as proprietor.

As it was with most communities, the store was a place to congregate and chat. This was magnified in little Rosseau Falls, since there was no other public building in which to socialize. Passed-down stories suggest many of these gatherings were enlivened with a healthy dose of alcohol, purchased in the store, of course. It was in fact perfectly legal at the time for general stores to sell liquor, provided it wasn't consumed on the premises. It seems, however, that more often than not this minor stipulation was overlooked and on hot summer days the booze flowed liberally on the store's shaded porch.

This unseemly behaviour may have been reined in a bit after the store was awarded a post office on December 1, 1880.[2] After all, as a federal facility certain standards had to be maintained, and postal contracts were

Courtesy Diane Rotz.

The Mutchenbacker House with its attached store/post office, shown here circa *1890, still stands today.*

simply too lucrative to risk losing. Mail was picked up and delivered by a steamer that travelled the fifty-kilometre distance from Gravenhurst, the nearest railhead, three times weekly. The first postmaster was William Snider, but the title was his in deed only. In fact, Snider never resided at Rosseau Falls, and the position of postmaster was filled by Peter Mutchenbacker.

When the Mutchenbackers later obtained complete control of the mill, Herman Mutchenbacker, one of Peter's two sons, began running the store and post office, leaving the milling to his brother, Asa. After the family sold out to the Kaufman Furniture Company, a string of store proprietors came and went: S.F. Gordon served for a single season, 1906, while E. Whitmore lasted only three years, until 1909. At the same time, the post office was reduced to a seasonal affair, open from the breakup of the lake in March until the end of October. The store lasted longer in Rosseau Falls than perhaps its dwindling population deserved, simply because its isolated location meant transportation to larger centres remained impractical for a great many years.

The final foreman to reside in the house was Albert Fry. He was also the last store manager and postmaster, and to him fell the responsibility of boarding up the little shop when it was closed in November 1928.

When the lucrative logging era ended, the village of Rosseau Falls was no more. The foreman's home and general store, which had once served as the centre of the hamlet, changed hands and became a cottage.

Today, seventy-five years on, the building is just a shadow of its former glory, aging and weathered and badly in need of repair. It's no longer even used regularly, the owners having long since built a majestic summer residence alongside that more accurately reflects their wealth. With all the luxurious modern cottages along Lake Rosseau's shoreline, this lonely house sits and ponders years gone by, back before neglect set in, to a time when it was the most breathtaking home in the area.

Though the current owners likely aren't aware of the details of its unique history, their summer residence is the sole surviving relic of one of Muskoka's smallest and most obscure ghost towns. That's why, when we had the privilege of actually visiting the home, we were pleasantly surprised to hear that the owners weren't going to erase this piece of history despite the toll the years have taken on it. Rather, they plan to restore the home so history can live on.

Rosseau Falls Mills

At the very heart of Rosseau Falls, both literally and figuratively, stood the imposing structure that was the sawmill. The very reason for the community's being, the mill was obviously the most important building in the little hamlet and as long as its saw continued to run the community was assured of an existence.

In the latter half of the nineteenth century, with Muskoka experiencing a lumber boom, sawmills sprang up along lakeshores and riverbanks like trilliums in a springtime forest. There were literally dozens of them. Most were small, employing only a handful of men and cutting lumber for local needs, lasting perhaps a few decades. In contrast, the mill at Rosseau Falls was the largest industry on Lake Rosseau's northern shores for more than fifty years.

The sawmill was originally water-powered, but being tied to the whims of nature was frustrating and not good business practice. For much of the year, the sluggish stream was incapable of turning the heavy machinery of the mill, so the typical operating season ran from around the beginning of April until the winter runoff was exhausted at the end of May. In years in which there was little snowfall, the already brief operating window would be further shortened. Even during the wettest of summers the river wouldn't flow strong enough to allow for more than the occasional day of sawing beyond May.

To increase productivity and eliminate any reliance upon nature, a steam boiler was built on the west bank of the river. Large overhead pipes brought steam to the mill, powering the whining saws. The switch to steam power, more than any other change, was responsible for the mill tripling its output from about half a million board feet per year to 1.5 million board feet.[3]

A wooden chute was set into the falls, preventing logs from jamming against the rocks or crowding into the pools that formed along the river's

Courtesy Diane Rotz.

Even at its peak, Rosseau Falls was never large. It was little more than a sawmill and a shingle mill (seen in the foreground), a building that served as both home to the Mutchenbackers and post office (seen at rear), wharves (seen here with the Theresa at dock), and a collection of worker's cabins.

western side. The chute also prevented the logs from being damaged as they descended this turbulent stretch. According to Doreen Nowak of Rosseau, parts of the chute were still evident in the 1940s when she played in the area. All that remains now, however, are drill holes in the rock that would have anchored the sides.[4]

Logs congregated by the hundreds in Mutchenbacker Bay and Cardwell Bay. A chain, drawing power from the turbine, would drag each log from the water, ready to be rolled onto a carriage and then fed into the circular saw. Cut lumber would be transported by carts running along narrow-gauge rail tracks and pulled by horses to the extensive wharves around the bay. This lumber would be transported by barge to the railhead at Gravenhurst.

Men employed in the mill really didn't have an off-season once it became steam-powered. They'd saw from late spring to late autumn, and then when the snows came, they'd kiss their families goodbye and head off into the bush camps to fell trees over the winter. Oftentimes they wouldn't return again until the spring drive in late March and April.

In addition to the sawmill, there was also a small shingle mill on site, likewise steam powered, which produced cedar shingles for Muskoka homes and businesses. Shingle mills were, as a rule, far less rewarding than sawmills, but they allowed an operator to make a profit from lower-grade lumber. It certainly helped that, with Muskoka growing by leaps and bounds in the late 1800s, there was a ready market at hand.

By the early years of the twentieth century the logging industry was rapidly receding in Muskoka, yet the sawmill at Rosseau Falls soldiered on for a time. It was the Depression that drove the nails into the Kaufman mill's coffin, as it did to so many others across the region. Hope dies hard, however, and attempts were made to keep the mill running and profitable into the 1940s. Ultimately, all such efforts to revive the dying enterprise were in vain.

Today, there are few clues that hint at the existence of either mill. The crumbling concrete foundation of the mill, still standing but largely obscured by foliage, is the most obvious. In addition, peering into the shallows at the mouth of the river will reveal pieces of rust-encrusted machinery and even the occasional cut timber.

Like so many other small communities across northern Ontario, the existence of a sawmill brought life to an area of wilderness that otherwise would never have been settled. Consequently, when the mill closed down, it meant the end of the hamlet of Rosseau Falls as well.

Steamboats That Served Rosseau Falls

With Rosseau Falls completely isolated amidst the dense forest of Lake Rosseau's northern shore, its only lifeline to civilization was provided by steamship. Though mail ships arrived as often as three times per week, it fell to overworked tugs to perform the daily chores that kept the mills fed with logs, the railcars at Gravenhurst full of lumber, and the community stocked with supplies. They were thankless, tedious tasks, but they were necessary nonetheless. Without these important work boats, Rosseau Falls simply would not have existed.

The first of two vessels that served the community was the *Rosseau*.[5] Built in 1879, she was originally part of the expansive fleet of steamers belonging to A.P. Cockburn that allowed him to claim the title "King of the Lakes." Later, she was sold to the Beardmore Tannery in Bracebridge for which she was predominantly employed pulling scows loaded with tan bark (tannic acid found in hemlock bark was used extensively at the time to cure leather). Then, in 1889, the *Rosseau* was sold to the Snider Lumber Company.

Under the Snider banner, the tug spent most of her time towing logs from the mouth of the Shadow River, located west of Rosseau, to Mutchenbacker Bay, and towing barges bearing finished lumber to the railway. Each barge, which measured about 15 feet long and 4 feet deep, could carry enough lumber for two or three railway cars, so it's easy to imagine the strain the steamship was constantly subjected to.

After the Snider Lumber Company pulled out of its partnership with Peter Mutchenbacker, the *Rosseau* was no longer available to serve the mill or its village. She continued in the service of the Snider Lumber Company for a while, but when the struggling business began shedding its assets the *Rosseau* was sold off. In 1907, she became the property of Gravenhurst tug captain William Henshaw, and two years later was sold to Captain Mortimer of Mortimer's Point. But the years of labour had worn her out, and she seems to have operated only a few more seasons before machinery problems and hull stress confined her to the docks. By 1915 she was rotting and no longer seaworthy, and she was dismantled shortly thereafter.

The lifespan of the second steamship to serve Rosseau Falls, the *Theresa*, was even shorter.[6] Built at Rosseau Falls in 1890 by David Abbey of Gravenhurst, the *Theresa* was the personal yacht of Peter Mutchenbacker and was named in honour of his wife. The vessel was only 49.5 feet long and 26 tons, and not ideally suited to the drudgery of the lumber trade. Still, when pressed into service she acquitted herself well.

A tragedy occurred aboard the *Theresa* that would cloud memories of carefree afternoons spent sailing aboard her. On July 9, 1900, Herman

Mutchenbacker was at the helm of the little yacht. Accompanying him were several members of the family, including his nephew, Clarence Groh, the ten-year-old son of his sister, Maria. After watching his uncle pilot the craft from the wheelhouse, young Clarence decided to climb down the steel ladder to the main deck. He must have slipped and fallen into the water, but no one saw the accident occur. It was some time before anyone knew Clarence was missing. Those in the wheelhouse thought he was on the main deck, and those on the main deck thought he was still topside. By the time his absence was eventually noticed, no sign of Clarence could be found. He had simply disappeared beneath the waves, swallowed by the lake. It wasn't until several days later that his body was finally recovered.[7]

In 1904, the *Theresa* was sold to the Magnetewan Hardwood Company and in April was shipped north by railway flatcars. Again, the vessel found itself employed as a tug for a lumber company. It was destined to change hands several times over the years, before finding a permanent home with Albert Alexander Agar of the Magnetewan River and Lakes Steamboat Line in 1910. The *Theresa* helped Agar to dominate both the transport and the towing business from Burks Falls to Ahmic Harbour.

After nine years of further sailing, she had started to deteriorate and was unceremoniously discarded and left to rot in a weedy elbow of the Magnetewan River. Presumably, she lies there still.

Neither the *Theresa* nor the *Rosseau* were ideally suited to handling heavy tugboat duties, but nonetheless both proved invaluable to the Mutchenbackers' success. They were hard-working ships over the duration of their careers, but the heavy toil probably hastened their final demise, sending them to early, watery graves.

The Mutchenbacker Family

Leaving one's homeland and immigrating to a foreign country is not the easiest of moves. Unfamiliar language and customs, strange climate and terrain, and an uncertain fate all await the prospective settler. Yet, many people are willing to face these obstacles in the hopes of making a better life for themselves and their families. This was never more true than in nineteenth-century Canada, when tens of thousands of predominantly poor Europeans poured into the young country in search of a fresh start and perhaps a shot at true prosperity.

The Mutchenbackers of Rosseau Falls were amongst this wave of hopeful humanity. For them, Canada proved to be a mixed blessing, providing both incredible highs and heartbreaking lows.

The Mutchenbackers originally came from Bavaria, in Germany, where Peter was born on April 14, 1837.[8] His family immigrated to Canada a year later and settled near Kitchener, Ontario, a region with a large number of German settlers. Here he met and in 1860 wed Theresa Bube (or Buby), who was born in Saximing, Germany, in 1838. The couple would have five children: sons Asa and Herman and daughters Maria, Clara, and Lizzie.[9]

In 1877, Peter brought the family to the wilds of Muskoka and hitched their fortunes to the success of the sawmill. The family thrived. Asa and Herman enthusiastically embraced the lumber industry, while Theresa sought to bring a semblance of civility to the untamed region — even planting a thriving flower garden against a backdrop of Muskoka bedrock.

Two of the three Mutchenbacker daughters married local men. Clara wed career lumberman Adam McPeak, who later followed Asa and Herman to Manitoba and remained there. Maria married Jonathon Groh in 1889. Seven years later they moved to West Gravenhurst, where they operated a general store and post office and prospered. A prominent man, Jonathon Groh was the mayor of Gravenhurst in 1905–06.

By about the turn of the century, the once harmonious and united family began to fragment. The drowning of young Clarence Groh off the tug *Theresa*, business differences between father and sons, and economic problems brought on by the decline of the timber industry in Muskoka all contributed to growing discontent.[10] As a result, it probably came as a surprise to no one when Asa, Herman, and brother-in-law Adam McPeak packed up their families and headed to the rich timberlands of northern Manitoba in 1904.

After the mass departure of his children, Peter sold the mill and retired to Gravenhurst. Both his health and that of his wife, Theresa,

Rosseau Falls lived and died with the prospects of the Mutchenbacker family. They owned the mills and the steamships that served them and operated the hamlet's post office and store. Peter Mutchenbacker, the patriarch of the family, is seen standing at back.

declined rapidly thereafter. He died on September 21, 1908, and she passed away just over a year later, on October 15, 1909. One can't help but wonder if broken hearts, the result of seeing their precious family broken apart, hadn't played a part in their deaths.

Meanwhile, Asa and Herman had firmly established themselves in the wilds of Mafeking, Manitoba. Their mill there, and the timber rights that fed it, dwarfed their prior operation at Rosseau Falls, and over the next decade they made a veritable fortune (Herman's diary notes he had made half a million dollars by 1911). But disaster struck on May 8, 1911, when a hellish fire raced through the forest, consuming everything in its path. With no road to provide a means of escape and the flames spreading too fast to even contemplate outrunning them, the Mutchenbackers and their mill hands huddled around the railway tracks, hoping beyond hope that a train would make it to extract them. With the flames closing in and no salvation in sight, the end seemed near at hand. Luckily, and at the last minute, the winds suddenly shifted and blew the flames back upon the burned-out terrain. Starved of fuel, the fire burned itself out.[11]

The families were saved, but the devastation had been complete. The mill, the supporting infrastructure, and 65 million feet of standing timber had all been reduced to ash. Asa and Herman had lost it all. After a few years of desperately trying to salvage something of their fortunes, they called it quits and returned to Ontario. On January 15, 1916, Herman wrote in his diary, "Lost half a million dollars — yes, lost our life's work. These were the days when it was harder to live than it was to keep from dying."

Asa fades from history at around this point. He worked as a munitions worker in Orillia for the duration of the First World War, but he never again came close to approaching his previous prominence or wealth. He died in 1950 at the age of eighty-two.

Herman, however, began rebuilding his life immediately upon his return to Ontario. After managing the Holt Timber Company operations near Parry Sound for a few seasons, he purchased a mill and extensive timber rights (47,000 acres) at Bigwood along the French River.[12] Not only did his operation cut lumber, but he also received a lucrative contract to provide telephone poles for Ontario Hydro. Prosperity followed in short order.

It was around this time that Herman changed his surname to Baker. Part of the reason, according to his granddaughter Diane Rotz, was that few people could pronounce or spell Mutchenbacker, an obvious detriment when in business. However, it's equally likely that with anti-German sentiment running rampant as a result of the First World War his Germanic name was the cause of some discomfort or embarrassment.

With the mills at Bigwood thriving, it surely must have seemed that the future was bright indeed. But trouble seemed to stalk the family. In 1922, it was discovered that Herman's partner, Milton Kaufman, was embezzling from the company. "He had juggled the books $34,400," wrote Herman on June 23, 1922. "He got to jail." Herman recovered from the betrayal, and the company continued on despite the lost resources, but worse was to come.

The Depression hit the mill hard, just as it did most of its kind across Ontario. Overnight, it seemed the market for lumber had disappeared.

Then, Ontario Hydro cancelled the contract for poles. By 1936, the company was teetering on the brink of destruction, and Herman on the edge of personal and financial collapse. On July 1, the Mutchenbackers lost their timber limits because they couldn't pay the taxes. On the same day, Herman noted in his diary that he lost his life insurance policy of $7,600 as well. "These two troubles almost sent me across," he wrote.

Though he had rebounded from setback and tragedy many times in the past, this time there was no recovery. Herman was too old, too tired, too despondent. He passed away ten years later, on November 20, 1946, at the age of seventy-five.

We are often deceived by the popular image of Canada as the "land of milk and honey," the promised land for early settlers. One would have thought that coming to a new country would have made things easier than they were back in the homeland; that was the plan, after all. But it didn't always work out that way. For the Mutchenbackers, Canada was a land of extremes. On the one hand, life here was often difficult and cruel, and there were times when it felt as though "it was harder to live than to keep from dying." But, as with all pioneers, they persevered through the upheavals in their lives, finding success in spite of the turmoil they endured. Many of these dramas — the feast and famine of their family fortunes — were played out in tiny Rosseau Falls.

3

FALKENBURG JUNCTION

Falkenburg Junction occupies a spot in what is today a forgotten corner of Macaulay Township, hiding along a dirt back road that, after only a short drive, becomes impassible to vehicles and fades into the forest. About 130 years ago, however, this same road was part of the busy Muskoka Colonization Road, a highway designed to open up the rugged and inhospitable hinterlands to settlement. Lured by false hope, hundreds of unsuspecting immigrants took up land along its length, attempting to establish farms in a region never intended by God to be put under the plough.

The land around Falkenburg Junction was unspectacular. The forests were just as dark and gloomy as elsewhere in Muskoka, and the soil similarly threadbare. But the location did have one thing going for it: it was here that the Muskoka and Parry Sound Colonization Roads met. As a result, this otherwise insignificant spot became a vital crossroads, carrying commerce and settlers to points throughout the district. The formation of a community was inevitable.

It was slow getting off the ground, however. For several years, about the only thing Falkenburg Junction could boast of was a crude log tavern, called the Junction Hotel, operated by Thomas George. Here settlers could drown their fears of failing in this unforgiving land, and in their drunken haze they might imagine that the maddening swarms of mosquitoes and the ever-present rock that was sure to hinder cultivation simply did not exist.

When Thomas George opened his primitive hotel, there was hardly a community to speak of. Falkenburg's population stood at only a couple of dozen spread out over roadside farms, and besides the tavern the only other buildings of note were a small shingle mill, also owned by George, and a post office operated by William Holditch that catered to nearby homesteads.

But as the tides of settlement began to push newcomers into the northern reaches of Ontario, traffic along the colonization roads began to increase, providing a much-needed boost to Falkenburg's fortunes.

In fact, the village that subsequently emerged subsisted largely by catering to the needs of the road-weary, providing especially the respite and nourishment that only a hotel could provide.

While Thomas George had by 1868 been put out of business by local officials, his tavern was soon up and running again under the new and completely legal proprietorship of William Brown. Another establishment, the Wellington Hotel, had been built a year earlier by Charles Percival, about a third of a mile north of the crossroads along the Muskoka Road.

The two taverns did steady business and provided the nucleus of a village, but it fell to newcomer Matthias Moore to ensure Falkenburg Junction would be stamped indelibly on the map. In fact, promoting the village and its development seemed to give his life purpose.

Matthias Moore, a recent immigrant from England, was probably the single most important individual in Falkenburg's history. He owned most of the land directly adjacent to the crossroads, and it was his decision to subdivide it into half-acre residential lots that allowed Falkenburg Junction to grow and take on the true appearance of village.

Moore was confident that the community would prosper and continue to develop, and for a time he was right. Continuous traffic along the roads did indeed spur growth. Dozens of folks were attracted to the bustling little hamlet, which soon came to include three stores: David Galloway's shoe shop, an Orange Lodge, and John Jackson's smithy. By 1872, Moore was running the village post office. But by far his most lucrative enterprise, and the largest industry in Falkenburg Junction, was the sawmill he erected later that year.

Despite having no previous milling experience, Matthias Moore was a man with ambition and threw himself into the role of lumberman with unbridled enthusiasm. The sawmill employed about a dozen men, all of whom were area farmers struggling to cultivate crops in the thin soil and who desperately needed an additional source of income.

Courtesy Muskoka Heritage Place Collection, Huntsville, Ont.

Matthias Moore built a sawmill in 1872 that sustained his family's fortunes, and that of the community at large, for many decades. As can be seen in this image, it employed many area men until its fiery demise in 1914.

Because the bush farms could barely support sustenance agriculture, Moore's mill literally bore the weight of the town's hopes.

Despite harsh terrain, unforgiving weather, occasional outbreaks of famine or disease, and unrelenting hardships, the people of Falkenburg never lost their faith in God. As it was in almost every nineteenth-century community, it wasn't long after settling in that they began to turn their thoughts to building a house of worship. Matthias Moore was the driving force behind this movement. When he subdivided his land into lots, he made sure to devote one acre for a future church, and as one of the original church wardens, he was also involved in organizing the congregation, planning the building's design, and raising the funds for its construction.

Within months of the survey, construction began on a church measuring 40 feet by 20 feet. Lumber and shingles were provided by Moore from his sawmill. Work was finished before snowfall, and on February 7, 1875, St. George's Anglican Church was officially consecrated and opened for services in a ceremony conducted by the Bishop of Algoma.

When the church opened, Falkenburg Junction was at the peak of its communal fortunes. In addition to the two hotels, the sawmill, the blacksmith, the Orange Lodge, and the shoemaker, the village now boasted three general stores and a schoolhouse.

But as quickly as prosperity had come to Falkenburg, it was stolen away even faster. The culprit was the Northern and Pacific Junction Railway (later the Grand Trunk, and later still Canadian National). Incorporated in March 1881 to construct a line north from Gravenhurst through to Bracebridge and on to Callander, and eventually perhaps to Sault Saint Marie, the railway inexplicably spurned Falkenburg by running its tracks and building a station three kilometres to the south of the village. When the tracks were opened in January 1886, it was the death knell of the village.

A new village, called Falkenburg Station, sprouted around the railway stop and like a weed sapped the vitality from Falkenburg Junction. Soon this upstart overshadowed its neighbour to the north, and businesses from Falkenburg Junction began to relocate there. Those shops that didn't migrate slowly withered away from a drought of both business and hope. Even St. George's Anglican Church was moved to the new townsite, dismantled and rebuilt in November 1886.[1]

A further blow was struck a few decades later when even the roads were diverted past the village, further hastening its demise into a backwater. By the turn of the century the population had dwindled from a high of about 250 to less than 40 as the pioneer-era buildings rotted and the lots were reclaimed by forest.

But even though Falkenburg Junction was growing quieter with each passing year, life had not yet been completely leached from the community. Arthur Moore continued to operate his father's sawmill until it burned to the ground in 1914, and three years later he agreed to allow his nephew, George Bernard Moore, to move his own sawmill to the old pond in return for $75 per month in payment.[2] George Bernard's operation remained here for thirteen years, at which time the lumber in the immediate area had been completely played out and the sawmill closed. Falkenburg Junction had run its course.

Today, the mill serves as one of the more ghostly relics of Falkenburg's past. It lies behind the weed-choked millpond, partially hidden by a regenerating forest. Overlooking the mill is the former home of George

Bernard Moore, standing atop what is known locally as Moore's Hill. This building, nestled among old trees, is still inhabited and is the only home still surviving from Falkenburg Junction's pioneer era.

St. George's Anglican Church is gone from the community, but the pioneer Moore Cemetery remains. Only four forlorn headstones occupy the grounds, pitifully few for a village that lasted for nearly half a century. Records suggest at least four or five additional souls were buried here as well. Could there possibly be more gravestones lying beneath the ground that have not yet been uncovered? It's a question that haunted us as we paid our respects to those whose graves were marked.

Teams of horses no longer pull heavily laden wagons bearing settlers and goods along the colonization roads, and it's been decades since the frenzied whine of saw blades has cut through the forests. Falkenburg Junction is eerily silent, funereal, and those few souls who remain have little clue that this forgotten back-roads location was once a thriving village.

Falkenburg Junction Hotels

Though Moore's sawmill was undoubtedly the largest industry in town, Falkenburg Junction's fortunes were really tied to the traffic that trudged along the Muskoka and Parry Sound Colonization Roads. It was a crossroads hamlet in the truest sense of the word, existing solely to cater to the needs of the road-weary.

The most basic needs, respite and nourishment, were provided by inns and taverns. With stagecoaches and wagons capable of no more than perhaps twenty or twenty-five kilometres per day travelling along the stump-ridden and rutted routes, roadside taverns sprang up like weeds in a fallow field. Strategic locations, such as important crossroads, wouldn't be complete without a watering hole or three.

Falkenburg was no exception to this rule. In fact, the first inn emerged even before there was a community. In 1865, Thomas George opened a crude log establishment called the Junction Hotel that catered to travellers making their way northwards from Bracebridge. Booze offered an escape from the harshness of frontier reality; it might have been temporary, but it was all the settlers had.

Thomas George was eager to profit from his land any way he could. Having settled there in 1860 and experiencing little luck in farming, he decided to try his luck as a businessman. Of course, it didn't matter to him or to his patrons that the whiskey he served up was manufactured in a back-lot still, or that lacking a tavern licence his entire establishment was illegal. Even the township council turned a blind eye to George's tavern.

But the provincial government cared. When they took over the mandate for issuing liquor licences in 1875, Thomas George's days as an innkeeper were numbered. When the axe finally fell, he turned to his Falkenburg Store and shingle mill to provide for himself and his family. In 1871, he left Falkenburg Junction for Parry Sound.[3]

The Junction Hotel carried on, however, under the ownership of William Brown. After purchasing the property from Thomas George in 1869, he applied for a liquor licence and, unlike his predecessor, was granted one. A man barely twenty years of age, only two years a resident of Muskoka, and a plasterer by trade, Brown would have seemed to be ill-suited to the task of operating a rough-and-tumble frontier saloon. Yet he did so for many years, and by all accounts with considerable success.

As late as 1888, the Junction Hotel was still in operation, after which point it fades from history. Though no definitive account of its ultimate demise exists, one can assume that with traffic along the Muskoka Road dwindling to a mere trickle, the business was no longer viable and soon thereafter simply closed its doors.

The other hotel in Falkenburg Junction, the Wellington Hotel, had a more dramatic final act. Located just a few hundred metres north of the Junction Hotel, when Charles Percival opened in 1868 it was actually the first tavern in town to be legally licensed. By the mid-1870s, the Wellington was under the stewardship of Robert Howard, and it was at this time that one of the more colourful and amusing tales associated with the community emerges.

In March 1875, Howard was travelling home by sleigh when a furious snowstorm descended upon the darkening landscape. Already struggling through the dune-like drifts, his horses began to tire as the full weight of the blizzard made itself felt. One of the horses, an old mare, began to show obvious signs of exhaustion, so rather than push the animal beyond her limits, Howard unhitched her and rolled her into a hole he made in the snowbank. Satisfied that the horse would remain warm until morning, he continued his journey home.

Later that evening, another traveller struggled along in Howard's wake. Suddenly, the snowbank erupted and with a snort a great dark head emerged to look the man straight in the eye. In the dark, the creature looked like anything but a horse, and the man recoiled in fear. He ran for the safety and solace of the Wellington Hotel, and upon arriving aroused the guests and staff alike to relate his tale of terror and announce to one and all that he had seen the devil and lived to tell of it. Henceforth, he declared, he would never touch another drop of "the demon-drink." Robert Howard apparently didn't have the heart to tell the man the truth.[4]

Customers, frightened or otherwise, became increasingly rare after the railway passed through the area in 1886, and so Howard sold the failing business to village blacksmith J. Roscoe. But the change of ownership and a new name, Roscoe House, did nothing to save the hotel's flagging fortunes.

Unlike the Junction Hotel, which simply faded away, Roscoe House went out in style. In April 1889, in what was an unusually dry spring, a fire broke out in the nearby blacksmith shop. Burning embers were carried aloft by gusts of warm wind, and soon flames were consuming Roscoe House as well. Desperate efforts to save the building were ultimately in vain, and within a few hours all that remained of the hotel were blackened timbers and smoking ash.[5]

On the surface, the fire that claimed Roscoe House seemed to be the defining moment that ended the era of the tavern in Falkenburg Junction, when in reality it simply put a final exclamation point on an event that had already occurred. The true demise of the village's hotels can be traced to 1886, to the very instant when the final stake in the railway built north from Bracebridge was driven. From that moment on, the inns of Falkenburg Junction were on borrowed time.

The Mills of Falkenburg Junction

The rumble and whine of sawmills would have been a familiar sound to those residing in the crossroads village of Falkenburg Junction in the latter half of the nineteenth century. Though little remembered today, and in the grand scheme of things insignificant enterprises, these mills were important locally and demonstrated the industriousness for which our pioneer forebears are known.

These mills may have been pitifully small compared to those operating along the large Muskoka lakes, but they were vitally important to the village's economy and were the largest industries in Falkenburg.

First to be built was a small shingle mill operated by Thomas W. George. Arriving in Falkenburg as an eager thirty-year-old in 1860, George began clearing a farm from the ominous forest and established the Falkenburg Store to cater to settlers and travellers alike. Not content with being a shopkeeper and postmaster, he also erected a steam-powered shingle mill to provide roofing for the homes and businesses being built around the busy crossroads.

Perhaps impatient with the slow growth of the community, George sold his businesses in 1871 and ended up in Parry Sound. The new owner of his mill was Matthias Moore. Moore, like George before him, was a man with ambition, and despite having no previous milling experience threw himself into the role of lumberman with unbridled enthusiasm.

While the shingle mill might have been a convenient means of easing himself into the industry, it wasn't profitable enough to sate Moore's thirst. Since he was already clearing his six-hundred-acre farm of trees for cultivation, and recognizing that the settlers who were joining him at the crossroads required lumber for building homes, barns, and businesses, Moore decided to build a steam-powered sawmill as well. This was where the money was at.

Construction began on November 11, 1872, a date that Matthias marked simply in his diary with the line, "cutting rafters and logs for mill."[6] The mill was unique in that it incorporated some of the conventions of traditional water-driven mills and others of the more modern steam-powered variety. Because it was steam-powered, the mill was freed from the constraints of requiring a ready water source to run the machinery, and yet Moore still painstakingly dug a millpond to serve it.

In the autumn, the water was drained from the pond by a pipe in the south end. Over the course of the winter, logs that had been felled from the surrounding forest would be hauled by horses into the drained pond by the dozen. Prior to winter melt-off in the spring, the exit pipe would be blocked and the pond would fill naturally as the snows began to thaw. The logs floated in this artificial pond and, as would happen in a water-powered mill, would be pulled up a chute by chains to the awaiting blades when needed.

It was a unique setup, one rarely seen, but it worked.

Together, the two mills employed almost a dozen men, most of whom were area farmers struggling to cultivate crops in the thin soil and who desperately needed an additional source of income. Moore's reliance on farmers as mill hands meant the mill's operation was dictated to a large degree by crop seasons. Peak periods, therefore, were after planting in the spring and after harvesting in the autumn. Product was sold mostly locally, though some shingles and lumber may have found their way to Bracebridge.

The mills took on increased importance when the Grand Trunk Railway (later still Canadian National) passed by in 1886, greatly reducing traffic along the colonization roads and thereby depriving Falkenburg of its main source of income. Because the soil could support sustenance agriculture at best, Moore's mills literally bore the weight of the town's hopes.

Unfortunately, the industries were too small and too isolated from important markets to keep the town afloat for long. By the time of Matthias Moore's death in 1893, many villagers had moved away. Still, the mills remained profitable and his widow, Susan, and sons, Arthur, Saxon, and Chad, and grandson George Bernard carried on in his absence.

It was familiar strife more than any other factor that undermined the business. When Susan died, she deeded over all of her property and assets, including the sawmill, to Arthur. Understandably angered by this slight, Saxon and George Bernard refused to work at the mill (Chad was dead by then, killed in a hunting accident).[7]

From 1917, George Bernard Moore, Matthias's grandson, operated a sawmill on the site of the original Moore mill. By 1930 the timber in the area was completely played out, so the machinery was moved out of Falkenburg to untapped woods.

Arthur ran the sawmill on his own for two more decades, though in a greatly reduced capacity and by some accounts not very successfully at any rate. The end came in November 1914, when the mill burned to the ground.

It was not yet the end of milling in Falkenburg, however. In 1912, George Bernard built a sawmill of his own nearby,[8] but in 1917 he approached Arthur for permission to move his machinery to the old millpond. Arthur agreed, for a monthly rent of $75. George Bernard remained here for thirteen years, at which point the lumber in the immediate area was completely played out. The machinery was moved again, to untapped woods and out of Falkenburg.

For the first time in more than half a century, the frenzied whine of saw blades didn't cut through the forests around Falkenburg. The village was eerily silent, funereal, and those few souls who remained knew that the mill's demise rang the death knell for their community.

Today, the millpond still exists at the southern end of Falkenburg Junction, just before the old Muskoka Road fades into the regenerated forest. Just visible beyond the stagnant water and through the trees are the sagging remains of George Bernard Moore's sawmill, though it's barely recognizable as such. It serves as one of the more ghostly relics of Falkenburg's past, a once very active operation reduced to a mere shell. Behind a collapsing wooden frame lies a stone and brick room that once encased the boiler, protecting the mill from fire, a constant hazard of running steam machinery. Old machinery remains scattered about, hinting at the complexity of the operation.

Like an old man tired after years of backbreaking toil, the mill barely stands upright, leaning unsteadily on a crooked frame. It's taking a well-deserved rest from a lifetime of toil. And yet, despite its sad condition, there's defiance there, as though it proudly remembers back to its youth, to a time when it was vibrant and useful. In that way, the mill is symbolic of the entire Moore lumbering legacy. All it has left are memories of past glory.

St. George's Anglican Church

To passing ramblers St. George's Anglican Church in Falkenburg Station is probably a picturesque but unremarkable little building. Few perhaps realize there is 150 years of Muskoka architecture, worship, and society embedded within it, or that the church represents the sole remaining building from the heyday of the nearby ghost town, Falkenburg Junction.

When settlers first began taking up lots around Falkenburg Junction in the 1860s, they did so sight unseen.

They held to a steady faith that God would provide them with rich fields if only the trees were cleared away, that prosperity would be theirs. Such faith proved misplaced. Life in Falkenburg was a constant struggle. The thick forest and bare soil hindered attempts at cultivation, while famine and disease ravaged the people as they fought to adapt to wilderness life.

Though the pioneers of Falkenburg may have been depressed by the poor quality of soil that represented the sum of nature's bounty, it certainly wasn't reflected in their devotion to God. As it was in almost

St. George's Anglican Church was spared the tragic fate of Falkenburg Junction as a whole. It was moved to the newer community of Falkenburg Station, where it remains in use today.

every nineteenth-century community, soon after settling in the people of Falkenburg began to turn their thoughts to building a house of worship.

Matthias Moore was the driving force behind this movement. When he subdivided his land into town lots in 1874, he made sure to dedicate one acre as the site for a future church. As one of the original church wardens, he was also involved in organizing the congregation, planning the building's design, and raising the funds for its construction.

It was a rapid-fire process. Within months of the survey, construction began on a church measuring 40 feet by 20 feet, with an eight-foot porch.[9] Lumber and shingles were provided by Moore from his new sawmill. Work was finished before snowfall, and on February 7, 1875, the church was officially consecrated and opened for services in a ceremony conducted by the Bishop of Algoma Diocese.

As it was in so many small communities, the church hosted functions beyond Sunday religious services. Baptisms, weddings, town meetings, Sunday school, and other gatherings vital to creating community spirit were held within. In a very real sense, within the church's walls beat Falkenburg Junction's heart.

That's why its loss only thirteen years later was so devastating. When the Northern and Pacific Junction Railway (later the Grand Trunk, and later still Canadian National) decided to extend its lines north from Bracebridge, it inexplicably decided to bypass Falkenburg and instead built a station two miles to the south.

In that instant the fate of Falkenburg Junction was sealed. Almost the entire community up and moved to Falkenburg Station, St. George's Anglican Church included. In November 1886, the church was dismantled and then reassembled at the new townsite.[10]

It's still there today, and is the only original Macaulay Township church remaining in use. Of course, alterations have been made over the years, some subtle, others — such as the excavation of a basement in 1964 to serve as a community hall — more obvious. The one constant throughout these renovations has been the love and sensitivity with which they were performed.

Back in Falkenburg Junction, the church may be gone but the graveyard remains. Amongst the weathered and leaning stones are found those of Matthias Moore, his wife, Susan, sons Arthur and Harold, daughters-in-law Annie Hueber and Jane Samway, and granddaughter Ida Louise. Their gravestones are eerily symbolic of the fate of the community they called home.

Falkenburg Junction Orange Hall

Since time began, men have congregated in secretive clubs to fraternize, establish business dealings, and pool their resources to shape their communities to their liking. The number of these groups exploded during the nineteenth century. For every recognizable society, like the Lions Club or the Freemasons, there were dozens of obscure ones. The list was nearly endless, and even small communities like Falkenburg Junction had their own.

Falkenburg Junction was a staunchly Protestant community, inhabited almost solely by Englishmen. In nineteenth-century Ontario, the expression of English ideals — Protestantism, Patriotism, and Imperialism — was made concrete in the form of Orange Halls, built and maintained by local branches of the Loyal Orange Lodge.

The Loyal Orange Lodge was a secretive and mysterious fraternity of gentlemen who conducted their meetings and affairs in private, away from the limelight. Only rarely, during anniversaries of important events in Protestant history, would the members make public appearances together, often in parades or other shows of solidarity. But while the Lodge was insular by nature, it looked outwards by quietly performing acts of benevolence and welfare. Families burned out of homes would receive assistance in rebuilding, farmers who suffered from poor crops were provided with food to sustain them through the harsh winter months, and the gravely sick were assured of medical attention regardless of their financial status.

In Falkenburg Junction, the Loyal Orange Lodge emerged around 1865, meeting in the darkened loft of a barn behind the Wellington Hotel. By 1868, this had been replaced by a dedicated Orange Hall built nearby.[11] The Orange Hall, like others of its kind across the province, was a small, wooden, starkly plain building with shuttered windows to keep out prying eyes.

Most of the wealthiest, most prominent men in town were members. Charles Percival, one-time owner of the Wellington Hotel, donated the land for the hall, and Matthias Moore was said to be the Lodge's master. Other businessmen and craftsmen would have donned robes and joined

A decaying barn that seems to encapsulate the fortunes of Falkenburg Junction. This turn-of-the-century building stands on the site of the Wellington Hotel/Roscoe House and the Orange Hall, both of which were destroyed by fire in 1889.

the secret society as well. The highlight in the social calendar was apparently Guy Fawkes Day, when the members joined for a raucous, celebratory dinner.

Besides hosting the mystery-shrouded meetings of the Lodge, the hall also served as a polling station during municipal elections until 1880. Why place a polling station inside such an insular building, instead of a more open location such as the school or one of the hotels? The answer might be political in nature. In many of these elections, Matthias Moore was on the ballot for the local council. English Protestants, who could be expected to vote for him, would have little problem entering an Orange Hall, but Catholics or members of foreign nationalities would be intimidated by this building so infused with patriotism and fraught with mystery. In effect, the elections were rigged.

When Falkenburg Junction began to atrophy after 1884 and businesses began to close or move to Falkenburg Station, membership in the Lodge began to dwindle. It was no longer active by 1890, and while its demise is not recorded it is likely to have been consumed by the fire of April 1889 that destroyed several nearby buildings, including the adjacent hotel.

Falkenburg Junction School

As Falkenburg Junction's population swelled, the need for a local school became increasingly evident. Settlers began talking privately among themselves about building a school to save their children the walk into Bracebridge. The initial meetings to that effect were held in 1867 and were attended by many concerned locals. Matthias Moore, having himself benefited from a thorough education, was a strong proponent of schooling and played a prominent role over the ensuing years in guiding the Falkenburg School.[12]

The local schoolhouse, SS #3 of Macaulay Township, was established sometime between 1868 and 1870, and was located half a mile north of the Junction on the eastern side of the Muskoka Road. No one knows exactly what it looked like, as no photographs or descriptions have survived. Matthias Moore kept a detailed diary of events in Falkenburg Junction and makes no mention of a school being erected, an event that he, as such a strong advocate of both education and his adopted community, surely would have taken part in. Therefore, we can surmise that the school probably occupied an abandoned settler's cabin — a common enough occurrence in those days.

The number of children attending would have fluctuated by the season. Older boys would have been required to help with farming and logging efforts for much of the year, which obviously was to the detriment of their schooling, but the average class probably numbered between thirty and fifty students.

Matthias Moore remained active in school affairs, becoming a school trustee in 1873 and then being elected to the Macaulay Township school board in 1875. Later, he became the board's chairman, while his son Arthur served three terms as trustee for SS #3. Some of the school board's instructions directed towards schoolmasters provide a valuable insight into education in pioneer Muskoka. In 1878, for example, the board recommended "a strict investigation by the teachers to be carried out every morning, and in the case of uncleanliness, to send the children home."[13] This type of discipline was probably inspired by the outbreaks of illness (such as measles and influenza) that occasionally swept through the region and were believed to be the result of poor hygiene.

In 1883, the board instructed that "it will be part of their [the teachers'] duty to give one Scripture lesson each day to all children under their charge, whose parents don't object, as they consider it the best text book."[14] This, obviously, was before the separation of Church and State was mandated into the public education system.

Beyond educating Falkenburg's youth, the schoolhouse also hosted all manner of community functions. Everything from dances and Christmas plays to village meetings were held inside. It's also been suggested that area Methodists might have held religious services here.

When the Northern Railway decided to run its tracks well south of the village, the impact was immediately felt throughout Falkenburg Junction. The schoolhouse might have been the sole exception that carried on as before. It would take several years for the migration to the new village of Falkenburg Station to have any appreciable impact on class sizes, and even then numbers still warranted a school at the Junction.

In fact, a new schoolhouse was built in 1887. By this date the original structure was showing its age, so it was replaced with a frame structure. The lumber came from Matthias Moore's mill, while money for its outfitting was raised by public donation.

This school was the last vestige of Falkenburg Junction's pioneer past to close, graduating its final class in June 1938. By that time the village had virtually disappeared, the student body was less than a dozen, and the move to centralized schools was well underway; the day of the one-room schoolhouse had come and gone.

Trying to find any evidence of the school today is a vain quest. The building itself has long since gone, likely dismantled by wood salvagers, and its site overtaken by regenerated forest. There's nothing, except for old black-and-white class photos of sullen-looking students, to mark its existence.

Falkenburg Junction's Post Office

It was often said in the nineteenth century that a community had come of age when it acquired a post office of its own. The opposite can be said as well — you could mark a community's demise by the date on which the local post office was closed. For Falkenburg Junction, the time between these two milestones was only thirty years.

The post office of Falkenburg Junction opened on August 1, 1863, making it the first post office in Macaulay Township.[15] William Holditch was the first postmaster, performing his duties from his own home, but he remained in the position for only two years. On May 1, 1865, Thomas George took over.

Thomas George was something of an entrepreneur, and at the time he was the most important man in town, with the hotel, store, and shingle mill under his ownership. Assuming the position of postmaster only cemented his prominent status in Falkenburg Junction. Unlike William Holditch, George didn't have to operate out of his residence. Instead, the post office occupied a rear corner of the Falkenburg Store.

In late 1871, Thomas George sold most of his assets to Matthias Moore and relocated to Parry Sound. The government quickly confirmed Moore as the new postmaster, and he ran the post office from an addition purposefully built onto his house.

Less than a year after changing hands, the post office was robbed by a masked desperado who burst into the building and levelled a pistol at the clerk, demanding all the cash, money orders, and stamps (history doesn't record who was operating the post office on that notorious day). The valuables were quickly handed over and the bandit raced from the building, vaulted onto an awaiting horse, and beat a hasty escape. It was a scene more familiar to residents of the American West than those in Muskoka, but it aptly demonstrates the frontier nature of Falkenburg at the time.[16]

Since there weren't any stages regularly frequenting Falkenburg Junction, it fell to members of the Moore family to pick up and deliver the mail. Typically, this was the responsibility of the younger boys who were not yet old enough to work full-time in the mill. Their frequent travels by buggy over the rutted roads may have been uncomfortable and time-consuming, but certainly they had a leg up on Falkenburg Junction's first postmaster, William Holditch, who trekked on foot to and from Bracebridge every week for the mail.

In 1879, mail service was extended to the village of Bardsville, located about ten kilometres west of Falkenburg Junction. A contemporary mail schedule tells us that a round trip by the Moore boys took the better part of five hours: they would leave Falkenburg at 10:00 a.m. and Bardsville at 12:30 p.m.[17]

Though it was the Moore children who handled the mail run, and Matthias's name was on the postmaster title, it was Susan Moore, Matthias's wife, who dealt with the day-to-day operation of the post office. She was well educated and by all accounts a good businesswoman, so Matthias was probably more than willing to let her handle its affairs while he devoted his time to the mills and his farm.

As a result of her prior experience in handling the post office, when Matthias died suddenly in April 1893, the government willingly transferred the title of postmaster to Susan's name and there was a smooth transition. But with Falkenburg Junction's fortunes already in a steep and unrecoverable dive, and the population dwindling rapidly, there was no longer any justifiable reason to maintain a post office in the village. As a result, on October 6, 1894, after more than thirty years of existence, it was closed.

The loss of the post office was just the latest in a string of blows that humbled this formerly buoyant community.

The Moore Family

Matthias Moore probably deserved a better fate than that which awaited him in the wilds of Muskoka. He was a truly good man, generous and caring, but in true pioneer mould he was also hardy, enterprising, and a tireless worker. Success should have been his right; few would have been more deserving. Instead, however, the railway snatched away his prosperity and indeed his legacy just before they could be cemented. It must have been devastating for the man.

Courtesy Patricia Evans.

Matthias Moore was not the first person to settle in Falkenburg, but he was the most important. In addition to farming, and ably assisted by his extensive family, he ran the village post office and operated the sawmill that provided jobs for struggling homesteaders. Many proud descendants of this industrious pioneering family continue to live in Muskoka to this day.

Although Matthias Moore was a prominent individual in his time and his descendants are represented in considerable numbers about the region, the man is little remembered in Muskoka today.

Matthias was born in Aston Leicestershire, England, on February 24, 1825. His family must have been comfortably wealthy, because he was commissioned an officer in the Life Guards Regiment in 1845 in an era when commissions were still purchased, not earned, and did not come cheap. He had the honour of riding in the Duke of Wellington's funeral procession in 1852.[18]

But, of course, military service consists of more than performing ceremonial functions, even in the British Army famed for its love of pomp and pageantry. Occasionally, one must go off to war, as Matthias did against Russia in the Crimean War of 1854–56. This conflict saw a total of twenty thousand British soldiers die, the majority from cold and neglect rather than on the battlefield. Moore shared the privations and dangers of the campaign with his men, gaining their trust and respect. But perhaps more importantly, the experiences of the war hardened him considerably into a tough, self-reliant, and spirited man, traits that made him ideally suited to thrive in the wilds of Muskoka.

By 1864, Moore was due for a promotion to captain, but he was passed over by a younger, inexperienced officer whose wealthy family simply purchased the rank. Moore was embittered, promising then that this would be the last the army would see of him, nor would it have his sons. Turning his back on Britain, Moore headed for Canada.

In tow were a wife, Susan Fielder, a woman who stood over six feet in height and weighed 250 pounds, and eight young children (two more would be born in Canada).[19] Matthias proved to be a loving father, and he was actively involved in raising not just his own children but also, as situations later dictated, several of his grandchildren as well.

Their first season in Canada was nearly disastrous. Upon arriving at his Muskoka land grant, Matthias pitched a tent, naively believing it would be sufficient to house his family for the winter. When a neighbour inquired as to when they intended to build a log cabin, Matthias replied that he had plenty of "good English blankets" to keep his family warm until spring. The man smiled at the newcomer's innocence and rode off, only to return a few days later with a crew of men who proceeded to erect a cabin for the Moores. If not for the chance encounter with the neighbour and the assistance of other settlers, it's likely few of the Moores would have survived the winter.[20]

They did survive, however, and after that there was no turning back for the industrious family. Within a few years they had established the second-largest farm in the township, at 589 acres, and were growing a wide variety of crops.[21] At the time, there was precious little else in Falkenburg, but with the trained eye of a military man Matthias immediately grasped the strategic importance of the new crossroads and decided to profit by it. He built a sawmill nearby to supply the lumber for the thriving village he knew would emerge there, and he subdivided his land into residential lots for the expected influx of settlers.

When his optimism proved misplaced and Falkenburg in fact did not develop as he had anticipated, Moore was forced to work that much harder on the farm and in the mill to provide for his ever-growing family. Sadly, this punishing workload and the privations he endured during the Crimean War took their toll. His health began to suffer in the late 1880s and he was forced to pass off much of the mill operations to his son Albert.

Matthias Moore died in 1893, at the age of seventy-one. Were his final days embittered by the twist of fate that doomed his town to obscurity and that undermined his fortunes? He had every right to be bitter, and surely no one looking back at his life of toil and tragedy would have blamed him if he was. Yet, the man doesn't seem to have been capable of self-pity. His diary entries present a person who was resigned to his fate but in no way despairing over it. "In God is my trust," Matthias wrote in 1886, at which point his health was already fading and his beloved village in decline. "Nothing shall make me afraid."[22]

But the Moore legacy didn't end with Matthias's death. There were, after all, ten children to carry on his name and, in some cases, his work.

Eldest son Francis (Frank) married Jane Samways, and together they had four children, one of which, Ada Louise, died of measles at age three and is buried in Moore Cemetery. Their son George Bernard would go on to play a prominent role in the Moore sawmill industry. Sadly, Jane died at the age of twenty-four, leaving three youngsters behind. With her death, something snapped inside Francis, and he was never the same again.

Soon, in Matthias's own words, "rows about money were becoming more frequent" between him and his son.[23] Then, inexplicably, Francis put spurs to his horse and fled to Toronto with new flame Marion Roscoe, leaving behind his worries and his children. Matthias took in his three grandchildren, raising them as his own.

Francis wasn't the only child to run away. Daughter Fanny eloped with James McNab and resided in Victoria, British Columbia, where they were blessed with eleven children. Matthias was not amused by this carefree act of love. He did, however, approve of Emma's marriage to Scottish tailor Alexander Cleghorn, whom she met while working as a seamstress in Toronto. The couple later moved to Los Angeles and had one daughter.

George worked for many years in the lumber shanties, supervising the harvest of trees for the family mills, but later moved to Toronto, where he built pianos for the Nordheimer Piano Company. Later, he went into business for himself. He wed Elizabeth Jane Clark and had four children.

Saxon Moore, the first child born in Canada, also worked for many years at the sawmill and in the lumber shanties. He was also a talented blacksmith, and was shoeing horses and repairing wagon wheels in Falkenburg well into the twentieth century. He married Jessie Keal, and the union resulted in ten children. Saxon was best friends with his nephew, George Bernard, who was actually only seven years his junior.

Tragedy struck down two of Matthias's sons. Harold died of an inflamed lung while still a child, and Gilbert (known as Chad), who drove the mail cart to Ullswater, was mortally shot by a cousin in a hunting accident. Before Gilbert was killed, he had married Maude Mills and had a daughter.

Nellie, or Helen Maud, had a tranquil life. She married farmer James Jennett and lived on a farm near Orillia. The couple was never blessed with children. Alice Moore, by contrast, had anything but a quiet life. When the railway was being built nearby, she fell in love with an impoverished Italian labourer named Pasquale Chermola. Matthias didn't approve, but they married anyways. During the course of their long, happy life together they lived in Italy, Kentucky, and West Virginia, and had at least three children.

Matthias Moore might not have had the success he so desired with his varied enterprises — the mill, farm, and post office — but he was a wealthy man when it came to family. Many proud descendants of this industrious pioneer continue to live in Muskoka to this day.

4
DEE BANK

Researching Dee Bank was both challenging and rewarding. After discovering that this village was at one time "equal to any in the district,"[1] we began to wonder why it hadn't been featured as prominently, for example, as Swords and Falkenburg Junction in ghost town literature. In time, we came to understand why. The little hamlet was one of the earliest communities in Muskoka, and also one of its shortest lived. Memories of Dee Bank's heyday are several generations removed, fleeting, and often wholly incomplete.

It was almost more than we bargained for. But the fascinating story that emerged as the research unfolded made the frustrations all worthwhile.

The once bustling village of Dee Bank was both a crossroads hamlet and a mill town. In 1868, where the Dee River rushes down from Three Mile Lake, John Shannon bought two hundred acres of land and built a large gristmill and companion sawmill. At the time, Shannon's gristmill was only the second such operation in the whole of Muskoka (the first being Bailey's at Bracebridge), and to the early settlers it was a godsend. Dee Bank became an important community because of it.

A strategic position along Muskoka's primitive network of roads also ensured Dee Bank prominence, if only temporarily. The village was the hub for three roads, including one that ran to Bracebridge and another that linked with the Parry Sound Colonization Road. A steady stream of traffic passed through the village, and it wasn't long before an inn was built catering to road-weary travellers.

The Dee Bank Hotel's presence dates back to around 1878.[2] Establishments offering food and shelter were required at thirty- to fifty-kilometre intervals because of the bad state of the roads. In addition to travellers, the hotel could count on the patronage of locals. Hard-working

From Illustrated Atlas of Parry Sound and Muskoka District, 1879.

Dee Bank sketched in 1879. The artist, Seymour Penson, was noted for his accuracy, so this illustration is as close to a photo of the short-lived community as we have.

men such as mill labourers, farmers, and lumbermen would gather in the barroom on Saturday nights to quench their thirst and drink away the stresses of a long week.

With the mill and hotel providing prosperity, Dee Bank grew rapidly. From a handful of modest farmsteads, by the end of the hamlet's first heady decade it had grown into the largest settlement in Watt Township. In addition to the mills and hotel, the village included a store and post office operated by John M. Barber, a tannery jointly owned by James Barber and a Mr. Bowman, and several craftsmen, foremost among them a blacksmith.[3]

The early settlers of Muskoka were by and large God-fearing and determined that their children should have both a religious upbringing and an education. As soon as a cluster of homesteads began to come together as a community, some local citizen would usually step forward to donate an acre of land as a site for either a church or a school, and then the entire community would pool its resources to finance and build the structure.

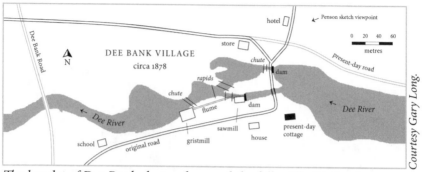

*The hamlet of Dee Bank clustered around the falls. All of its businesses —
the store, the mills, the cheese factory, the hotel — were located alongside
or near the waterway.*

Dee Bank was no different. By the mid-1870s it boasted both a
Presbyterian church and a schoolhouse. Wood for both came from
Shannon's mill, and bees (as gatherings for the purpose of performing
some task were then known) were called to throw up the walls and roof.

In its heyday, the proud population of Dee Bank numbered around
seventy-five, proud in part because many observers felt the community
had a bright and prosperous future. *The Gazeteer and Directory of the
County of Simcoe, including the District of Muskoka for 1872–73* noted
that "the soil in the vicinity is very productive and the township is rapidly
increasing its wealth and population."[4]

In 1883, John Barber sold the store and post office to his brother,
forty-two-year-old farmer James Barber. Whereas John was proprietor
for only a few short years, James would become an institution in Dee
Bank, running the businesses for the balance of the century.

Changing transportation patterns undermined Dee Bank's early
potential. First, the coming of the steamships inevitably stole the
spotlight from inland communities and focused it on those along the
shoreline. As a result, and despite boasting one of the largest gristmills
in the district, Dee Bank began losing its prominence to the nearby
port of Windermere. Businesses and settlers began to cluster there at
Dee Bank's expense.

But while the growth of Windermere was a severe blow, it was the
arrival of the railway, and the trend for industry to locate rail-side, that

ultimately doomed Dee Bank and dozens of little hamlets like it. Road traffic dwindled, depriving way station hotels of business. Industries that were not linked to rail lines found they could not compete and eventually closed.

The hotel closed, never having seen the twentieth century. The tannery, which never really found a niche and was overshadowed from the start by far larger factories in Bracebridge, lasted only a few short seasons. The mills fared somewhat better, but even they dwindled in importance with each passing year. By 1890 the sawmill was gone, and the gristmill was destroyed by fire around 1910. There was never any thought towards rebuilding it.

Many farmers were just as disillusioned. There was a disastrous grasshopper plague in 1873–74 that caused widespread crop failure, and several severe winters in the early 1880s led to famine-like conditions. By the time Canada West was opened for settlement, few Muskoka settlers required any encouragement to forsake their bush farms and head out to the Prairies.

Such, in brief, was the fate of Dee Bank. James Barber watched the village's steady decline unfold around him. He recognized that with each business that closed and every family that caught "Manitoba Fever," the day when he would have to give up his store and post office was closer at hand. The mercantile was first to go, closing in 1897. Six years later, in July 8, 1903, the government closed Dee Bank's post office.[5] Barber moved to Bracebridge shortly thereafter.

Gradually, those few residents who remained likewise drifted away. Today, only the sound of gurgling water greets visitors to the former village site.

Our search for Dee Bank took us to the waterfall, where it all began with Shannon back in 1868. We walked the rocks, looking for anything that would take us back in time. There was little to see, beyond the placid millpond that stretched out below us. Back along the road, our attempt to locate buildings that might have been part of the community was equally fruitless. It was only towards the end that our perseverance was rewarded by discovering the former church/school. This lone building is all that has survived of a once active community.

Maybe with our help, Dee Bank will be remembered for a little while longer.

Dee Bank Church/School

Homework has an entirely new meaning for the owners of Dee Bank's sole remaining structure, the once abandoned nineteenth-century schoolhouse. Instead of poring over books and struggling to stay alert during lessons, the homeowners have laboured lovingly to transform this former community building into a charming country home.

Private residence is actually the structure's third function. When built back in the 1870s, it initially served as a house of worship for the local Presbyterian congregation (Methodists had to travel to nearby Ufford for services). John Shannon had donated a parcel of land on the eastern outskirts of the community as well as the lumber from his sawmill for its construction. Shannon's neighbours had volunteered their time to help erect the building.[6]

This building, the only one remaining from Dee Bank's brief heyday, has had a varied career over the past century. It began as a church, was later turned into a schoolhouse, and has since become a private residence.

The church was a natural focal point for the community, and a place of much pride. That's why it hurt so much when, with each passing year, the congregation shrank as Dee Bank was slowly strangled by fierce competition from Windermere. It soon became evident to one and all that the church's days were numbered.

By the 1890s, the population of Dee Bank had shrunk to such a degree that it was no longer capable of filling the pews regularly. The congregation anguished over the decision but really had no recourse but to close the church and then travel to the up-and-coming village of Windermere for worship.

The building wasn't empty for long, however. While Dee Bank no longer had enough Presbyterians to support a house of God, the area farms were still home to enough children to require a school in the vicinity. So, with the original schoolhouse (built sometime in the early 1870s) showing its age, the trustees purchased the former church and moved classes there in 1895.

Class sizes in SS #5 of Watt Township were never large, partially due to the proximity of another schoolhouse in Windermere just a few miles down the road. Probably no more than twelve or eighteen students attended at any one time, most of whom walked five or six kilometres (or more) to and from school daily. Poorly served by children, the school was also a revolving door of teachers throughout its existence, with no schoolmaster lasting longer than a few seasons at most.[7]

One of the more memorable teachers was John Kaine, who served from 1934 to 1936. "He was a very good teacher, one of the best," remembers Dee Bank resident Aubrey Bogart, then a teenaged student. "I remember one of Kaine's eyes was at a ninety-degree angle, which allowed him to see kids fooling about even while his back was turned writing on the chalkboard. You couldn't get away with much with Mr. Kaine."[8]

As the years passed and the farms in the region dwindled in number, class sizes inevitably shrank. By 1938 the student body was so small that the school had to be closed. Rather than sitting empty, however, the building was used as a community centre. It was employed in this capacity for nearly two decades, but then in 1957, in a surprise move born of desperation, the school was reopened because of the sudden increase in the number of students in the area. The school was closed a second, and ultimately final, time in 1965.

Later, the building was sold and transformed into a private residence. During its near 140-year existence, the former church and school has seen few structural changes. At some point during its educational career it was bricked over, but beyond that it remained — and remains today — remarkably well preserved.

Dee Bank's Mills

The most lucrative profession in any nineteenth-century community was that of miller. Running a sawmill or gristmill was a dream job, the kind with which a man could make his fortune. Consequently, ambitious men were always on the lookout for fast-flowing streams to power such industries. In the late 1860s, this quest for riches brought one man to Dee Bank and set in motion a chain of events that would see the largest gristmill in Muskoka raised on this unexceptional river.

But the story begins rather humbly, when Scotsman Archibald Taylor raised a primitive sawmill on the falls in 1866. Little is known of the man himself, and he was as much a mystery to his contemporaries as he is to modern historians: "We never knew much of Taylor," writes Seymour Penson, "he was a dark-haired enigma of a man."[9]

Likewise, no one knows why he abandoned Dee Bank and moved a few miles downstream, to Clarks Falls, a mere year or so later. There the mill, which had been moved in its entirety, thrived for several years. "His whole outfit was pretty rough," writes Penson, "and the one-inch lumber that he sold was of many thicknesses. There was no sorting of lumber into classes at Taylor's. He knew but one price, and that was $8 per thousand feet all round."

In 1868, John Shannon was lured to Dee Bank by the sound of the rushing water as Three Mile Lake emptied into the Dee River. Shannon knew that there was wheat being grown in large quantities in the fertile fields nearby, and decided this was an ideal place to erect

Dee Falls in mid-summer. It's hard to imagine this was once the site of the largest mill in Muskoka; for most of the year water runs lazily down the chute and would have been incapable of powering machinery.

a flour mill. It was a sound idea. The closest mill was in Bracebridge, more than ten miles away over poor roads, so there was definitely a need for a local option.[10]

Shannon hired Frank Newel, an Englishman with considerable experience in bridge and other construction work in the old country, to build the gristmill's frame. Initially, work went well. "There was plenty of good pine to work with and good men to help," noted William Albert Shea in his book, *A History of the Sheas*, but below the surface trouble was brewing.[11] Newel was a difficult man who "stood for no interference from anyone" and resented any input from his employer. The mill would be built his way, or it wouldn't be built at all.

The two bull-headed men repeatedly locked horns. Shannon felt it was his right, as owner, to make his wishes known and offer advice. Newel considered any suggestions, no matter how tactfully expressed, to be stepping on his toes. The pent-up animosity eventually exploded in a heated argument that quickly came to blows. As curses were thrown back and forth, Shannon reached out, grabbed hold of Newel's beard, and ripped a chunk out of his face. The builder responded by swinging a two-by-four like an oversized baseball bat, narrowly missing his target. Had it landed, there is no doubt that Shannon would have been killed or gravely injured by the blow.

At wits' end, Newel packed up his tools and ran, not stopping until he reached Saginaw, Michigan. In his wake, he left the framing timbers lying about like the pieces of a giant jigsaw puzzle. No one could figure out how they were to go together, which left Shannon in a terrible bind. If he ever wanted his mill completed, he knew he'd have to grovel before Newel. It wasn't a prospect he relished, but there was no alternative. Work stopped for over a year while he tracked down the runaway builder, and it was only with great reluctance that Newel returned to his task.

The entire community had a stake in the mill, so they watched with interest for progress in its construction and anxiously awaited the call to assist in raising the frame. The settlers lent their assistance with no thought towards payment, "save for the service the mill would be for the area." Bees were always popular events, a time for the community to come together in work and play. The men would labour while the women cooked bountiful meals the likes of which were rarely seen in those days of hardship. George Summers, who as a young boy was present at the raising bee, vividly remembered the event even in his golden years: "There was three days of the event, and what a time. All you wished to eat."[12]

Despite its troubled construction, the completed gristmill was a marvel of workmanship. The imposing structure stood three storeys high, was well lit thanks to numerous windows, and had plank floors that were smooth and flawlessly laid. It was said that there was not a single mistake in the whole building. Shannon equipped his masterpiece with the best machinery money could buy.

At the time, the mill was only the second in Muskoka and for many years thereafter was considered the largest and finest to be found north of Orillia. Shannon didn't content himself with just this enterprise, however. Ever ambitious, he also added a sawmill built in the shadow of the gristmill.

Unlike the gristmill, his sawmill did not have the finest machinery. Instead of the more modern circular saw, he utilized the obsolete up-and-down arm band saw. There was no shortage of timber to feed the saws; farmers clearing their land for cultivation provided logs by the dozen, and would continue to do so for many years. Three Mile Lake provided an easy and convenient means of delivering the logs, which would be collected in the water and towed to the mouth of the Dee River by steamship.

The twin industries thrived for about twenty years, but by the late 1890s they both began to suffer, though for different reasons. The sawmill's demise was a result of the exhaustion of lumber around Three Mile Lake, while for the gristmill it was the flight of farmers from the region, which cost the mill most of its patrons. The once majestic building, reduced to a sad and largely lifeless shell, was put out of its misery in a fire (which many believed had been purposefully set) that burned the mill to the ground sometime around 1910.[13]

When the ashes had cooled, there was little remaining. Today, there's even less. The millpond is still evident both from the bridge over the Dee River and by scrambling down the embankment of North Shore

Road. When the water is lower, step across the rocks amidst the river and look carefully at your feet for the rusted spikes that once anchored some aspect of the operation imbedded in the stone. Most of the year, the river trickles rather than flows, working its way down the rocks so gingerly that it's hard to imagine it could ever power a gristmill, let alone one of the largest mills in all of Muskoka. Just one of many surprises Dee Bank pulls on us.

James Barber

The name James Barber might not mean much to you or me, and is all but forgotten in modern-day Muskoka, but in the small community that was nineteenth-century Dee Bank this name loomed large. James Morrow Barber — storekeeper, postmaster, miller, farmer, and tanner — was probably the most prominent individual in Dee Bank. So much so, in fact, that for most of its existence, he and his various enterprises seemed to define the community.

But this story doesn't begin in Dee Bank. It begins in Fingal, Elgin County, Ireland, where James was born to Phineas S. Barber and Susanna Marr in 1842. Hoping for a new start, the family fled the famine-ravaged Emerald Isle for Canada. Here, in 1866, James married eighteen-year-old Emma Margaret Johnson and began a family of his own.

In 1870 the young couple, accompanied by James's brother John, arrived along the shores of the Dee River to take up land.[14] James and Emma quickly turned the bush lot into a prosperous farm, complete with a large herd of cattle. James recognized that a great many of his neighbours likewise kept sizable dairy herds and came to the conclusion that a tannery would likely be viable.

With additional financing from a fellow settler named Bowman, Barber began construction in 1872 at a site on the north shore of the Dee River just to the east of the bridge. The tanning process depended upon hemlock bark, which is rich in tannin, for use in the chemical bath that converts animal hides into tanned leather. Thankfully, hemlock trees were once as common as pine in Muskoka's forests, so there was no shortage. Many farmers earned additional money by heading into the bush to harvest the bark, usually in June, a time when the bark peels easiest from the trunk and when the farmers were enjoying a brief hiatus between seeding and haying.

In 1880, John Barber had acquired the local post office contract and opened a general store.[15] Three years later, however, he caught "Manitoba Fever" and moved out west, but not before selling his business to James. Whereas John was proprietor for only a few short years, his brother would become an institution in Dee Bank, running the store and post office for the balance of the century. Later, he also added the gristmill to his business holdings, by which time he owned the entire business core of the little hamlet. James Barber's many contributions to the village earned him the respect and affection of nearly everyone.

His success was short-lived, however. Dee Bank had faded badly by the 1890s, and so too had Barber's prospects. The tannery had long since closed and the mill was running at far reduced capacity, leaving Barber to support his family almost entirely with the store and post office. Unfortunately, with each passing year, the clientele dwindled as people moved away in ever-increasing numbers. The shrinking customer base meant that each year Barber remained open was merely postponing the inevitable anguished decision. Finally, in 1897 all pretense was given up and the general store closed. Barber maintained the post office for another six years, but on July 8, 1903, the government closed it down as well.

At loose ends and too old to return to farming, James Barber sold his farm to Albert Briese and moved to Bracebridge. He died there in 1910 at the age of sixty-eight. His twelve children scattered, many ending up in the United States, and as a result the Barber legacy in Muskoka is largely forgotten.

James Barber had a hand in most of Dee Bank's enterprises and, as a consequence, in the community's success. But therein lay the problem. Barber's fortunes were so intricately linked with those of Dee Bank itself that when the village died so too did his ambitions. Sadly, James Barber had hitched his horse to the wrong wagon, tying his fortunes to a place with no future.

It was a tale repeated in ghost towns and vanished villages all over Ontario. We shun failure, and so the enterprising gentlemen who formed these communities are forgotten today. But for their fellow townsfolk, men such as James Barber were extremely important. Through their industries they provided prosperity for their respective communities (if only temporarily), and symbolically these self-made men represented the hopes and dreams that all settlers carried with them as they braved new frontiers.

The Bogarts of Dee Bank

Serene in idyllic surroundings as it is, it's hard to believe that scarcely 125 years ago Dee Bank was one of the busiest and most prosperous commu-

nities in all of Muskoka. In fact we probably wouldn't have believed it all, nor been able to picture the hamlet and its people, had it not been for the memories of Aubrey Bogart, an amiable farmer who has called the area home for all of his eighty-eight years.

It was through the memories of third-generation Dee Bank farmer Aubrey Bogart that the little-known community truly came to life for us. His grandfather, J.C. Bogart, was the first settler in these parts.

Bogart takes pride in the fact that he, his father, and his grandfather have all toiled over the same land, that Bogarts were here at the beginning to watch the village come to life, and that Bogarts are still here today long after Dee Bank became a ghost town. This family, humble and hard-working, has been here for it all.

James Cyrus Bogart, a former officer in the British army, and his wife, Eleanor Cook, arrived in Watt Township in 1861. They were the very first settlers in the vicinity of Three Mile Lake, and it was several years before anyone else came to join them.

When others finally did arrive in 1863, there was a moment of controversy as up to thirteen families erected temporary shanties along the shores of the lake on land claimed by Bogart. Two years later, when surveyors mapped Watt Township, it was discovered that the families were indeed squatting and that they would be forced to move on. It was a sad, painful moment for many of these settlers, as neighbours had developed into friends, but no record exists of any harsh words or hostility towards James Cyrus Bogart.

Perhaps one of the reasons these families were so reluctant to leave was that Bogart's land was some of the best farmland to be found anywhere in Muskoka, an unusually rich clay field ideal for cultivation. In fact, Bogart was enjoying bountiful wheat harvests within a year or two of clearing the fields.

"Before the mill arrived, my grandfather, J.C. Bogart, had to go all the way to Bracebridge to have his grain ground into flour," explains Aubrey, a faraway look in his eyes as he recalls stories told to him as a child. "He used a dug-out log canoe to take him across the lake and then walked the rest of the way. It was a twenty-mile hike along narrow footpaths — there were no roads then — so J.C. would head out in the morning with a bag of grain on his shoulder and not return until evening."

"One time," Aubrey suddenly chuckles, "J.C. was on his way home after dark. He came across this big wildcat, a lynx you see, standing smack in the middle of the path. The cat didn't move and held its ground. J.C. dropped his bag of flour on the ground and gave that darn cat the strongest kick he could. He got the worst of it though! He banged up his toes pretty good, because it wasn't a wildcat, just a punky stump!"

For reasons that are understandable, James Cyrus greeted the arrival of the Shannon mill in town with enthusiasm. The combination of bountiful fields, a determination to succeed, and a nearby mill allowed Bogart to prosper in a fashion many Muskoka farmers would have been envious of. But even so, life could still be harsh and cruel. Diphtheria, the scourge of so many settlers, claimed three of Bogart's children, two girls and a boy, all of whom were carried out of his home in the span of a week.

In time, the family farm was passed on to his son, and then to his grandson, Aubrey, who still runs it today.

By the time Aubrey took over the reins, the vibrant village his grandfather had a hand in founding was no more. In fact, he vividly remembers threshing hay in fields where rotting lumber piles and shallow depressions represented former homes and businesses, indicative of how rapid the community's decline truly was. But he attended the one-room schoolhouse, recalls the fiery demise of the mill, and watched as Dee Bank's last remnants fell prey to the passage of time.

The community is no more, and yet it remains alive in his memories. It's only fitting that a descendant of J.C. Bogart, the first settler at Dee Bank, should be one of the few still residing there and one of even fewer who remember anything of the vanished village.

5
GERMANIA

Like most ghost towns, Germania lives on only in the fading memories of those few who remember its glory days. With each passing year the community is disappearing as farm lots become overgrown, buildings sag, and the last ancestors of the original settlers leave our world. But the spirits of this former farming village are still with us, and if you stop to listen you might hear them whispering through the trees, reminding us of Germania's rapid rise and tragic fall.

Located deep in the heart of Draper Township, surrounded by dense forests and low, swampy lands, Germania is an odd location for a farming community. But with southern Ontario already occupied by sprawling farms, by the middle of the nineteenth century this wild and unforgiving land represented the new frontier of settlement, unsuited though it was for farming. Therefore, in an effort to accommodate the seemingly endless influx of immigrants eager for land, Draper Township, along with the remainder of Muskoka, was surveyed and opened up for settlement by the Free Grants and Homestead Act of 1868.

Looking back, it all seems like some kind of cruel joke. The land here is, in most cases, beyond the limits of reasonable cultivation. The soil is shallow and lacking nutrients; the rock upon which Germania rests is only a few inches below the surface. There are a few pockets of relatively rich soil, but callous surveyors did not confine the lots they laid out to these choice areas. Worse, prospective owners wouldn't have the opportunity to inspect properties before signing their names to the deeds. Lots issued in an office in Toronto all looked alike, and to the naive newcomers they were equally enticing. It was only when the families arrived at their lands that the truth sunk in.

One can only imagine the shock and dismay the immigrants felt when first laying eyes upon their new homes. Clouds of mosquitoes and blackflies gladly welcomed the newcomers, one's nearest neighbour would be miles away, and the bush was so thick and unruly that a person would be swallowed up after stepping only a few feet off the road. In the thin light that streamed through the dense forest the task of turning this rugged wilderness into the prosperous farms they had been promised must have seemed all but impossible.

And yet, the German immigrants who settled this part of Draper Township to establish Germania gamely set themselves to the task of replacing trees with golden fields of wheat. It didn't matter how wretched the land was, or how cruelly the government's betrayal stung, at the end of every day of seemingly endless labour the settlers' hearts still felt light. For them, the land represented the hopes of creating a new and better home for themselves.

It was a tough task, to be sure. The climate was unlike that which they were used to in the Old World, especially the desperately cold winters, while the Anglo language and culture were equally foreign and made

Courtesy Mary Fitzmaurice.

The first task upon taking up land was to clear it for cultivation. If this task was not completed settlers could — and some did — starve to death over their first winter. Women were not exempt from this labour; they worked alongside their husbands as equals.

integration difficult at first. They no doubt learned many harsh lessons in their first years in Canada.

Despite hardships, these hardy settlers defied nature through sheer determination. By the mid-1870s, farms had indeed replaced forest and Germania was surrounded by fields lush with wheat and oats. Ontario was then a major exporter of grain to the British Empire and beyond, so a decent crop would provide the farmer a handsome return. The community prospered and grew.

There were some fifteen to twenty families who initially settled Germania, but among the crowd two names seemed to stand out: Gilbert and the Weissmuller. These families, who were interconnected by marriages both in Germany and here in Canada, form a thread of continuity in the village's history and are notable for their varied contributions to the community. The story of Germania is, in a very real sense, the story of these two founding families.

Brothers George and William Gilbert, who hailed from Hesse-Darmstadt, were among the first to arrive in Germania. As fate would have it, their properties straddled the crossroads that would become the heart of the community, and it was largely through their generosity that Germania would come to boast both a church and school.

In 1876, the villagers decided to build a church as a sign of their faith in the Almighty. William Gilbert donated a parcel of land on the southeast corner of the crossroads, Herman Weissmuller provided lumber from the sawmill he operated on Weissmuller Lake several kilometres to the south, and the entire community came to erect the structure. Services were held in both English and German. For a time the village had a resident minister, who resided in a parsonage provided by the community. After that building burned down, ministers would be brought in from Gravenhurst, with members of the congregation providing both transportation and accommodations.

In 1888, a school (SS #2) was built for the sum of $405. By that date, the community of about seventy-five people also boasted a post office, one or two general stores, and Nick Weis's blacksmith shop.

The largest business in Germania was undoubtedly the sawmill of the Weissmuller Lumber Company, founded by Herman Weissmuller on nearby Weissmuller, or Germania, Lake. Though small in comparison to the huge mills ringing the larger Muskoka lakes, Weissmuller's steam-powered mill was a vital local industry. It provided the lumber needed to sustain Germania's growth, enabled farmers to earn cash or barter by providing the mill with trees culled from their properties, and offered winter employment to many local men.

Herman Weissmuller, the father-in-law of George Gilbert (through his daughter Katherina), was a weathered man in his fifties when he arrived in Canada. But despite his relatively advanced age, he set himself to the task of clearing fields with the energy and dedication of men half his age. It was probably while cutting down the vast forests to reveal the precious soil below that Weissmuller hit upon the idea of establishing a mill. Why not make use of all those trees?

The mill thrived and operated until the early 1920s, when it burned down. After flames claimed the mill, the Speicher family purchased the blackened steam engine and removed it to their property, where a new mill was erected. This too burned down, drawing a curtain on the lumber industry in the Germania area.

Herman Weissmuller didn't have all his eggs in the one basket, however. As early as 1880, he was operating a general store alongside his sawmill, selling all manner of goods to area residents. Short of making the trek to Uffington, about sixteen kilometres northwest along rutted and winding roads, this was the only shopping opportunity the villagers had.

This was the height of Germania's fortunes. Who could have known that within two or three generations, the community would for all intents and purposes have disappeared? There was no one dramatic event that spelled the doom of Germania as a community. Instead, it was just a slow sagging of fortunes that played out over half a century.

Despite the hard work and resilience of the farmers, fewer than half were able to establish farms that lasted into the twentieth century. The land simply would not support anything beyond subsistence-level farming, and many families decided to pull up stakes and seek new opportunities in the newly opened Prairies or find employment in the towns and cities. Slowly but surely, Germania began to fade away.

Yet the little hamlet would not die. The indomitable will of the pioneer descendants would not let it. While the population dwindled with each passing year, life in Germania carried on much as it did before. People still tended to family farms, some selling milk, butter, and cream to a local dairy or wool to a small woollen mill in Bracebridge. Horse and buggy remained the primary mode of transportation well into the 1940s. It was as if time had ground to a halt in the village.

But really, time stands still for no community. It advances onward, relentlessly, leaving relics of the past like Germania to shrivel like fruit on a rotten vine. By the 1950s the once proud village was a sad, withered shadow of its former self, home to only a handful of people. The post office closed in 1957 and the school only three years later.

Germania — the village of yesteryear, not the collection of modern homes that occupy many of the pioneer lots — is now all but forgotten. Most of the residents are only vaguely aware of the history that surrounds them. But one person can still wistfully remember a time when Germania was a going concern: Mrs. Velda Gilbert, a woman who has called the village home for all of her ninety years, was willing to share her knowledge and memories, and to guide us through what remained of the community.

One of the few original buildings still standing tall and proud is the Gilbert Lutheran Church. The building has not been appreciably altered since the day it was built, and the walls whisper stories of long ago. Music from the faithful pump organ still fills the room during services held monthly each summer. To enter this beautiful building is to step back in time.

Surrounding the church with the souls of bygone congregations is a small cemetery, the final resting place for the families that founded the community. We walked side by side with Velda Gilbert among the fading and cracked tombstones, she pointing out relatives who have left her, we soaking in the memories she shared. It was only then that we truly began to comprehend how tight-knit the community was a century ago. Neighbours weren't just friends, they were also quite literally family.

Directly across from the cemetery is a blue house where Mrs. Gilbert was born and raised. She stops and looks around to recall her father, who worked the very land that stood in front of us. "He did all his plowing by hand, and never once complained," she says and spreads her arms wide. "All of this was fields of wheat and oats and beans. We also kept cattle for milking. It was a hard life, and a good life."

But that was a long time ago. We got a sense of the time that has passed since Germania was a thriving community when we visited the former schoolhouse, located just west of the church. To look upon this weathered structure was heartbreaking. Unlike the church, it doesn't show any signs of being cared for. Its days of grandeur are long gone; time has taken a terrible toll on this former home of knowledge.

Elsewhere, former concession roads leading to bush farms are overgrown and often barely visible. Along them, one finds occasional hints of the farms of yesteryear — a fence post here, a lilac bush there. The mill that once served Germania disappeared long ago and left no traces behind. No longer does the whine of saws echo across the tranquil surface of Weissmuller Lake. Today, only residences line the shores.

The mill, like Germania as a whole, has disappeared into the past. Gone, yes, but not forgotten. At least not so long as people like Velda Gilbert keep the memories alive.

Schoolhouse

Muskoka is a land of wild and rugged beauty, unsurpassed for its glorious views of countless lakes and vibrant forests. But this visual splendour masks a land that proved obstinate to settlement, a land where simply surviving on a bush farm proved an endless challenge. With the unrelenting demands of the frontier farm, one would have thought that schooling would have taken a back seat in the minds of early settlers. As Germania aptly demonstrates, this was actually far from the truth. Instead, the pioneer settlers were eager to see their children educated and quickly built a schoolhouse to that end.

The school section that encompasses Germania, School Section #2 (SS #2), was formed in 1868 even before the Germanic settlers began to settle the lands in large numbers. The first school was held in the private home of a Mr. Hydman, located a mile or so north of Germania, which was rented for six months starting in May 1869.[1] This building was probably a crude log cabin that Mr. Hydman had abandoned after his farm was established and he found the means to build a more respectable frame home to reside in. Certainly, it was quite common for early schools to be located in empty settlers' shanties.

Mrs. Spence was the first teacher, hired for the pitiful sum of $70.[2] When she was subsequently rehired for the following year, she managed to pry an additional $10 from the tight-fisted school trustees, but it was still a terribly modest salary. In general, the life of a pioneer schoolteacher was anything but comfortable.

In 1872, a new log school was built on the Thomson property by D. Lamont and his brother for a total cost of $114.[3] Because it was located on their farm, this school became known as Thomson's Corners, but it served a far wider populace than just those in the immediate area. Children from Germania, for example, had to endure a daily two-kilometre walk both there and back. Perhaps enjoyable in summer, this

The bell no longer rings at Germania's schoolhouse, and the peal of children's laughter can no longer be heard from the overgrown yard. Built in 1888 and closed seventy years later, until recently it served occasionally as a community centre.

trip was inconvenient and uncomfortable in the winter. Nevertheless, the school seemed particularly well attended. An existing register shows that in January 1880, some forty-three students were in attendance.[4]

By the late 1880s, Germania had established itself as the centre of the school section, so it only stood to reason that the school itself should be located there. The situation was finally addressed with a new frame building, erected just west of the village intersection in August 1888. This handsome new building cost the proud community $405.

The Germania school had numerous capable and respected teachers, but the one who stands out the most is Mrs. Julia Weis. No teacher did more for the school than she, even though her period of service was only a few short years. Julia Weis was born and raised in Germania, the daughter of farmers John and Caroline Weis. At first she taught in Barkway, where she boarded, but in 1911 she got the school in Germania just across the road from her parents' home.[5]

"She was a wonderful person, so kind, always helping someone," remembers her niece, Evelyn Weis Lawrie. Her generosity was best felt by the children she taught. "The school had exactly one hundred books, bought and paid for by Julia. She also sent to Eaton's for a tennis set and marked out a court in the schoolyard. Every Sunday thereafter, all the young people would gather and play." The entire community, but most especially the pupils, must have been devastated when Julia married John Sullivan and moved to Michigan in 1916.

After the Second World War, centralized schooling saw the demise of the one-room schoolhouse. The end for the Germania school came in 1960, after which time children were bused to Bracebridge. The aging school sat empty and was virtually ignored. For reasons unknown, it didn't enjoy the same lavish care that the church just down the street did, and subsequently time began to take its toll.

So much so, in fact, that it's almost heartbreaking to look upon the sagging structure today. The paint has faded, the yard is overgrown, and the walls are beginning to lean wearily. All the hard work and sacrifice of the early settlers, men and women who attempted to bring knowledge and education to the young minds of the community, is slowly wasting away. As we strive to preserve the past with our words, it's difficult for us to watch an important historical building — one of the few examples of a pioneer schoolhouse in Muskoka that has yet to be converted into a residence — being so grossly neglected. Instead of cherishing it for future generations to enjoy, perhaps as a teaching tool, it is allowed to slip away.

When it's finally gone, we will have lost a valuable link to the past, as the schoolhouse reflects more than a century of Germania's history, tracing its development from its beginnings to its eventual demise. It's a profound testament to the values of those who came before us, showing that to these German settlers Canada represented not just an opportunity to acquire land but also, perhaps more importantly, to create a better life for their children.

The Blacksmith Shop

No pioneer farming community would be complete without a blacksmith shop, and Germania was no different. Around the crackling flames of the forge, hammering upon the anvil and pumping the bellows as he served the varied needs of the town, was Nicholas John Weis.

Nicholas (Nick) John Weis was born on October 27, 1870, the son of local farmers John and Caroline Weis. Instead of following in his father's footsteps by depending on the bounty of the land for his livelihood, Nick elected to take up the trade of blacksmithing. After a time apprenticing in a nearby community, he returned to Germania sometime in the early 1890s and set up a board-and-batten smithy on the corner of his parents' farm facing the road and almost directly opposite the schoolhouse. This represented the first time the village had the services of a local smith.

The blacksmith was an important man in a developing community. While it was the most important part of his job description, the blacksmith performed many vital tasks beyond the stereotypical shoeing of horses. He could make nails and essential wrought iron cooking ware, mend a harrow or a plough, and forge tools or hinges. If the machinery at Weissmuller's mill needed repair, the blacksmith was the one to call on. Rough roads would quickly wear down the iron

Courtesy Mary Fitzmaurice.

Nicholas John Weis, the village blacksmith, as a young man. He was the only blacksmith the village would ever know.

rims on wooden wagon wheels, forcing the traveller to stop at the smithy to have them repaired. Many blacksmiths would even make repairs on the wagons themselves.

There is some confusion about the identity of Germania's blacksmith. Many sources mistakenly list Paul Weis (or Wise, the later anglicized version of the name) as the artisan in question, but his niece, Mary Fitzmaurice, is quick to point out that not only did Paul never serve as village blacksmith, he didn't even reside in Germania! It gets even more confusing, because Nick Weis, who was in fact the blacksmith, was known locally by his middle name, John.

Nick was far from the stereotypical blacksmith — burly, brash, unkempt, and uncouth. Instead, he was slender of build, quiet, and unassuming. Even though he didn't talk much, everyone in town held Nick in high esteem. "He was our neighbour and a very friendly fellow, a real nice man," remembers Velda Gilbert.[6]

Nick Weis remained behind the forge well into the twentieth century and into the automobile age. Horse and wagon remained a principle means of transportation in much of Draper Township into the 1920s and beyond, ensuring a steady demand for the blacksmith's services. "Uncle Nick shod all the horses around, including Barkway, Uffington, you name it," remembers Mary Fitzmaurice. "But when he married he moved to Toronto and became a home builder. My cousin, Virginia Speicher, and I often played in the abandoned shop as kids."[7]

When Nick Weis moved away in the 1920s there were still some wagons upon the rural roads of Germania, but with each passing year they dwindled in number. Nick was among the last blacksmiths in Draper Township, the last of a rapidly disappearing breed of man. The closing of his doors seemed to represent the end of an era.

Nothing remains of the smithy today. The forge has long since cooled, the anvil no longer echoes under a rain of hammer blows, and the building has been torn down. The era of the blacksmith, even in Germania, has long since drawn to a close.

Weissmuller Lumber Company

It's hard for anyone coming to a new country, with a new language and lifestyle to learn. The young at least are able to adapt, but older individuals are more set in their ways. For them, it's particularly hard starting anew. Imagine, then, coming to this country as a middle-aged pioneer and finding yourself in the midst of an absolute wilderness. Overcoming nature, conquering a harsh and unforgiving land, was a young man's game, after all. So what do you do? Some might choose to live off the land, while others would seek to exploit it. Herman Weissmuller chose the latter.[8]

Herman Weissmuller was born in Ahlfeld, Hesse-Darmstadt, Germany, in 1816. He was already a weathered man in his fifties when he, his wife, Maria Dorothea, and their nine children arrived in Canada, but despite his relatively advanced age he set himself to the task of building a new future for himself with the same energy and dedication of men half his age. It was probably while cutting down the vast forests to reveal the precious soil below that Weissmuller hit upon the idea of establishing a sawmill. Why not make use of all those trees?

By the 1870s, the booming cities of the American East Coast and Midwest were rapidly depleting domestic lumber sources, creating a demand that Ontario lumbermen were eager to meet. The untapped wilderness of Muskoka became the centre of this thriving industry. Salivating lumbermen swarmed in, axe and saw in hand, and fell upon the tall, proud trees that dominated the landscape.

When Herman Weissmuller decided to join this frenzy by building his sawmill on the southwestern shores of Weissmuller Lake (also known as Germania Lake) and creating the Weissmuller Lumber Company, he also established the largest and most important business in Germania. Though small by comparison to the huge mills ringing the larger Muskoka lakes, Weissmuller's steam-powered mill was extremely important to Germania and its settlers.

While it provided the lumber needed to sustain Germania's growth, more important was the effect the mill had on the local economy, particularly as it generated wealth for area farmers in a variety of ways:

farmers could earn cash or barter by providing the mill with trees culled from their properties, find winter employment in the bush camps felling trees, rent out horses to drag these same logs to the mill, and sell oats to feed the hardworking logging horses. In short, the mill sustained farmers where the soil could not.

There were no chutes or falls to harness for power, nor was there a stream large enough on which to transport logs. These geographic realities shaped the mill and how it was run. Of necessity, the mill was steam-powered. While more efficient, steam engines had an unfortunate tendency to cause fires. Slowing the process immeasurably was the necessity of dragging logs through the woods and down primitive roads by overburdened and plodding horses. Nevertheless, come springtime, Weissmuller Lake would be clogged with bobbing logs awaiting their turn at the saws.

The lack of rail access had a dramatic impact on mill operations as well. Initially, most of the lumber sawed went to area residents for building their homes, barns, and places of business. When Draper Township was firmly settled, however, this market quickly dried up. Thereafter, logs and cut lumber would be laboriously transported to Kielty's Siding at South Falls, where they were loaded onto railway flatcars and shipped to urban centres in southern Ontario and the United States.

Initially, the Weissmuller Lumber Company employed as many as six men during the whole of the year, but as business eventually tapered off the mill would operate for only a few weeks every year.

The years of building his dream, establishing a lumber mill and homestead, finally caught up to Herman Weissmuller in 1905 when he died at the age of eighty-nine years. The business was left in the trust of his children.

The mill thrived and operated until the early 1920s, when it burned down. The threat of fire was a steam-powered mill's constant companion, especially one with an aging forty-year-old engine. The Weissmuller mill was just one of many that met a fiery demise across Muskoka. When the embers had cooled, Weissmuller took stock and decided against rebuilding. The costs just didn't seem to be worth the increasingly limited returns. Instead, the blackened steam engine was sold to the

Speicher family, who removed it to their property and erected a new mill. Eventually this too burned down, drawing a curtain on the lumber industry in the Germania area.[9]

When we visited Germania, we were disappointed to find there were no longer any Weissmullers in the immediate vicinity.[10] Sadder yet, no relics of the once thriving mill are visible. Today, modern residences line the shores where the Weissmuller Lumber Company once flourished. Through its name, however, Weissmuller Lake continues to be associated with this family that conquered all odds by finding a way to prosper in a harsh wilderness.

Gilbert Lutheran Church

The village of Germania is home to one of the most charming churches in Muskoka, a building of rustic beauty and historic significance. Huddled in a clearing amidst the dense forests of Draper Township, it represents generations of strong devotion to God. And yet, with thin soil, ever-present rock, and a sea of trees determined to foil attempts at farming, one must wonder exactly what the early settlers had to be thankful for. That's just part of the mystery of Germania Nazareth Evangelical Lutheran Church.[11]

It was in 1875, at a time when Germania was just newly established and home to a mere handful of struggling farmers, that the first tentative steps towards establishing a church in the village were made. A board of trustees was established, comprising the three most prominent names in the community: George Gilbert, Herman Weissmuller, and Nikolaus Wettlaufer. It fell to them to organize the building efforts, raise the necessary funds, and acquire land.

In most nineteenth-century communities, local landholders donated small parcels of land — generally half an acre of so — upon which to build houses of worship, and Germania was no different. It was William Gilbert who stepped forward to sign over a lot, and as a result the church became known unofficially as the Gilbert Lutheran Church in his honour.

Herman Weissmuller did his part by donating the necessary wood from his sawmill. Construction took place in 1876, and by the next year the church was complete. Building the church was a community affair, but so too was maintaining it. For example, all parishioners owning farmland were required to supply a quarter cord of wood per year for heating.

To provide a home for the preacher, a parsonage was constructed opposite the church on the northwest corner of the village intersection. This meant that for a time the community enjoyed the presence of a resident priest, an individual devoted solely to the spiritual needs of Germania's residents. When the building burned down, however, the village was forced to share its preacher with nearby Gravenhurst. Residents were required to provide him with transportation to and from Gravenhurst as well as accommodations while he was in town.

In keeping with the community's ethnic nature, services were initially held in both English and German. This continued until nearly the turn of the century, by which time a new generation of Canadian-born and fluently English-speaking residents began to take over communal affairs. The village's Teutonic heritage would always remain a part of its character, but no longer would it dominate religious matters. This was especially important because by this date several non-German families, notably of Scottish birth, had arrived to add diversity to the community.

The 1890s was arguably the heyday of Gilbert Lutheran Church. Attendance was at a peak, the congregation pooled its meagre resources to purchase an organ for $40 in 1892, and in 1900 new floors were laid throughout. The church was the beating heart of the community, and it shows in the attention the residents lavished upon it even while the substandard soil was providing little in the way of profitable harvests.

Sadly, this glory period did not last long. Germania dwindled in the twentieth century, with disillusioned farmers abandoning their lands for fresh opportunities elsewhere, and as it did the church naturally began to suffer from lack of resources and attention. Finally, with the congregation no longer large enough to sustain it, the church was closed. For many years it was neglected, and as time and the elements took their toll, the building began to fall into a state of disrepair. It was slowly being embraced by shrubs and trees, while the headstones in the cemetery were choked by weeds. It was a sad turn of events for a once proud church.

Thankfully, in recent years concerned citizens have saved the building from a tragic fate and painstakingly restored it to its former glory. The dull grey siding that once covered its exterior walls has been removed to reveal the original log construction. No one can fail to be impressed by the rustic majesty of the building, and its sturdy timbers seem to symbolize the strength and indomitable spirit of those who settled this difficult landscape. Gilbert Lutheran Church is one of the few examples of non-veneered churches in Muskoka, therefore offering a unique insight into pioneer construction.

The special delight of the church is in the interior. Despite the renovations, it has not been altered since the day it was built and the whole atmosphere breathes the spirit of a bygone era. The pews, altar, baptismal font, and oil lamps are all original, and one can't help but be struck by the "mouse-proof" pump organ, donated by Charlie Speicher in 1921. Heating is provided solely by an ancient wood stove. A unique historical artifact is a copy of the lot's original land grant, issued

Courtesy Mary Fitzmaurice.

The life of an early settler was not all work. Here, Germania residents pose after a local theatre production.

February 1, 1875, encased in glass and holding a place of prominence along the church's rear wall.

The cemetery adjacent to the building gives silent testimony of the many German families that once populated this part of Muskoka. These gravestones are signposts to futility, reminding us that despite the best efforts of the early settlers to forge a lasting future in Germania, the climate and terrain proved too wild to tame. Those who lie in rest here were broken, in mind or spirit, by the very land they sought to cultivate.

And yet, despite the tragedy that is Germania, the church continues to triumph. It is the only surviving pioneer-era Lutheran church in Muskoka, and services continue to be conducted once a month during the summer, keeping alive more than a century of tradition.

Germania's Stores and Post Offices

By the 1880s Germania was a community feeling good about itself. It boasted a growing population, a thriving sawmill, and a beautiful church. All that was needed was official validation, in the way of a post office, to demonstrate that the village had come of age. It wasn't long in coming, thanks to active campaigning by Herman Weissmuller.

On September 1, 1884, Germania was officially granted a post office by the government of Canada.[12] Herman Weissmuller's son, John, was named postmaster, and the Weissmuller home served as an improvised office. Intriguingly, in spite of the efforts expended in campaigning for the position, the Weissmullers remained involved with the post office for less than a year.

William Stamp assumed the role of postmaster in July 1885 and moved its operations to his home, located across the road from the Weissmullers'. While there was a certain prestige that came with the position of postmaster, for Mr. Stamp at least it was also a physically taxing job. In those days, mail arrived at Gravenhurst by train and was then conveyed by stage to Uffington, ready to be picked up and distributed by the rural postmasters of the region. Mr. Stamp would walk the five kilometres north to Thomson's Corners to meet the stage and carry the mail home on his back. Road conditions were so poor that oftentimes he did not return until 10 p.m., exhausted from hours of trudging through snow or mud. In later years, as the exertion became too much for his aging body, Mr. Stamp purchased a horse named Lucy to help complete his rounds.

In 1906, after more than twenty years, Mr. Stamp retired and handed over his postmaster duties to Julius Rossgar (or Rusker). The new appointee was an ambitious man, a man who had visions of prospering as a merchant. To that end, he opened a combined post office and store — the first in Germania — along the shores of Weissmuller Lake. To residents of the little farming community, who previously had to venture to Utterson to purchase any of the necessities of life, the store's opening was an exciting development.

What an exciting place the store was, full of barrels of salt and flour, with bolts of cloth jostling with tools and household items for space. Many tins and boxes lined the shelves and candy lay stacked on the counter, almost begging to be eaten. Everyone loved "going to the store," a weekly outing that offered an opportunity to explore the merchandise and to socialize with neighbours in an informal and spontaneous manner.

After three years, Rossgar sold the store to Willis and Mary Couke. For ten years the couple ran the store hand in hand, but in 1919 Willis died and left Mary to manage on her own. Few women of the time independently ran a business, so had they been in her shoes many women would likely have called it quits rather than face the intimidating challenge. Mary was a strong-willed woman, however, and had been an equal partner with her husband in operating the store. Instead of selling out, she continued on alone for several years as both store proprietor and postmaster.

By the 1920s, the decline of Germania's fortunes was already well underway. The mill had closed and many settlers had moved away. As a result, the store lost many customers and business naturally suffered. By the time the Couke property was sold to the Carleton family in 1923, the mercantile was no longer deemed profitable and consequently the new owners made no attempt to continue the business.

After the store closed, residents of Germania once again were forced to travel to Utterson, or even Gravenhurst, for their shopping needs. Some items could be purchased by peddler, as Mary Fitzmaurice remembers: "There was a man from Housey Rapids who came around to the different homes with a truck and he brought groceries for the families to buy. He in turn bought the farmers' milk and Aunt Mary always sold her cheese this way."[13]

There is no doubt that when the Couke store closed, the entire community felt the loss. Having a store in the village was more than a convenience; it was also a source of pride and communal identity. Its closure was a shock, revealing in the plainest of ways Germania's ill health. Surely some residents even recognized that the village would one day perish.

But that day wouldn't come for some time yet, and in the meantime, James Kirkhouse assumed the postal contract. He, as with all the postmasters who would follow him, performed his duties in the confines of his own private residence. Kirkhouse served until 1938, when he was forced to relinquish the role when he and his entire family took seriously ill. Patrick and Elizabeth Mary Carleton took over the duties briefly, until a new postmaster in the form of James Joseph Henry could be found.

A succession of postmasters followed in the last decade of the Germania post office, but on November 30, 1957, the local post office closed for good.

By this time, Germania had gone from an energetic and close-knit hamlet to a collection of scattered farms with a fading identity. The loss of the post office only hastened the erosion of the social fabric that had once bound neighbours together, as had the loss of the store some twenty-five years earlier. In a very real sense, after the post office closed Germania no longer existed, not even as a seal on a letter.

Prominent Families

There were some fifteen to twenty families who initially settled Germania, families who did their share of living, working, and dying in the little community. But among the crowd two names seemed to stand out:

Gilbert and Weis (later Anglicized to Wise). These families, who were interconnected by marriages both in Germany and here in Canada, form a thread of continuity in the village's history and are notable for their varied contributions to the community. The story of Germania is, in a very real sense, the story of these two founding families.

John and Caroline Weis

The Weises left their mark in Germania as farmers, teachers, and blacksmiths, all important but humble occupations. While materially they were far from the wealthiest family in town, their story is perhaps the richest of any who called this community home. Certainly it's the most entertaining.[14]

John Weis was the head of this founding family. Born in Luxembourg in 1845, he was the son of John Nicholas Weis and Margaretha Federspiel. Mid-century, the family left Europe and settled in New Oregon, New York. It was here, among a colony of German immigrants, that John Weis met and wed Caroline Rosa Vialkowitsch, an ethnic Pole hailing from Wurtemburg, Germany.

Caroline came from a remarkable lineage. Among her ancestors were members of the nobility, most notably the eighteenth-century aristocrat Prince Varauski of Poland. By the 1800s the family had fallen on hard times and in 1858 sailed for new opportunities in America.

The union of Caroline and John seems to have been a tempestuous one, with Caroline later telling her granddaughters that "she shouldn't have married John because she didn't like fish and he was an avid fisherman." There was more to the unrest than merely culinary preferences, however.

After marrying, the couple settled in Dunkirk, New York, and had a fine home and farm. But when John heard about Crown lands being given away freely in Muskoka he impulsively uprooted his family and headed north. The family set out for Canada in 1878 and got as far as Washago at the northern extremity of Lake Couchiching by rail, and then had to walk the rest of the way.

Upon arriving at their lot in the depths of Draper Township, Caroline's heart sank like a stone. There was nothing but bush and rock, and it was far removed from anything resembling the refinements of civilization to which she had grown accustomed. She hated it in Muskoka and kept her good dishes packed in a barrel for more than six months, hoping beyond hope that they would go back to New York and resume their previous life.

John, on the other hand, seemed invigorated by the challenge. He was an ambitious and determined man, and immediately set to work clearing the land. It seemed the more people told him something couldn't be done, the harder he toiled to prove them wrong. John grew vast fields of strawberries even though all his neighbours told him they would never grow. "There were no weather reports to go by," remembered granddaughter Evelyn Weis Lawrie, "but he seemed to know when a storm or frost was coming and would call on everybody to help him cover the field with straw, rags, paper, and anything he could get hold of and it saved the crop."[15]

Similarly, John boasted an orchard with peach, pear, plum, and apple trees even though fruit trees were difficult to grow in the harsh climate. When the temperatures dropped he would turn up the collar of his coat and head out into the orchard to build low smug fires to help save the trees and their invaluable crops.

John also grew conventional crops such as oats and wheat, and was known for his prizewinning potatoes and carrots.

Sadly, the farm he established didn't long survive him. "Grandpa must have been a good farmer," noted Mrs. Lawrie, "because after he died and John the second son took over, the strawberries all died and all the fruit trees died." Without the ability and drive of his father, John simply couldn't make the farm work and eventually had to concede defeat. The farm was sold and he moved away. In time, as Germania's fortunes sagged, his siblings followed suit and turned their backs on the pioneer hamlet.

The farm that John Weis founded is long gone, the fields reclaimed by the regenerating forest and several modern homes replacing the pioneer-era farmhouse. In retrospect, the land was simply too stubborn

Courtesy Mary Fitzmaurice.

Though the first few years in Germania were rough, soon prosperous farms had been carved out of the woods. Most lasted no more than a generation or two, such as the Weis family farm, pictured here, which stood across from the church. Nothing remains of it today.

to be farmed with any real success. John probably should have listened to his long-suffering wife and remained in New York.

The Gilberts

The Gilbert Lutheran Church is among the most charming historic buildings in Muskoka, a landmark beloved by many. It graces magazines and newspapers, and it's a favorite attraction in the annual Gravenhurst Open Doors festival. Yet the family for whom it is named, the family whose patronage made the church possible, is almost completely forgotten.[16]

Wilhelm (William) Gilbert and his wife Margaretha (Margaret) hailed from Hesse-Darmstadt, Germany, where they were born in 1839 and 1848 respectively. Fleeing economic hardships in Germany in search of new prospects, the young couple set sail for Canada and the newly opened Muskoka District.

Accompanying them were William's brother Georj (George), two years his junior, George's wife, Katherina, and her parents, Herman and

Maria Dorothea Weissmuller (who later established the Weissmuller Lumber Company). Together, these hardy individuals would bear the weight of establishing the village of Germania.

William and George Gilbert established farms across the road from one another at what would become the heart of the community. Literally carving homesteads and fields from the dense forests was difficult work, but they persevered and their toil eventually paid off with rich fields of wheat, oats, and beans.

Even though they worked tirelessly and in the early years success was by no means certain, the Gilberts still found it in them to give to the growing community. In 1875, George provided land for the Lutheran church and cemetery at the southeast corner of the village crossroads, while William donated land for a parsonage to house the resident minister on the northwest corner. Later, in 1888, George gave further land upon which to build a school.

In 1917, exhausted by a lifetime of labour, George Gilbert passed away. He did so just as Germania was beginning its slide into obscurity. George's farm didn't long outlive him.

William, meanwhile, had predeceased his younger sibling by many years. He died in 1896, at the relatively young age of fifty-seven, leaving the farm to his son Henry and his daughter-in-law Rachel. It would be in good hands. The farm he had carved quite literally from the wilderness carried on, and indeed prospered, for another three decades under his son's able stewardship.

Henry was an excellent farmer, skilled at both raising crops and animal husbandry. His daughter Velda Gilbert, a resident of Germania for most of her ninety years, recalls, "Dad had some of the best fields around, which he ploughed all by hand. He planted wheat, oats, and beans, and we kept lots of chickens and thirty head of cattle for milking. The wheat went to feed the chickens, and the oats to feed the cows. Dad would raise calves up and sell them. It was hard work back then, but they didn't seem to mind."

To house his family, which eventually grew to include four children, Henry built an attractive home opposite the church, a home that still stands today. Its fine workmanship demonstrates that the builder's skill with a hammer and saw equalled that with a plough and harrow.

When Henry retired from the farm, there was no one willing to take up the mantle. For the first time in more than sixty years, visitors to Germania would not be greeted by the sight of golden grain swaying gently in the wind or the sounds of cows braying off in the fields.

Like so many in Muskoka, the Gilbert farm didn't survive beyond two generations. In the years after Henry's passing, fields became overrun with weeds and eventually encroached upon by forest, while the barn and outbuildings either succumbed to the elements or were torn down. Only the charming home Henry built remains, but it seems oddly out of place today, a farmhouse without a farm.

6
ASHDOWN CORNERS

The Nipissing and Parry Sound Colonization Roads, both of which were intended to open up the interior of northern Ontario, intersected a few miles west of Rosseau. As a busy crossroads, it was inevitable that a community would spring up here. This village, called Ashdown Corners, earned the distinction of being the first settlement anywhere on Lake Rosseau's northern shores. Ironically, it also became the first settlement there to die.

The first settler at Ashdown Corners was Ebenezer Sirett, locally known as "Squire Sirett," who emigrated from England in 1859. Six years later, he arrived in the wilds of Muskoka–Parry Sound District to take possession of a free land grant on the northwest side of the intersection where the Parry Sound Road crosses the Nipissing Colonization Road. There, he and his sons attempted to carve a farm from the endless rock and trees covering the precious, though threadbare, soil.

Next to arrive were Benjamin Sowden Beley and his brother-in-law Thomas Dawson, who came to Canada in 1867. Both men settled their families at Ashdown Corners, clearing land for farms and raising homesteads. Beley even ran a store that first year, located on the southwest corner of the intersection.

James Ashdown, for whom the community would take its name, arrived in the spring of 1868. Ashdown purchased the Beley store and called it the Cheap Cash Store. Its name prominently painted on the sidewalls like a latter-day billboard, the store was the most notable business in the area and a landmark of sorts — it was natural that the crossroads hamlet be named after the store's owner.

Ashdown quickly became the wealthiest man in town. In 1868 Dick Irwin built a hotel in the village catering to weary travellers. When it burned down a few short years later, Irwin uprooted and moved farther north, but James Ashdown, recognizing the strategic importance of the crossroads, built a second hotel on the same spot. He proved far more successful than his predecessor, thanks partly to his wife, who was "a good hostess and housekeeper," and the business thrived for many years.[1]

Arriving the same year as did the Ashdowns were Charles Martin and family. Their daughter, the future Mrs. Alfred Clubbe of Rosseau, wrote her reminiscences later in life, which provide an insightful description of the ordeals settlers went through simply getting to Ashdown Corners: "We landed at what was known as Cameron's Bay, the only landing at the head of Lake Rosseau. Rosseau itself was not on the map at that time. From there we had to walk three miles through a narrow brush trail to my uncle's and the mosquitoes were in the thousands to give us a welcome."[2]

By 1870, Ashdown Corners was a small but thriving hamlet, with a population of between fifty and eighty souls. At the time, it was easily the largest community for many miles. Despite the constant struggle to scrape out an existence from their bush farms, the hardy settlers found the time and resources to build several community buildings that would serve to bind the families together. The first erected was a church, followed shortly by an Orange Hall used for dances and public meetings, and then a schoolhouse in which students were educated under the stern, watchful eye of headmistress Rickards.[3]

While most settlers were farmers, Ashdown Corners boasted a surprising number of businesses. In addition to the aforementioned store and hotel, there was a sawmill, McCan's blacksmith and carriage shop, Thomas Scott's planing mill, and a sash and door factory operated by Cyrus Lawson.

The toil and turmoil of founding their village behind them, and with a solid core of businesses to build upon, there was no reason for anyone in Ashdown Corners to believe the future would be anything but bright. Indeed, most looked towards the future with confidence, sure that the little village would develop into something special.

Unfortunately, fortunes changed fast in that era, and before anyone knew it those of Ashdown Corners were mired in the quicksand. The end might be slow in coming, and people might make desperate attempts at rescue, but once immersed in misfortune a community's fate was already sealed. There wasn't one single event that doomed Ashdown Corners, but rather a conspiracy of several working together to undermine its future.

The first blow was struck when William H. Pratt decided to build a major resort at the north end of Lake Rosseau called, appropriately enough, Rosseau House.[4] When it opened for business in July 1870, it was immediately hailed as the finest wilderness resort in Ontario and wealthy people from Toronto and the United States began to flock to it every summer. The hotel became the new focus for the area, and soon businesses and settlers alike began to gravitate to it. In the process, a new community called Helmsley (now Rosseau) arose to offer competition to Ashdown Corners.

Other blows followed. Pratt disliked having to travel several miles to Ashdown Corners to pick up his mail, so he petitioned vehemently to have a post office built at his hotel. When he proved successful, it eroded more of Ashdown Corners's significance and provided yet more incentive for settlers to gravitate towards Helmsley. Then came a disastrous forest fire in 1881 that burned out many farms in the Ashdown Corners area. Rather than start anew, many families simply moved on.

The final blow came a few years later, when traffic along the colonization roads began to dwindle. This was a result both of the widening reach of railways, which inevitably reduced road traffic, and the general realization that the settlement of the wilds of northern Ontario had been a disastrous failure. Consequently, what had been only a decade before a busy crossroads was now a lonely and isolated locale of no intrinsic value, its one resource of note — servicing the traffic along the two roads — rapidly disappearing. Ashdown Corners was, in a word, obsolete.

Some futile attempts to stop its fall were made. For example, in 1893 gentlemen by the names of Anderson and Mills opened a cheese factory in the community, and in one month alone they shipped 2,800 pounds of produce to Toronto. In fact, the quality of the cheese was so high that in 1894 the industrious pair won a bronze metal in a competition that included Britain and all her colonies.[5] Their success was short-lived however, and within a few years the business had closed. It had been a last, desperate attempt to save Ashdown Corners.

By the turn of the century there was little left of the crossroads community, all businesses and most residents having long since relocated the short miles to Helmsley or left the region entirely.

The Church and Cemetery

Almost as soon as Ashdown Corners was established, its residents gathered together to build a house of worship. Such was their devotion to God that no matter how deprived they were, or how much sacrificing they did to work their new lands, their belief kept them strong. So it only seemed right that all the pioneers should donate valuable time, energy, and resources to the construction of a church. The building they erected would come to symbolize the pioneers' faith that all of their hard work would eventually pay off.

Ultimately, and tragically, it was faith misplaced.

The church was built by 1869, a plain board-and-batten structure whose simple appearance did little to reflect the important role it played within the community. The planks came from a local sawmill, and the entire congregation came together in a bee to raise the frame.

Inside, the church was unsurprisingly without the array of fine furnishings that could often be found in nineteenth-century churches. There were no stained glass windows, no elegant baptismal fonts, no statuary or screens, and no finely crafted altar. The congregation simply never had the time to mature, to acquire treasured artifacts, to grow beyond the most humble of beginnings.

But that isn't to say that the church was neglected. Far from it, the church was actually at the heart of the community. Few missed Sunday services, and a wide array of important communal functions — weddings, baptisms, funerals, and religious festivities — were held within its hallowed walls.

In October 1885, Alfred and Eliza Sirett provided a plot of land several kilometres north of the crossroads to serve as a local cemetery.[6] It's likely that this piece of land was already a family plot and that several burials had previously occurred there, but it was only in the autumn

Ashdown's demise was a boon for the hamlet of Hekkla. The residents purchased the empty and silent Ashdown Church at a cut-rate price and painstakingly moved it to their community where, more than a century later, summer services are still held.

of 1885 that the area was fenced in and consecrated as the Church of England Burial Ground, Rosseau.

Interestingly, despite being consecrated, it was only in 1897 that the land was officially deeded to the Bishop of Algoma. By this time, Ashdown Corners was well past its prime, a sad shadow of its formerly vibrant self. Its church, which had been built with such hope for the community's future, was an empty and silent shell, no longer home to faithful followers. Twisting the knife further, in 1899 the congregation at Hekkla bought the abandoned church and moved it to their community. Men arrived during the winter to dismantle the building and haul the lumber back by sleigh. Pensively watching them work was a handful of Ashdown Corners's older residents, men and women who fondly remembered a day when the church was a source of local pride and piety. Watching the building torn down must have been a painful experience.

In its new life, the church served Hekkla for nearly three-quarters of a century until it closed again in 1965. This time, there would be no reprieve; the closing was permanent. And yet, the church still breathes life, thanks to a single memorial service held every summer and tender year-round care provided by the community.

Likewise, the cemetery at Ashdown Corners continues to operate even a century after the village disappeared. Still open to the public, it lies north of the former village site, off the Nipissing Road at the end of Cemetery Road. During 2005 and 2006, the cemetery underwent major maintenance work by concerned residents from as far away as Rosseau, restoring it to working order and thereby allowing burials to resume.

The sanctity of the burial grounds is once again being respected after decades of neglect. As a result, the memories of Ashdown Corners's founding families, the men and women who died trying to tame this wild land, are being preserved and honoured.

The Nipissing Road

The wagon bounces over yet another rock before coming to a sudden, jarring halt. Cursing, the settler inspects the wagon for damage. He fears

The Ashdown Cemetery is secluded and few today know of its existence. Amongst the pines are the headstones of most of the village's early settlers, including Benjamin Sowden Beley and Alfred Sirett.

the worst. Mile after mile of ruts, mud holes, and rocks have taken its toll on the wagon, and if it has broken down, he and his young family will be forced to carry all their worldly possessions to their land grant. Good news. The wagon is fine, but thoroughly stuck. The settler swats at the mosquitoes gorging on his neck while surveying the situation. He looks around, seeing nothing but endless trees. There'll be no help forthcoming out here; the last farmstead he passed was miles back. With darkness approaching, he suddenly felt very small and very alone.

Scenes such as this played out numerous times along the Nipissing Road in the nineteenth century. Far from being a road upon which dreams were built, as it was labelled by government officials, the Nipissing Road was far more likely to lead to hardship and heartache than to prosperity.

In 1864 the government of Canada elected to open up the vast, untracked interior of Parry Sound District to settlement by creating a colonization highway that would cut through the heart of this wilderness frontier. Surveys were completed in 1865 and construction on the road began in earnest the following spring.

Commencing at the north end of Lake Rosseau, the road ran 108 kilometres northward, through inhospitable forest and swamp, over rivers and rocky highlands, before terminating at Lake Nipissing.

For much of its length the Nipissing Road, as it was known, was little more than a rough trail. And yet it was busy, very busy. Contemporary accounts record as many as thirty to forty wagons laden with immigrant families and their belongings passing through on a single day.

To serve these travellers, taverns and inns, often little more than log shanties but occasionally quite refined, sprung up along the Nipissing Road. There were dozens of them, so many in fact that at one point an only slightly exaggerating newspaper correspondent noted that there was a watering hole located every three miles. If the comforts of civilization were hard to find out here in the wilderness, then at least a shot of whiskey to chase off one's fears at failing in this harsh land wasn't.

Also developing along the Nipissing Road were tiny hamlets, each one located about sixteen to twenty kilometres — or an average day's journey — apart.[7] Like the taverns, these communities existed almost solely to cater to road-weary travellers. Here, settlers could find a store to purchase goods, a blacksmith to shoe a horse or repair a wagon, a post office to mail off a letter to concerned relatives, or a church in which to pray that the decision to uproot their family and settle them in this frontier wasn't a terrible mistake.

Though the road remained primitive, it remained in steady use for two decades. But the arrival of the railway in Callander in 1886 diminished its importance. It was far faster, to say nothing of more comfortable, to travel by train than in a bone-rattling wagon for days on end. Predictably, use of the Nipissing Road began to dwindle, and as it did the taverns and villages along its length withered away like fruit on a winter vine.

As decades passed, the forest began encroaching upon the road, in time overwhelming vast stretches. With a few exceptions, the Nipissing Road is today accessible only by off-road vehicles. Its length is littered with abandoned cemeteries, overgrown farms, and broken dreams.

McCans's Carriage and Wagon Shop

The Parry Sound and Nipissing Colonization Roads, the lifelines of the region along which thousands of settlers struggled on the way to their forest homesteads and upon which all local trade depended, were, despite their importance, in most cases hastily constructed and poorly maintained. They were pitted with potholes, protruding rocks, and quagmire-like mud patches and inevitably took their toll on the wagons and horses passing over them.

Early Ashdown Corners settler Henry Hugh McCans correctly surmised that a blacksmith shop located in the crossroads hamlet would do steady business from broken-down vehicles and animals.[8]

Hugh McCans was born in 1826 in Dunmore, County Newry, Ireland. The infamous Potato Famine, during which tens of thousands of impoverished Irish perished from starvation, caused a tide of desperate immigrants to sweep up against Canadian shores. McCans was among this wave of humanity, arriving in the 1840s and settling in Merrickville, in eastern Ontario.

On December 25, 1849, he married Jane Nelson of Montague Township, Lanark County. The couple resided a few years in Merrickville, then moved to Madoc, and eventually found themselves lured by the promise of the free land grants to the hamlet of Ashdown Corners in 1870.

Hugh was a blacksmith by trade who supplemented his income by farming his two hundred acres of land. It's easy to equate blacksmiths with horseshoeing and nothing more, but that would provide an incomplete picture of their value to the community and detract from their expertise. In addition to forging horseshoes, blacksmiths repaired farm equipment such as ploughs and furrows, rimmed wagon wheels, made a variety of tools and farm implements, and crafted household items such as pots and hinges. In short, if the product was metal, a blacksmith was expected to be able to make and repair it.

A man of energy and vision, McCans recognized the growing need for wheel transport in the area, and as a result by 1879 he had expanded his business from a simple smithy into a carriage shop where he made wagons, buggies, carts, and cutters. Even in its heady early days Ashdown Corners was still a small community, so beyond building perhaps a few vehicles every year most of McCans's time would have been spent repairing wagons and performing the traditional functions of a blacksmith.

McCans prospered as long as traffic along the colonization roads remained steady. His home life, however, was troubled. He and Jane had ten children together, but only three reached adulthood. The others perished from diseases such as smallpox and influenza, two — twelve-year-old Elizabeth Ann and nineteen-year-old Henry — dying in 1876 alone.

The three surviving children led disparate lives. Sarah (1850–1907) married John Mainprize and moved to Penetanguishene. Robert (1867–1941) inherited the family farm and remained in the area; his descendants live in the Rosseau area to this day. John (1861–1941) was also a farmer but had to move away in search of land of his own to cultivate.

By the late 1880s, traffic along the colonization roads had dwindled considerably as the web of railways spread further across northern Ontario. It was likely around this time that Hugh McCans, by now approaching seventy years of age, closed his smithy and carriage shop. Too old to tend to the fields, he retired to Rosseau, where he died on December 19, 1908.

His legacy, in the form of the still-standing carriage shop, constitutes the most vivid reminder of Ashdown Corners's brief existence.

Sawmills of Ashdown Corners

Sawmills played an important role in most northern communities. Lumber was a vital commodity and milling a lucrative business, so it followed that someone would step forward to seize the opportunity to fill local needs. Ashdown Corners was no different in that respect.

In fact, many of the businesses that formed Ashdown Corners's core depended on the nearby sawmill at Shadow River for their survival.

The Shadow River (at that time called White Oak Creek), a winding river that begins near the hamlet of Hekkla and empties into Lake Rosseau, is hardly impressive in its size but nevertheless runs deep and strong enough to have sustained milling operations for many decades.

The first mill at Ashdown Corners was erected shortly after the first settlers arrived, likely in 1869 or 1870, and was built solely to meet local demands for lumber. Just who established this sawmill is lost to the mists of time.

We do know the mill was located near the second bridge along the Nipissing Road that spans the Shadow River. We also know there was a shingle mill attached, and that the mill supplied wood for Cyrus Lawson's sash and door factory, Hugh McCans's carriage and wagon shop, and Thomas Scott's planing mill.

Beyond these few details little about the mill is known. Sometime later, a newer mill was built by a Mr. Bennett and a Mr. Hunstein on the site of the original mill. Some logs came from as far north as Turtle Lake and were driven down the river come springtime, though most were harvested from local farms and hauled along the Nipissing Road by horse and sleigh during winter. As with the first miller before them, Bennett and Hunstein made lumber only for local consumption.

When the timber in the area began to run out around the turn of the century, the millers moved their operation to the shores of Turtle Lake.

Beyond these two rather modest mills, the Shadow River witnessed logging on a much greater scale. Every spring from around 1880 to 1900, hundreds of logs would be driven down to Lake Rosseau from the heavily forested interior, every one of them destined for the Mutchenbacker Mill at Rosseau Falls. It was an operation that dwarfed the mills at Ashdown Corners in scope and in wealth.

Charles Beley, who was raised on a farm near the mouth of the river, vividly recalled in his later years the spring drives he witnessed as a child: "When I was a boy I have seen White Oak Creek full of board timber from the Lake two miles up, without a knot of shake in any of the pieces, all virgin pine."[9] These logs, which could have come from as far away as Long Lake, would be towed by tug east to Mutchenbacker Bay, cut into lumber, and then shipped to the railhead at Gravenhurst for delivery to American markets.

The demise of the Mutchenbacker sawmill in 1904 spelled the end of logging operations on or along the Shadow River. Today, the idle mill site at Ashdown Corners is long overgrown and no trace remains of the operation. For its part, the Shadow River reveals nothing of its brief fling with fame and its role in the frenzied lumber industry of yesteryear.

Hotels of Ashdown Corners

When people think of Muskoka's hotels of yesteryear, the image of one of the grand old resorts — perhaps Windermere House or Clevelands House — is automatically conjured up in the mind. But as enchanting as this picture might be, it represents only half of the total picture.

Less well known, but just as vital to the development of the region, were the humble roadside establishments that catered to common travellers. In a day when roads were poorly built and rarely maintained, travel was limited to a bone-jarring sixteen to twenty kilometres per day. At each interval, one would be sure to find a hotel or two. Accommodations might not have been lavish, but to road-weary people it would have felt like heaven. Most of these establishments have long since been forgotten, among them Ashdown Corners's Humphrey House, Junction Hotel, and Nipissing House.

As soon as the Nipissing Road was established, hotels catering to travel-worn traffic sprung up all along its length, providing food, drink, warm beds, and welcome respite after a day's long journey. According to a contemporary newspaper account, "there was now a beer agent [a hotel or tavern] every three miles" along the Nipissing Road.[10] In many cases, these establishments provided one of the last comforts of civilization, in the form of companionship or drink, before the settlers disappeared into the untamed land to take up their isolated homesteads.

The Humphrey House, the first inn to appear in Ashdown Corners, was one of the more important of these stopping places, thanks to its strategic location astride the crossroads of two busy colonization roads — the Nipissing Road and the Parry Sound Colonization Road.

The hotel's founder was William Irwin, a fiery Irish immigrant who had apparently previously tried farming without much success. He did, however, know his way intimately around a barroom. In a day when hotels existed largely on the sale of alcohol, it was therefore perhaps natural that Irwin should try his hand at the hospitality trade.

Irwin arrived in Ashdown Corners in 1868 and immediately built Humphrey House (sometimes called the Humphrey Hotel) on the northeast corner of the crossroads. Humphrey House stood an imposing three storeys tall — though the third floor was probably given over to the Irwin family quarters — with a large and "well-appointed" dining area capable of seating twenty. As many as a dozen guest rooms occupied the second floor.

The hotel featured a separate barroom; after all, it was unseemly to drink in front of women and children. Unlike many in his era, Irwin did not consider alcohol to be the devil's drink. In fact, according to some accounts, booze flowed so readily at Humphrey House that it seemed as if Irwin might be trying to make up for all those establishments that had gone dry. This barroom surely must have seen its share of drunken antics, but unfortunately none survive to be retold.

Behind the hotel stood a large stable to accommodate the horses of overnight guests and a sizable garden where Mrs. Irwin grew all manner of vegetables.

If in 1870 or so Irwin had taken the time to reflect upon the hotel he most certainly would have swelled with pride. Humphrey House was a fine establishment and a thriving business. A constant stream of travellers marched into the hotel and headed straight to the bar to flush the dust from their throats. The only known photo of the hotel shows at least five or six wagons hitched out front, and it was said that Irwin's sons were kept busy all day pumping pails of water to refresh weary horses.

Success would be short-lived, however. Around 1871 or 1872, a fire broke out in the hotel and began to spread rapidly, flames licking hungrily at the wood. The Irwins and their neighbours fought desperately to control the fire, but it was a losing battle. Despite their efforts, the inferno soon engulfed the entire building.

The fire marked the death of Humphrey House; Irwin never rebuilt. Instead, he pulled up stakes and moved farther north along the Nipissing Road to the village of Dufferin Bridge.[11] Here he built a sawmill and a new inn, called Irwin House, but he could never recapture the success he had achieved with Humphrey House.

With Irwin's departure, a void emerged in Ashdown Corners. There was still a need for an inn, both to serve travellers and to serve as a social heart for the community. Town founder and tireless entrepreneur James Ashdown stepped forward to fill the void with a new hotel, built upon the foundations of its predecessor, which he dubbed the Junction Hotel.

Like Humphrey House before it, the Junction Hotel did steady business selling liquor and providing accommodations. Mrs. Valettia Ashdown was noted as "a good hostess and housekeeper."

By the late 1870s, Ashdown Corners began to be eclipsed by the village of Rosseau to the east. Businesses and settlers began to gravitate towards this rising community, and it was only a matter of time before the shrewd James Ashdown relocated to this new centre of economic activity.

But the hotel didn't die with his departure, at least not yet. It continued into the late 1880s or early 1890s, lastly under the name Nipissing House and run by Benjamin Ross. But by then the opening of the railway as far north as Callander had siphoned away most traffic on the Nipissing Road and there was simply no consistent business to be had.

Ashdown Corners and its hotel soon disappeared from history.

Today, the forest has reclaimed the former hotel site, but for a few short years the lively inn — under its various identities — had been a bustling centre of activity. Its star had glowed brightly, if briefly.

Ashdown Corners School

During Ashdown Corners's earliest years, there was no school to educate the children of the handful of settlers who had taken up residence at the frontier junction. But it's not as if the youngsters were running wild; they were desperately needed, boys and girls alike, on the homestead. Education was a luxury these hard-pressed people could not afford.

Around 1871, Georgina Rickard (later Mrs. Harry Sirett) took it upon herself to open the first school in the region. It was a private venture, unsupported in any way by government funding, and may have followed the traditional British model of elementary education that saw parents paying for the privilege of sending their children to school. The school was located two hundred metres north of Ashdown Corners at the west side, but lasted only a few short years.

As the population in the northwestern area of Lake Rosseau increased and the families had settled in, a larger community school was built to provide free education to the children of both Ashdown Corners and nearby Rosseau.

SS #1 was built in 1873 and opened that fall. At that time, township councils had the power to tax only those with children, and only to raise sufficient funds to pay for the teacher's salary, not construction. As a result, money for building the schoolhouse was raised by public donation, with storekeeper James Ashdown providing the lion's share

There were only three teachers in the thirty-year history of the school, which was unusual in an age when most rural schoolhouses saw a new teacher almost every year. The first headmaster was Mr. Harper, followed by Miss Walker, and then finally Mr. Heatherington.

In 1903 the school section was divided into two and the Ashdown Corners school closed. While the village of Ashdown Corners had all but disappeared by this date, there remained numerous farms in the area and few parents were pleased to discover that their children now had to walk to Rosseau and back every day.

To remedy this intolerable situation, the locals elected a board of trustees (including secretary-treasurer Arthur Redfern, Robert McCans, and Joseph Philips) and began to raise money for a new school. By

1909, $750 had been raised and local carpenter W.C. Stoneman was hired to erect a frame school, measuring 30 feet by 20 feet, on Lot 76, Concession 2.

The school was a true community effort, so it was fitting that several of the teachers over the years came from the immediate area. Elizabeth Jane McCans, the granddaughter of blacksmith and carriage-maker Hugh McCans, occupied the position for a brief period in the 1920s, while the final teacher before its April 3, 1947, closure was S. Amy Beley, a descendant of one of Ashdown Corners's founding fathers.

With the exception of the addition of a larger porch and new coats of paint, the schoolhouse had remained virtually unchanged from the time of its construction. Another sixty years has passed, and it still hasn't changed a whole lot, despite the fact that it now serves as a private residence.

Ebenezer Sirett

Though the community would take the name of another man, the first to settle at Ashdown Corners was Ebenezer Sirett. Far from being

Courtesy Rosseau Historical Society.

resentful of the newcomer, Sirett embraced him. He went so far as to encourage a union between the two families.

But while "Squire" Sirett was willing to allow another man to enjoy the spotlight, there was no doubt that it was he who was

Ebenezer Sirett was the first settler at what would become Ashdown Corners. Such was the respect in which he was held that neighbours began to refer to him as "Squire," an English title indicating a certain level of status and prominence.

Ashdown Corners's true founding father.

Born in England, Ebenezer Sirett brought his family to Canada in 1859 and settled in Etobicoke (in present-day Toronto) on a rented farm. While Sirett proved to be a capable farmer and more than able to extract a comfortable lifestyle from the soil, he felt restless there. After all, it was every man's dream to own land to call his own.

The Free Grants and Homestead Act was a godsend for men such as him. No sooner was Humphrey Township surveyed and opened for settlement than Ebenezer Sirett arrived, sons in tow, to stake his claim. He was so eager that when he arrived in September 1865 he was the first settler anywhere on the northern shore of Lake Rosseau. He found himself in virgin wilderness, a true pioneer.

Sirett and his boys became the owners of five lots, composing a total of one thousand acres, along the north side of the Parry Sound Colonization Road and astride the Nipissing Road. They spent several months clearing land and building a log cabin before returning home to wait out the winter months. Spring thaw found them back in Humphrey Township, and by summer they were soon joined by Mrs. Sirett and her daughters. One can only imagine how intimidated the women must have been by the towering trees, the strange sounds of the darkened night forest, and the harshness of the climate. It was not a lifestyle for the faint of heart, certainly.

In these early days of northern settlement, it fell to the homesteaders to perform winter labour along the roadways. Ebenezer Sirett and his sons helped complete the Parry Sound Colonization Road during the winter of 1866–67, cutting down trees by the dozen so that an overland route between Parry Sound and Muskoka would become a reality. Prior to the completion of this important work, Parry Sound had depended solely on lake transport for communication and was therefore totally isolated from the time the ice set in sometime in November to its breakup the following April.

Others followed the Siretts to the region, among them the Ashdown family. Ebenezer Sirett and James Ashdown had been neighbours in Toronto and were fast friends. In fact, it might have been Sirett's encouraging words that lured Ashdown to Humphrey Township. The relationship was cemented when Sirett's son, Alfred Tom, married

Ashdown's daughter, Eliza Marsh Ashdown, on October 12, 1878.

Despite being trailblazers, individuals whom others followed, the Siretts never really profited from arriving first at Ashdown Corners. They were farmers, good ones at that, and their farm was widely considered to be the best in Humphrey Township, with decent crops and supporting prime beef cattle. But the soil here, as elsewhere in the north, was too poor to give up any riches. Ebenezer Sirett literally wore himself out attempting to transform the forest into something resembling the pastoral lands he remembered from his youth in England.

Disillusioned with what Ontario had to offer, Ebenezer's son, William, moved out west in 1881. There, he found his way into the Manitoba Agricultural Hall of Fame. Though the honorifics were his, they reflect knowledge and skills passed down to him by his father, experience that was put to good use in the fertile lands of the Prairies but had been wasted on the harsh expanse of northern Ontario.

James Ashdown

One hundred and thirty-nine years ago, in the spring of 1868, James Ashdown joined several settlers at the crossroads of the Nipissing and Parry Sound Colonization Roads. Like his fellow settlers, he had been guided here by the hope that a prosperous future could be built upon the rocks that seemed ever present in his harsh landscape. Little could he know that that soon he and the new community he would help found would become inexorably linked, that the little crossroads hamlet would take his name as its own.

Within just a few years' time, the obscure crossroads James Ashdown settled upon would be known as Ashdown Corners, an honorific symbolizing this man's importance within the growing community.

James Ashdown was born in Britain in 1829, but by the 1860s he had immigrated to Canada and was living in the village of Weston (now part of Toronto). Blessed with a solid formal education, Ashdown was serving as a clerk in a local store but dreamt of his own establishment and his own fortune.

The Free Lands and Homestead Act, which, as the name implies, offered free land to prospective settlers as a way of opening up the Muskoka–Parry Sound District, caught Ashdown's attention. Here was an opportunity too good to pass up, a chance to start fresh and be the man he always aspired to become. So in the spring of 1868, thirty-nine-year-old James Ashdown packed up his family and headed north, starting anew for the second time in his life.

He had no intention of being a farmer, however, so with a trained eye he began scouting out locations for establishing a store. Ideally, it would have to be in a growing community, a place that saw heavy traffic, and yet one not already served by a rival merchant. When Ashdown happened upon the hamlet at the crossroads of the Nipissing and Parry Sound Colonization Roads, he knew instantly this was the place. It met all his criteria: the community was small but growing rapidly thanks to its position astride two busy roads, and there was no store for dozens of miles.

There was one problem, however. All of the land adjacent to the crossroads had already been spoken for. Ashdown would have to purchase the lot for his store if it was to be located in a prime roadside location. Thankfully, Benjamin Beley agreed to sell half an acre of land on the northwest corner.

Before the end of the year, Ashdown's store was up and running, and by all accounts doing a thriving business. The building was a large, two-storey structure emblazoned with huge lettering along the side that read "Cheap Cash Store." One thing is for certain, Ashdown wasn't subtle in his advertising.

James wasn't the only Ashdown prospering in the role of shopkeeper along the Nipissing Road. His eldest son, William, had opened a general store of his own in the hamlet of Spence, located about thirteen kilometres south of Magnetewan, where he did a brisk business among trappers, Indians, and lumbermen.[12] He, like his father before him, was born to operate a general store — both men were amiable, astute, enterprising, and most important of all, willing to work long hours.

In 1871, Humphrey House in Ashdown Corners burned to the ground and its owner turned his back on the ruins. Ever the entrepreneur, James

129

Ashdown seized the opportunity before him by building a new hotel upon the still-warm ashes of the first. The new Junction Hotel proved to be prosperous, with Mrs. Ashdown — who seems to have managed its daily affairs — earning a reputation as an outstanding hostess.

By this time, James Ashdown owned two of the crossroads' corner lots and both of the most important businesses in town. It was perhaps natural that the community would therefore become known as Ashdown Corners.

It wasn't long before the hours began to take a toll on Ashdown, undermining a body that was already fragile to begin with. As James's health began to fail, William returned from Spence to assist in running the businesses. As the years passed, William took on an increased load, allowing James to ease himself into restful retirement.

Though no doubt honoured to be the namesake of the village and proud of all they had accomplished there, the Ashdown men were first and foremost businessmen. So when Rosseau began to overshadow Ashdown Corners in the 1880s, neither had any hesitation about abandoning it for greener pastures.

James sold the store to move to Rosseau, and while he was only one of many to do so, it was his loss that the community felt the most. James Ashdown was its leading citizen, after all, an astute businessman, the one individual around whom all activity seemed to gravitate, and a man whose success reflected the health of the village. When he left, not only was it a blow to the morale of the villagers, but it was also a clear sign that Ashdown Corners was in trouble.

In Rosseau, James purchased another store on the property now occupied by Hilltop Interiors (circa 2007), but he was an absentee owner. In his stead, his brother Charles managed the business. In an ironic twist of fate, the shop was later assumed by the same gentleman who had earlier taken over the Ashdown Corners store, James Brown.

When James Ashdown died, his funeral was one of the largest the area had ever seen. There was a general outpouring of praise for the man whose entrepreneurial spirit had been instrumental in not only establishing the community named in his honour but also transforming it — for a time at least — from a sleepy hamlet into a bustling village.

Benjamin Beley

The village of Ashdown Corners was born in the throes of a crazed land rush, among a throng of desperate and hopeful immigrants who flooded into the newly opened area in search of free land. During those early years, it was as a primitive community, a settlement of hastily constructed log cabins built by men willing to do anything, work to any lengths, to secure a new future for themselves.

Benjamin Beley was among this wave of humanity, but he was cut from a different cloth than most.[13] Educated, privileged, and from a wealthy background, when Beley came to town he brought with him a sense of civilization. In a day when most settlers were concerned only with growing enough food to feed their families, Beley was an experimenter, growing different types of crops while also cultivating all manner of flowers and shrubs in his garden.

But despite differences in background and manner, he shared the same diligent work ethic as his fellow homesteaders, faced the same trials and tribulations, and was driven by the same fierce determination to succeed in this alien land.

Benjamin Sowden Beley was born in 1841 in Liverpool, England, the second of two sons born to George and Eliza Beley. His father, George, was a merchant and was involved in an import/export business specializing in trade with Argentina. Benjamin's elder brother was likewise a merchant, so it was assumed that he would follow in the family footsteps. When George Beley learned Benjamin had no intention of entering the world of buying and selling, and instead had his heart set on farming, he was angry and confused. It drove a wedge between the two men that would never fully be bridged.

Benjamin proved successful as the manager of an aristocrat's Devon estate, and in 1865 found an advantageous union when he married Lucy Dawson, the daughter of a Welsh clergyman. But while he had some wealth and standing, Benjamin still lacked the one thing he truly desired: land to call his own, to do with as he pleased, to pass on to his children. He realized he would never find land in Britain, so he began to look elsewhere.

For a time it looked as though Benjamin might settle on New Zealand, but the glowing praise contained in letters from Lucy's brother, who came to Canada to work on the survey of the Nipissing Road, convinced the young couple to immigrate to Canada instead. They made the fateful move in 1867.

Benjamin ventured up to the junction of the Parry Sound–Nipissing Road first in order to pick out the lots for his homestead and improve the shanty on the property he had chosen. He then returned to Toronto for Lucy. Together they took the steamer *Waubuno* to Parry Sound, and then climbed aboard a stage for the final leg of the journey.

Benjamin makes mention of the journey in his journal: "After a great deal of needless delay, we started for Rosseau Junction [Ashdown Corners]. Lucy and the driver in front, Brooke and I behind. It was very hot and the flies troubled us badly towards evening. We dined at Matheson's and arrived at the junction a little after 8 p.m., very tired with

Courtesy Mary Beley.

Benjamin Sowden Beley transformed his crude settler's cabin, known as Oaklands, into a home of refinement and culture. When it became clear that Ashdown Corners was being eclipsed by nearby Rosseau, Beley moved to that community, where he farmed and ran a popular tourist resort, Rossmoyne Inn.

the jolting of the journey, and for my part thankful to get home into the woods again."[14]

The Beley home was little more than a log cabin alongside the banks of the Shadow River. It must have been a shock to Lucy when she first laid eyes on it, but they soon they transformed it into a centre of refinement that belied its rustic appearance. The interior was furnished with fine tables, chairs, and beds brought with them from England, and the home was renovated to include glass windows, a second floor, porch, a kitchen addition, and partial plank siding. It was transformed from a simple shanty to a comfortable home called "Oaklands" in just a few short years.

Benjamin believed in the old adage about idle hands, and worked tirelessly to improve his lot. He farmed, sold logs to mill operator A.P. Cockburn for two dollars each, and even operated the village store during his first year and a half in Muskoka. His example was an inspiration to all residents of Ashdown Corners.

Despite his industriousness, Benjamin was powerless to defy the trends that were working against the village he called home. After a decade, it became obvious to him that Ashdown Corners was in a death spiral and that Rosseau was emerging as the going concern in the area. Painful as it may have been, in 1878 the Beleys turned their backs on Oaklands and moved to a farm at Beley Point, on Lake Rosseau, just across the bay from the village of Rosseau. The home they built there, which they called "Ferncliffe," remained in the family until 1987, and Beley showed typical enterprise by both farming and running a resort called Rossmoyne Inn.

Benjamin Beley died June 11, 1896. Whereas Muskoka was a disappointment for many settlers, for Beley it delivered upon its promise. He owned land of his own that was indeed passed on to his children and their children, enjoyed considerable financial success, and perhaps most importantly, established a name and identity for himself out from under the shadow of his father.

7
MILLAR HILL

During the heady days of settlement, when land was cheap and hopes were high, rural communities grew up in even the remotest areas of Muskoka. In most cases, the soil in these frontier areas was utterly unfit for farming, the terrain rugged and unforgiving, and the sense of isolation almost overwhelming. Even the most iron-willed farmer was eventually brought to his knees by the hopelessness of the situation.

Such, in brief, was the experience at Millar Hill, quite possibly the most forlorn and isolated settlement anywhere in Muskoka. Located in the wild highlands of Sinclair Township northeast of Lake of Bays, the community — which was more a rural settlement than a recognizable village — struggled vainly to establish roots in threadbare soil and amidst an imposing forest. It also struggled with an identity, being known at various times and by various people as Millar Hill, Limberlost, the Quinn Settlement, and perhaps the most appropriate of them all, Stoney Lonesome.

The first man to attempt to tame the wilds here was David Millar, an adventurous Scotsman known as "Roaring Davie," who came to Muskoka in the late 1870s and settled along the Sinclair–Franklin Township line.[1] What possessed this man to settle so far beyond civilization is unknown, but it was certainly not in his nature to back down from any challenge and he took to the task of carving out a homestead with characteristic enthusiasm.

Within a decade, a dozen or so families had joined him in taking up land along Millar Hill Road (also named Stoney Lonesome Road). These included the Blosses, Burnses, Deans, Lasseters, Lees, Langmeades, McCanses, Quinns, Rhodes, and Shepherds. They were a disparate lot; some were Irish or Scottish, others English, but all had in common an unbreakable resolve to make something of their new homes.

Courtesy Bob Constable.

This image of the David Millar farm suggests something of the bleakness of the landscape. Millar, the first to arrive at the hamlet that bore his name, was an adventurous man who was invigorated by the challenge of taming this wilderness.

It was a hard life. Wealth in terms of dollars and cents was almost unknown, and scratching enough food from the soil to feed one's family was always a chore. Winters were unusually harsh, and far removed from civilization the community was shrouded in a cloak of isolated obscurity even at the best of times. And diphtheria epidemics were a constant threat, striking the community several times over its brief existence.

But these shared travails only brought the settlers closer together, bonding them in ways unseen in more prosperous communities. Joys and sorrows were shared alike, and neighbours were always there to lend a hand or share whatever meagre possessions they might have. To say the settlers were close-knit would be an understatement; they were family.

One of the first settlers to arrive was Joseph Langmeade, another hardened Scotsman who became almost an institution in the community. He was among the earliest to arrive, the last to leave, and in between helped Millar Hill forge an identity for itself.

Langmeade was one of the primary movers behind the founding of a school (SS #3) to serve local youth. Even though the school operated only in the summer months, it served to enlighten students who otherwise would not have received an education. Furthermore, the building provided a venue for Anglican church services and a place to hold communal meetings, both of which were important in creating the ties that bound neighbours together.

Langmeade, who lived across from the school and served as a trustee for the duration of its existence, also served as Millar Hill's one and only postmaster. He received the position in 1912 and operated the post office out of his home for the next two decades.[2]

Every community has its share of characters, quirky individuals around whom colourful tales are inevitably woven. The most unusual resident of Millar Hill was undoubtedly Robert Burns, the son of early settlers Thomas and Sarah Burns. Born in 1886, Robert was a farmer, ranger, and accomplished trapper. Local lore says that he had somehow mastered the power of hypnotism, and that he would use his mystical abilities to put other trappers into a trance and steal their pelts.[3]

Fred Quinn was quite probably the most important man in the community's short existence, and his mill, located on the Boyne River, was its lifeblood. Quinn came to Millar Hill with the intention not of cultivating the soil but rather of reaping the forests for the valuable lumber they represented.

His arrival was a godsend to the settlers of the region because the logging industry offered the promise of guaranteed, if modest, incomes that were not dependant upon the co-operation of nature as crops were. In the wintertime, dozens of men would head deep into the woods to seek employment at Quinn's bush camps, where they would spend months on end away from their families and in near total isolation. There were always enough jobs to go around, from sawing trees to cutting trails, skidding logs, and driving horses.

In April, the logs that had been cut and collected all winter would be driven downstream to the sawmill, where other jobs could be had as soon as spring seeding was completed.

For a decade or more the Quinn mill provided an economic

foundation for Millar Hill. But when it closed and moved to Dwight in the early 1910s, it left the settlers who depended upon it for their livelihood in a lurch. Destitute, many of these families faced starvation if they remained, and so they packed up their meagre belongings and turned their backs on their farms.

Behind them, the fleeing farmers left only their barns, the shells of simple frame homes, the log schoolhouse that was at the heart of the community, and the lonely figure of Henry Langmeade, by now a weathered and gnarled old man who stubbornly refused to join the exodus. His eventual passing marked the death of the community he helped establish.

It's difficult to believe today, as you walk through dense forest, that farm fields once stretched across these same hills. But every once in while you stumble upon a little clearing or pile of stone, and you realize that farms once existed here.

Courtesy Bob Constable.

The Lee House was one of the first plank homes in the area, replacing hastily constructed log shanties. This comfortable home masks the hardships faced by people settling this inhospitable corner of Muskoka.

Millar Hill School

By the late 1880s, enough families had taken up lots along Millar Hill Road that residents could for the first time begin to contemplate raising buildings to serve various important communal functions. There were now sufficient children in the area, for example, that a school was clearly required. Arrangements were duly made to fill that important niche: a convenient roadside parcel of land was acquired by school trustees, Quinn donated lumber from his sawmill located on the nearby Boyne River, and money was raised by public subscription to outfit the building.

Millar Hill's school was somewhat unique in that it operated, at least initially, for only a few short months during the summer. There were two reasons for this unique circumstance. First, the settlers at Millar Hill simply could not afford to lose their children — vital labourers even at a young age — from their farms for more than a short spell. The land here is rocky, the soil poor, the forest dense and seemingly endless. Carving out an existence in this rugged, primal landscape was a struggle during even the best of years and required dedication and sacrifice from the entire family. While everyone surely appreciated the value of an education, it was obviously of secondary importance to survival.

The other reason Millar Hill's school was limited to summer classes was the difficulty in recruiting full-time teachers. Few were willing to move to such an isolated, economically depressed region so far from the trappings of civilization. Attracting teachers for a few months in the summer, perhaps while on leave from full-time appointments elsewhere, proved far easier.

Finding that all-important first teacher was challenging, and when no one initially stepped forward to fill the position the settlers began to grow restless. In desperation, they approached Henry Reazin, a young medical student and the son of the local school inspector, to take up the appointment during his summer vacation. Eager for a challenge and looking to raise money to continue his education, young Reazin agreed.[4]

He couldn't have known what he was in for. Upon arrival, he was shocked to discover his schoolhouse was still nothing more than a pile of logs and lumber. Undeterred, Reazin worked alongside the settlers to raise the building. It took half a day to lay the foundation, and another day and a half to raise the walls and add a roof. On the third day, the first class was held in what was still a doorless, windowless building.

The students at Millar Hill School benefited from the closing of another schoolhouse near Dwight, from which a blackboard, desks, and other vital equipment were secured. It's doubtful that the settlers of the area, most of whom survived on a modest existence, could have otherwise afforded these items initially; it might well have been years before the school was as well equipped as it actually was.

This humble backwoods school was the beating heart of Millar Hill. Not only did it provide the education by which local children could secure their futures, but it also served as a social centre and as a church for the Anglican population in the vicinity.

Henry Reazin served only a single season as the teacher. There were four others over the ensuing years, including Lucy Emberson, Gertrude E. Fox, Edna Ochs, and finally Lida Pearson.[5]

By the time Lida Pearson accepted the position in 1916, Millar Hill was a community in a steady decline. The mill had closed and moved to Dwight, and most of the farmers had accepted that they could not coax a living from their stump-studded, nutrient poor fields and had gone elsewhere in search of new beginnings. During that final year, Mrs. Pearson taught no more than half a dozen children, the offspring of diehards who had not yet conceded that the village was doomed.

But even the most stubborn individual would eventually have to accept that Millar Hill's demise was pending. Most apparently did so quite quickly, because the school did not reopen again in 1917.

The schoolhouse likely would have crumbled and rotted away, if not for the intercession of Dr. Henry Reazin, who held a warm fondness for the building where he had spent a summer teaching so many years ago. Rather than watch it slowly collapse under the weight of time and elements, Dr. Reazin had the building dismantled and then floated across Lake Solitaire to a secluded spot where it was rebuilt and served as a cottage for many years.

Unfortunately, the schoolhouse-turned-cottage eventually burned down, depriving us of the last tangible reminder of Millar Hill.

The Lasseter Family

Hard labour. Extreme hardships. Privation. Tragedy. Such was existence for the settlers of Millar Hill. But amongst the trials and tribulations, there could also be moments of triumph, successes that showed just what man was capable of with perseverance and faith.

The story of the Lasseter family seems to encompass the entirety of the pioneer experience in this harsh, unforgiving corner of Muskoka.[6]

News of the Muskoka's free land grants spread far and wide, reaching across the ocean to Europe and south into the United States. One of those who found himself hooked by the promise of prosperity was Cleveland, Ohio, native Henry Lasseter.[7] For a man who spent his days in the drudgery of working in a factory, the thought of venturing into the Canadian wilderness and staking claim to hundreds of acres was exciting and adventurous. Perhaps naively, he decided to take the plunge.

His young family in tow, Lasseter headed for Canada in 1876. Upon arriving, he found the lots adjacent to or near the newly cut roads had already been spoken for, and as a result he had to go further afield than he would have liked. The land Lasseter ultimately received as his own was Lot 13; he later added Lots 11 and 12.

This was a remote, tough area, isolated from the nearest towns by miles of crude roads cut through dense forest. It would be hard work just getting to his land, and harder work to extract any bounty from the rock-hewn soil. Yet Lasseter, like the other settlers of Millar Hill, took up the challenge.

Leaving his family in Bracebridge, the eager homesteader made his way to his new land claim and, with the assistance of some neighbours, erected a simple log cabin. Only when the home had been built did he return for his wife, Hannah, and two sons, Walter and Samuel Valentine (Val).[8]

It took them three long, weary days to reach their destination, and when Mrs. Lasseter first saw the cabin that would be her home tears came to her eyes. "Do you think we are doing the right thing bringing the children here?" she said with voice cracked with emotion. Her husband consoled her. "The first appearance is always the worst," he said stoically.

Henry Lasseter settled into the role of farmer. The next four years were an endless cycle of clearing land, burning brush, plowing fields, and picking rocks from the soil. Every chore was made miserable by the clouds of mosquitoes that seemed to hover over the landscape like dark rain clouds.

Despite working tirelessly, however, Lasseter struggled with transforming his land into a sustainable farm. He had come to Canada with visions of lush fields and perhaps a herd of fat cattle, but all he seemed to find was heartache as he attempted to scratch a living from the rock-hewn terrain. Two new children came, representing more mouths to feed.[9] Many times, his family went without proper food, and the hardships they endured took a toll on his wife.

July 1, 1881, saw the family in dire straights. It had been days since they had any meat, and Henry grew frustrated watching his loved ones subsist on meagre portions. He decided to go hunting with a neighbour, a man named Wilder, hoping to bag a deer that would carry them through for a few weeks. It was an ill-fated decision. There was an accident, and Henry was shot and killed by his companion.

The blow was too much for the grieving widow. Already pushed past endurance by the demands of the bush farm, Hannah made

Courtesy Bob Constable.

Haying on an unidentified farm at Millar Hill.

arrangements to rent the land and then took her children to Toronto to live with her sister.

By 1887, Hannah had remarried and Walter and Val were now old enough to assume greater responsibility in the care of the farm, and so the family returned to Muskoka. Though little more than boys by today's standards — neither of them was yet old enough to grow true facial hair — they succeeded where their father had failed by taming the land and making the farm habitable.

The younger Lasseters were tireless, driven to succeed on behalf of their father. They offered their services as labour to other area farms, sold logs to lumber companies, and cut hundreds of cords of firewood, which they peddled around to resorts and in Huntsville. Val, the elder bother, worked winters in the logging camps.

Together, Walter and Val built a fine stone home to replace the original log cabin, using rocks harvested from their fields.[10] Within a few years they had one hundred acres under cultivation or cleared as grazing land. They also erected a solid stone fence that entirely enclosed their farm and subdivided it into smaller twenty-five-acre fields. At the time, the Lasseter farm was the only one in Muskoka that could make this claim.

But while the Lasseter boys worked tirelessly to build a future for themselves and their own families, they never forgot their ill-fated father. While most people celebrated July 1 with fireworks and festivities, for them it was always a sombre day of reflection.

Walter ultimately took over stewardship of the farm and operated it until advancing age forced him to give up the land he so dearly loved. He passed away in 1946, and with his death the Lasseter farm died also.

The Quinn Sawmill

For as long as lumber camps and sawmills operated, bush farmers such as those at Millar Hill were promised a guaranteed if modest income. It was enough on which to survive, if not actually thrive. But after the trees were exhausted, the millers and logging operators inevitably moved on, leaving the settlers who depended upon them with a choice to make: Do they remain on the farm for which they had struggled for so many years, or do they simply admit defeat and start anew elsewhere?

In most cases, the decision wasn't actually a difficult one to make. Without the hard cash promised from yearly employment in the lumber industry, farmers would face destitution and starvation if they remained on their unyielding land.

With this in mind, it's easy to see why the Quinn sawmill meant so much to the residents of Millar Hill. It was more than just an important village industry; it represented the very key to their survival.

The man behind the mill and upon whom the community's fortunes depended was Thomas Quinn, a hard-working but otherwise unspectacular individual. Born in 1845, he spent the first thirty-odd years of his life in Cartright Township, Ontario, where he married around 1870, watched with pride as a daughter was born in 1874, and then grieved when he lost his wife shortly thereafter.[11] In 1877, thirty-two-year-old Thomas wed eighteen-year-old Caroline Bailey, and four years later — with the family having swelled with the addition of two more children — moved to Muskoka in search of a new life.[12]

Thomas was a farmer, first and foremost. Like the rest of the settlers at Millar Hill, his initial years on the homestead were devoted to securing the necessities of life: a home, a barn for livestock, and cleared land for crops. It was only after completing these vital tasks that he turned his thoughts towards erecting a sawmill.

The Quinn mill was located along the banks of the Boyne River, which flows rather lazily from the highlands of northern Muskoka down to Lake of Bays. There was no waterfall near Millar's Hill, so by necessity the mill was steam-powered. This was for the better, at any rate, allowing operations to continue much later in the year than would otherwise be possible. And certainly throughout the 1890s its services were in constant demand as the settlers graduated from temporary log cabins to frame homes and barns, resulting in a steady stream of customers in need of lumber.

The sawmill was by far the largest building in Millar Hill and provided jobs for numerous local men, both in the form of cutting trees in the bush during winter months and labouring at the mill itself. As many as

Courtesy Robert Constable.

Threshing grain at the farm of Thomas Quinn, who also operated a sawmill that employed many local men. Pictured here are Richard and Tom Quinn Jr., John Low, and Frank Millar.

six men might work at the mill at any one time. One man was responsible for starting the steam boiler in the morning and keeping it running all day long, maintaining a steady pressure of steam to keep the machinery operating smoothly. Another might operate the bull chain that brought logs up from where they gathered in the river, several others would run the saws, and then one or two men would stack the freshly cut lumber. On a good day, the mill might cut ten thousand board feet of lumber.

Pine was the wood of choice, but much of the forest in the area consisted of magnificent stands of maple and yellow birch, so the mill cut significant quantities of these woods as well. Hardwood logging presented an interesting problem because hardwood logs were known to sink rapidly, meaning a great many logs would be lost being driven to the mill. It was eventually discovered, however, that if logs were peeled and allowed to dry they would remain afloat much longer. This naturally reduced loss, allowing smaller mills like that belonging to the Quinns at Millar Hill to remain viable even after the stands of softwood had been depleted.

Thomas Quinn's decision to build the mill paid off handsomely, rewarding him with a degree of comfort that was almost unheard of in the area. But while he may have been able to more consistently put food on the table and afford finer clothes, his relative affluence didn't mean he or his family was immune to the trials and tribulations common in the area. In fact, Thomas Quinn was no stranger to despair, losing four children to diphtheria within days of each other in 1894.[13]

Throughout the 1890s, sound and steam emanating from the mill filled the air around Millar Hill on routine basis. It was comforting for the settlers to hear the whine of the blade or see plumes of steam creeping across the landscape. They knew that as long as a fire remained in the boiler, life remained in their community.

But time was against these small, independent operations, and the Quinn sawmill was no different. By the late 1890s, settlers were giving up on their failing farms, abandoning partially cleared lots that were soon purchased by logging companies. This meant that the Quinns began losing not only customers but also access to timber. Inevitably, this took a toll.

It was the death of Thomas Quinn in 1913, however, that truly spelled the end of the sawmill. Like so many of the second generation of settlers, his sons saw little future in Millar Hill and didn't hold the emotional attachment to the land that their parents had. As a result, sometime around 1916 they moved the mill downstream to Dwight, a much larger community with a brighter future, where the industry enjoyed better access to markets and timber. Here, the mill continued to prosper for another twenty years before being claimed by fire in 1938.[14]

Langmeade and the Post Office

If David Millar was the namesake of Millar Hill, Henry Langmeade (also spelled Langmaid) was its heart and soul. Langmeade devoted as much energy to seeing to the welfare and spirit of the community as he did to working his own land, serving as postmaster, school trustee, and beloved community patriarch. He was there at the beginning, helping Millar Hill rise out of the wilderness, and remained there alone at the end, long after all his neighbours had given up on the land that had once held such promise.

Langmeade was born November 29, 1844, in the highlands of Scotland. The bleak hills of his homeland offered no prospect for the future and he had but two choices: seek work in the oppressive, black, and demoralizing industrial centres of Britain or flee the bleak agricultural landscape by immigrating to a new land. For Langmeade and his family it was an easy choice.

Though Muskoka was hardly idyllic farmland, for some it seemed the last chance to claim a piece of their own, and so they eagerly took up the challenge. Langmeade was one of the countless determined, naive, and desperate individuals to do so, arriving around 1879 to settle a land grant adjacent to David Millar's parcel in Franklin Township.

Langmeade was tough and inventive. Clearing the forest and breaking the rock-hewn soil for planting was miserably hard work, and unpredictably harsh weather plagued farmers, but Langmeade persevered and succeeded where so many others failed. He may never have prospered, but he survived and claimed more than the six feet under him that would have been his meagre due back in Britain.

As the number of families joining Langmeade and Millar in this corner of the township multiplied, the need for a school soon became apparent. Langmeade was one of the movers and shakers behind efforts to build and, later, maintain the schoolhouse and served as a school section trustee for its entire existence. Since trustees were elected by their peers, his twenty-four years in this position are representative of the high esteem to which he was held by the people of Millar Hill.

Besides serving as school trustee, Langmeade was also Millar Hill's postmaster, the only individual ever to lay claim to this title. The post office, which operated out of Langmeade's home, was opened May 1, 1912.

Mail was serviced by the Huntsville and Lake of Bays Navigation Company during summer months. Steamers would pick up mail from the railhead at Huntsville and deliver it to Grassmere on the Lake of Bays, where it would be collected by Langmeade. During winter months, Langmeade or a proxy would have to make a cutter ride into Huntsville for mail pickup and delivery.

Langmeade was an ideal postmaster, appearances aside. He was a tall man, thin and gaunt, with a rough, unruly beard the colour and texture of a wire scrub pad — to some he might have looked untamed and perhaps ornery. But nothing could have been further from the truth. Behind his bushy eyebrows were eyes that twinkled with good humour, and his creased face was all too ready to stretch into a smile. He loved to tell yarns, loved listening to them nearly as much, and to him people weren't neighbours or customers, but rather friends.

In his advancing years, after he had been widowed and when his health no longer permitted him to engage in the full measure of farming activities, it was said that Langmeade's one true joy was to watch the high-spirited children playing at the school directly across the road from his home. Perhaps their zeal for life reminded him of himself in his younger years, when he arrived in Canada full of optimism and enthusiasm.

The post office was closed October 16, 1928. Henceforth, all mail was serviced through the Hillside post office. Henry Langmeade, the last inhabitant of Millar Mill, watched sadly as bush reclaimed one-time farm fields and slowly swallowed up the remnants of the community he so loved.

The Millar Family

David (or Davie, as he was warmly known) Millar had a sense of adventure beating in his soul, driving him to explore the frontiers of the world and to seek out challenges and adventures. This wanderlust would eventually bring him to the wilds of Muskoka, specifically to Millar Hill, which he spent the latter half of his life trying to tame.[15]

He was born in Dumfries, Scotland, in 1838. Life in this small, quiet community seemed restrictive to the adventurous youth, and so at very young age he threw off the shackles of this dull existence and went to sea aboard a schooner. During his years spent as a sailor Millar voyaged to the Far East on several occasions, where he saw countless exotic lands and stopped at mysterious ports of call.

Perhaps tiring of the nomadic life at sea, Millar came to Canada with the intention of purchasing land and starting a family. He spent a few years near Georgetown, Ontario, where he met and wed his wife, Susan, but life in southern Ontario was too dull and uninspired to hold his attention for long. Lured by the prospect of free land and new adventures, Davie Millar set out for the great northern country of Muskoka in 1878.

His new land was located far from civilization, and at that time he had no neighbours for many miles. Yet, the challenge of making a home in this vast wilderness didn't scare him in the least. In fact, it seemed to invigorate him, and soon he had cleared several acres for crop fields and built a homestead for his wife and ten children.[16]

In time, other settlers would join him in what seemed to many to be the middle of nowhere, each man trying to take advantage of the free land grants being offered to provide a brighter future for their families. This small collection of farms slowly took on the appearance of a community, which became known as Millar Hill in honour of the area's first pioneering resident.

The early settlers had many challenges to overcome, not only those stemming from the harshness of their land but also epidemics that occasionally swept through like a forest fire, burning away the young and the infirm. Among the most feared of these illnesses was diphtheria, serious and highly contagious bacteria that would, if left unchecked, rapidly infect an entire community. In children, fatality rates were often as high as 20 percent.

When an outbreak occurred, the entire community would come together to help each other in whatever way they could. One Millar Hill woman (whose name unfortunately has been lost in history) who had lost a child of her own to the dreaded illness unselfishly offered her home to a neighbouring family to protect them from their own sick child. This was just the way it was back then; you did what you could to help each other through these horrible, trying times. Sometimes, however, this selflessness came with a price, as the Millars found out in a tragic manner.

During one of these occasional diphtheria outbreaks Susan Millar volunteered to nurse the suffering Quinn children through their sickness.[17] She was thinking of her neighbours and probably not of herself

Courtesy Bob Constable.

The Millars and Quinns were among the dozen or so families that made up Millar Hill, and there were several intermarriages between these two prominent families. Pictured here are Jack Quinn and Lil Millar, married in 1903.

or her own kids, demonstrating a remarkable sense of compassion when one considers what was at stake. She spent countless hours caring for the children, ignoring her own fatigue, which grew with each passing day.

On an extra tiring day, her mind numbed by lack of sleep, she forgot to do one simple thing and it cost her dearly. Her routine upon leaving the Quinn home was the same every day: she'd go to the outhouse, change her clothes, and thoroughly wash to rid herself of bacteria. On this day, however, she forgot to wash her hair, and within a matter of days three of her youngest daughters contracted the illness and died. How does one ever overcome something like this? The guilt, the sorrow, the loss. In those days, one had no choice. Susan Millar had other children to think of and, hard as it was, she had to move forward.

While Susan Millar is best remembered for this tragic episode, Davie Millar is remembered in a more jovial light. He was well known for cursing in a particularly colourful manner that he must have picked up while at sea, but his salty tongue didn't discourage the area children from looking upon him with fondness. Seemingly every day, "boys would often gather at Davie's gate after school to beg a yarn from the old seaman, and there was usually an apple or a carrot or such delicacy to make the visit doubly worthwhile."[18]

Davie Millar was only too glad to regale them with a story or two, for he was as fond of the children as they were of him. He was devoted to the youth of the community, spending years as chairman of the school board and superintendent of the Sunday school. A tireless worker, Millar tended to his farm, laboured in lumber camps over the winter, rented the services of himself and his oxen to anyone in need, and helped dig the canal that links Fairy Lake and Lake of Bays.

Undoubtedly exhausted from a lifetime of toil, David Millar died August 8, 1922, at the age of eighty-five. With his death, Millar Hill's light — already dimming from years of depression — was finally extinguished.

8
COOPER'S FALLS

By the middle of the nineteenth century, when many of southern Ontario's sawmill towns had become mere ghost towns, Muskoka remained a remote wilderness thick with pine. The rich bounty of its forests was becoming widely known and it drew considerable attention from the lumber companies that were increasingly anxious for new stands of timber to harvest.

There were problems, however. While forest in Muskoka was described as being "as thick as grass," there was no practical means of getting to it. There were no roads into the region, no navigable waterways, and no communities to support logging operations with the food and manpower they would need. The provincial government responded to this dilemma by devising what they called the "Colonization Road Scheme." Under this project, the government would survey and build as many as two dozen roads leading into the wilderness from the settled south. For anyone willing to build a cabin and clear a few acres, the land along these roads would be free.

The colonization roads, it was safely assumed, would open up the north to civilization and thereby allow the logging interests to profitably harvest the timber they so desperately coveted.

One of the first of these colonization roads was the Muskoka Road. Beginning at Washago at the northernmost point of Lake Couchiching, this rough trail twisted northward around hard rocks, over foaming rivers, and through unpleasant swamps. From the Muskoka Road ran a network of concession roads that disappeared into all corners of the district. Along the most southerly of these roads, the first one beyond the Severn River frontier, lay the village of Cooper's Falls.

Cooper's Falls was one of the first communities to emerge in Muskoka (though in truth, half lay within Simcoe County's Rama Township), and was the product of a dream shared by husband and wife Thomas and Emma Cooper. The couple was ostracized in their native England because their union broke the class barriers upon which Victorian society was based: quite simply, a wealthy girl of good standing should not marry a common man of low breeding. Desiring a home where they could live happily together without stigma or gossip, they immigrated to Canada in 1864 and headed for the free land being offered in Muskoka.

Thomas and Emma settled upon a lot in the southeast corner of Muskoka, alongside the Black River that ran from the eastern highlands in Haliburton down to Lake Couchiching. They couldn't have known it at the time, when they were huddling for warmth in a drafty log cabin and struggling to clear enough land to grow crops, but their land was strategically located to be at the centre of a future logging boom and their fortunes would therefore be assured.

During the 1870s, the Severn and Black River watersheds became thriving highways of the lumber industry, along which countless logs were delivered to bustling mills at Washago and Orillia. The demand for lumber was insatiable; the Dodge Lumber Company alone had more than a thousand lumberjacks cutting over 80 million feet of pine in Morrison and Ryde Townships.[1]

Thomas Cooper decided he could profit from the logging boom by opening a general store that supplied the bush camps. Later, he would add a small sawmill of his own alongside a waterfall on the Black River, providing lumber for area settlers. The privation experienced during their first years in Muskoka was replaced by prosperity and comfort.

Soon, a little hamlet started to come to life around the Cooper businesses. Several cabins lined the winding wilderness road, a log schoolhouse was built in 1874 using logs from the surrounding forest, and by 1878 Thomas Cooper had opened the community's first post office and officially named it Cooper's Falls.

With growth came the need for a house of worship in which the settlers could meet their religious obligations. An Anglican church was therefore built in 1884, and a Methodist church followed in 1894.

Cooper's Falls added a school in 1872, with Thomas Cooper as trustee playing a pivotal role in its organization and construction.

Courtesy Richard Mount.

Logging was big industry along the Black River watershed, and every winter bush camps (such as the one pictured here) sprung up in the depths of the forest. Cooper's Falls sustained itself on the logging industry, and when the timber was inevitably played out it began to atrophy.

During the 1880s and 1890s, there was an undeniable sense of optimism in the air. The population rose to more than fifty, Cooper's Falls boasted an annual fall fair that drew participants from all over the region, and there was even a brief prospecting craze when rumours (unfounded in the end) began circulating that the rock was rich in valuable minerals.[2]

Businesses began to flock to the growing community. These included a second store run by Joe Kehoe, a blacksmith shop, and James Gouldie's short-lived shingle mill. William Cooper, Thomas's son, attended the Agricultural College in Guelph and sought to diversify the local economy by establishing a cheese factory. The venture, well intended though it was, ended in failure after only a few short years.

The most contentious businesses in town were the hotels, since they did most of their trade serving alcohol to bush-weary lumbermen and became dens of boisterousness as a result. Thomas Cooper, a deeply religious man and a noted Temperance advocate, had hoped that his town's residents would live good and clean lives and was therefore far from pleased when lumbermen would loiter around in various stages of intoxication. He held nothing but disdain for the drunken, careless lifestyle of these individuals, but also blamed the hoteliers who profited from selling them booze.

Cooper needn't have worried, because the problem eventually solved itself. By the turn of the century the woods along the Black River had been depleted of pine, bringing an end to the wild and woolly days of the lumber boom. The shantymen whose behaviour had so concerned Cooper disappeared almost overnight.

Unfortunately, the loss of the local lumber industry meant hard times were ahead for Cooper's Falls. The hotels had depended upon the sale of alcohol for their very survival, and so they closed up shop in the first decades of the twentieth century. In short order, their closure was followed by the smithy, the cheese factory, the school, and the Methodist church. With nothing else to sustain the community, Cooper's Falls began a slow decent into obscurity.

Despite the loss of the logging industry and the businesses that fed off of it, and the general unsuitability of the area for agricultural pursuits, Cooper's Falls fought doggedly to stave off death. It seemed, even as buildings were being boarded up and families leaving for greener pastures, that the village was unwilling to join the ranks of Muskoka's ghost towns without a fight.

Much of this tenacity is seen in the form of eighty-six-year-old Frank Cooper, the grandson of Thomas Cooper and the last proprietor of the general store. It was a painful decision for Frank to close the store in 1968, and he regretted that it would be he who put an end to a century-old tradition. Frank knew that the business was no longer profitable — in truth, it hadn't been for several years — but he had literally grown up in the store and found it difficult to let go.[3]

The building still stands today, with the spry Frank running his construction business from within the attached living quarters. He's left the store itself virtually intact from the day he turned the key and closed up for the last time: product still lines the shelves, the storeroom is still full with stock that will never be sold, and the tools of early storekeeping — a cheese cutter and weight scales, for example — rest on the countertop.

Frank isn't alone in Cooper's Falls, but close to it. At last count, only a dozen or so people live in the faded hamlet; they are outnumbered by the derelict buildings that line the roadway. Most of these tired structures are cabins and farm outbuildings, but there are a few of particular note.

Across from the store, for example, is the old community hall, which many mistakenly refer to as a blacksmith shop.[4] Home to many social events, the hall was also where justice of the peace Thomas Cooper presided over legal proceedings. To the east are the twin churches, literally side by side, St. George's Anglican and the Free Methodist. Both are well tended, though only the former still sees occasional services. Finally, there's the schoolhouse, now transformed into a private residence.

Cooper's Falls may not be a ghost town — "I'm still here," Frank Cooper points out — but it's certainly a shade of its former self, a village that exists more as a spectre of the past than a part of the present. And it was, for a time at least, a glorious and exciting past.

Thomas and Emma Cooper

Many people lived and worked in Cooper's Falls over the years, each of them contributing something to the community's development. But nobody meant more to the village than its founders and namesakes, Thomas and Emma Cooper. For this devoted couple, Cooper's Falls represented a true labour of love — their love.

Thomas Cooper was born in Fawkham, Kent, England, in 1836. Emma was born a year later in the same community. But while technically neighbours, they might as well have been born a world apart, for Thomas came from common stock and Emma was born with a silver spoon in her mouth.[5]

Emma and Thomas Cooper started to notice each other twenty years later when Thomas, the son of the local butcher, began to deliver meat to Emma's privileged household. The two exchanged shy glances that said more than any words could, but Thomas, being the hard-working and humble man that he was, knew better then to socialize with the upper class. Emma was clearly out of his reach, a young woman reserved for the son of some blue-blooded aristocrat.

However, Emma had different plans. She was attracted to Thomas, and found a way to escape the watchful eyes of her protective family by hiding herself in the backyard where he could not help but notice her on his way out after making his deliveries. In these stolen moments a warm relationship formed.

Despite the fleeting nature of their rendezvous, over time their friendship grew stronger and eventually Thomas and Emma began to talk of marriage. When they finally did wed, on March 24, 1859 — both at the young age of twenty-two — Emma's family disowned her over the scandal. It was simply not proper for a girl of her station to marry someone so simple.

Thomas and Emma's first child was born within a year of their marriage, and the second child a year later. Emma continued to be shunned by her family, who would cross the street to the other side if they were unfortunate enough to run into her in town. This miserable situation pained Thomas so much that when he saw posters advertising Canada as the place to make a new life, he saw an opportunity to free his young family of the stigma that haunted them.

Emma and Thomas emigrated with pitifully small means, leaving Britain on July 31, 1864, aboard the steamship SS *Hector*.[6] After a short stay in Toronto, they headed for the free land grants of Muskoka. They took a train to Barrie, which was then the end of the line, and then proceeded by boat across Lakes Simcoe and Couchiching to Washago. From there, they headed off into the bush in search of their allotted land — Lot 12, Concession 13. When night overtook them, Emma held the children close to her and covered them with her long skirts, while Thomas fed a blazing fire to keep the packs of lurking wolves at bay.

The next morning they reached their land and eagerly started to build what would be their new home. Four days later, their primitive cabin was complete. Afraid that wolves would jump into the cabin and kill his children, Thomas cut the windows high above the ground and would jam them with logs at night.

The early years were extremely hard for the Coopers. They planted potatoes and turnips in between the stumps of fallen trees, but often had to rely upon the region's natural bounty to survive — fish, venison, small game, nuts, and wild fruit. When illness or weather made hunting and fishing next to impossible, many times they would go hungry.

Because their nearest neighbours were miles away and rarely seen, and the closest community was more than a day's walk, the Coopers were isolated and had to be self-sufficient. They had to improvise by making their own yeast, and in the darkness of night the only light they had came from candles that Emma made from animal fat.

Every six months, Thomas would take animal hides to Orillia to trade for supplies. He started out in the early morning to walk the twenty-five miles, leading a milking cow that would haul the supplies back. While in town, he would purchase a barrel of molasses, maybe some oatmeal and flour, and whatever other necessities he needed and could afford at the time. He'd stay overnight and head out again the next morning. Because of the poor conditions of the narrow tracks that then served as a road, it was difficult for Thomas to be back at his homestead before dark, especially if the weather was foul. But it was important that he was, because at dusk wolves would begin to emerge for their evening hunt and Thomas didn't intend to be on their menu.

On one trip, however, he very nearly was. Thomas found himself caught in the forest after nightfall, coaxing the nervous heifer along with one hand and holding aloft a lit cedar torch with the other. Suddenly, dark shadows began to prowl around the edge of the torch's meagre glow, becoming increasingly brazen with each passing moment. Without warning, the wolves attacked in a frenzy of bared teeth and spine-tingling growls. Thomas scrambled up a tree as the wolves closed in on him, but there was no escape for the poor cow. Thomas watched helplessly from his perch as the wolves killed his heifer and ate their fill. When the pack disappeared, Thomas fled to the cabin and waited for sunrise to return for the supplies.

Thomas was a kind man who admired and cherished his small cultured wife. Emma was a courageous woman who weighed about a hundred pounds but nonetheless braved the wilderness alongside her husband and gave birth to five more children in that small cabin.

All of the hardships eventually paid off, however. By 1876, Thomas and Emma had established themselves well enough to build a proper house, a sawmill on the Black River, and a general store to serve the settlers that had joined them in southeastern Muskoka.

This was the beginning of the village of Cooper's Falls. Thomas and Emma Coopers' dream of a prosperous new existence had come to life. Most importantly, they had accomplished it together.

Some of their children continued to embrace their dream after Thomas and Emma had passed. They lived in the town, worshipped at the church, attended the school, ran the store, and operated a sawmill. Even today, many of Thomas and Emma's descendants still reside in the area, providing a tangible link to the founding of Cooper's Falls.

The Schoolhouse

Most early Muskoka settlers came from humble stock in the Old World. Conscious of their own generally inadequate education, they made sure that their children were better taught. Even young girls, who traditionally were taught little more than docility and the skills inherent in running a household, received practical educations.[7]

Of course, these idealist immigrants could be excused if in the first few years of settlement schooling was not of immediate importance. Providing the necessities of life — food, shelter, warmth — took precedence over providing an education. But as soon as farms were up and running, settlers would band together to create school boards, hire teachers, and raise schoolhouses. That important event in Cooper's Falls's existence came in 1872.

Early that year, residents of the area began to organize themselves for the task at hand. Thomas Cooper, as usual, was at the forefront. At a township council meeting on January 15, 1872, which Cooper attended on behalf of his fellow settlers, the council paid the sum of $30 towards building a school in School Section #4. Ratepayers provided the remainder of the necessary funds themselves.

The village schoolhouse has been transformed into a private home and is almost unrecognizable. But eighty-six-year-old Frank Cooper, who continues to live in Cooper's Falls, fondly remembers youthful years spent in this one-room schoolhouse.

It would be two more years before any real movement was made towards realizing the dream of a school in Cooper's Falls. Finding a suitable piece of land was the principal holdup, as it had to come at a reasonable cost and needed to be central to the intended student population. Finally, in early 1874, the trustees purchased a quarter of an acre from Matthew Parks (Lot 10, Concession N) on which to build, and later that year a log schoolhouse took shape.

The log schoolhouse served well in its intended purpose for more than a decade, but the primitive building eventually became obsolete and was too cramped for the large classes that resulted from the growth of Cooper's Falls. Clearly a larger, more modern facility was required. To that end, an additional adjacent half-acre was added to the school premises and a new frame building was erected alongside the original log school. In 1890, a final half-acre was purchased to create a lot large enough to allow the children to comfortably play during recess.

Teachers in those days had it rough. Large classes, the need to juggle lessons for grades one through ten, unruly students, and a job requirement that saw teachers serve as both educators and school janitors (cleaning the building, stoking the fire first thing in the morning, bringing in firewood, and more) strained their time and patience. But worst of all was the mere pittance most were paid for their troubles; at SS #4, the average annual salary of a teacher in the late nineteenth century was usually between $250 and $300.

But what's interesting to note is that class sizes for the period could be misleading, creating a false impression of the number of students a teacher would have to contend with. The registers for Cooper's Falls still exist and are remarkable for what they reveal about pioneer-era schooling.

A careful examination of the books reveals that few children attended school every day in that time period. For instance, in 1890, teacher Australia B. McBrien had fifty-five students registered, but only one child had perfect attendance and came 191 days. There were twenty-two students who attended school fewer than forty days in total, while one child attended only once during the entire school year and another two attended only twice. In other words, pioneer-era teachers were not as harried as we might initially be led to believe.

These registers also reveal something about Cooper's Falls itself: even in what was arguably the village's heyday (the 1880s being the period of the most frenzied lumbering in the area) its inhabitants were still preoccupied with day-to-day existence and required the labour of their children more often than not to make farms and businesses work.

SS #4 served the community and those children lucky enough to attend regularly for nearly a century, finally closing in 1965 when Rama Central School was built. By this point, classes were down to fewer than ten students most often, not so much because children were required at home but simply because there were so few children in what was by then a rapidly diminishing community.

The Cooper's Falls school is still there today, serving as a distinctive private home. Although the building is currently undergoing extensive renovation, certain telltale features remain, most notably the bell tower that once summoned children to class.

The Sawmills

A faraway look appears in eighty-six-year-old Frank Cooper's eyes as he remembers the days of his youth and brings up the mental image of a sawmill along the river wreathed in steam as it slices logs into lumber. It's a bittersweet memory, because while like most young boys he was fascinated with the noisy machinery as a child, it was that very same machinery that brought about his father's untimely death. He was only three years old at the time, but somehow the memories are vivid in his mind's eye.

The sawmill Frank remembers was the last in a string of mills operating in Cooper's Falls, and it marked the final demise of the lumber industry that had sustained the community for so long.

Village founder Thomas Cooper is credited with being the first sawmill operator in the area. Though some claim there is little evidence to support this assertion, Frank is convinced his grandfather ran a mill. First, there is the oral tradition as passed on by his family, but perhaps more convincing is the log stamp (used, like a branding iron on cattle, to mark possession of cut logs) bearing the initials "T.C."[8]

The mill would have been located alongside the Black River falls, where it could capture the energy of the rushing river as it plunged over the rocks in order to power its saw. Built sometime around 1878, it would likely have been a small and rather primitive industry, and always tied to the flow of the river.

The mill would have been a boon to settlers. Trees that were chopped down and then dragged to where they could be dumped into the water would earn a settler a welcome bit of cash when cash was rarely seen. All the trees on the property — with the exception of the most valuable pine, which remained Crown property — belonged to the homesteader, and in most cases the annual winter harvest of forest products yielded a larger reward than did field crops and livestock.

Thomas Cooper's mill wasn't the only option in the area for farmers wishing to sell logs. In 1885, a sawmill owned and operated by a man named Bothwell was up and running along the banks of the Black River, and before long James Gouldie started a shingle mill that used lower quality lumber to produce roofing shingles.[9] None of these mills were particularly enduring, however, and by the early years of the new century all had disappeared.

That's not to say that lumbering in the area had come to an end. Far from it, in fact; as late as the 1920s sleighs and cadging teams hauling hardwood logs were still routinely seen in the area. Recognizing there was still some life in the lumber industry yet, Thomas Cooper's son, William, purchased a steam sawmill in 1921. He had the machinery shipped to Washago by train, then by wagon to Cooper's Falls, where it was set up alongside the Black River.

Unlike Thomas Cooper's mill, this one was no longer at the mercy of the weather and the river's flow. Converting logs, formerly useless slab of wood, and sawdust into energy to power its saws, pulleys, and conveyors, the mill could cut merrily away, uninterrupted, in all seasons. The riverside locale was selected primarily because it was more convenient to deliver logs by way of water than by hauling them overland.

The mill ran successfully until 1925, but operations came to a sudden and tragic end. "Dad was working down at the mill one day, when he had an accident with the machinery," remembers Frank Cooper. "It was early spring when roads were bad, almost impassable. He had to be taken out by boat to Washago and then by train to the hospital. When he died, it left my mother alone with nine kids, the oldest my sixteen-year-old brother."[10]

The death of William Cooper drew a curtain on milling in Cooper's Falls. Never again would the scent of fresh sawdust linger in the air or plumes of steam coil around the river. Not coincidentally, never again would the community enjoy any prosperity.

Blacksmiths

As early as 1877, Cooper's Falls was reported to be looking for a blacksmith. Thomas Cooper, a tireless advocate of the community that bore his name, put out a call for skilled artisans to provide for the needs of his fellow settlers. If the village was to grow, he knew a blacksmith would be required.

Cooper succeeded in his search, but while attracting a blacksmith was one thing, retaining him proved to be something else entirely. The village experienced a revolving door of smiths over the years, and several times Cooper was forced to search anew to fill a vacant forge.

The first blacksmith lasted only a decade, and on November 4, 1887, the *Orillia Times* reported the need for a new one: "There is a good opening for a blacksmith here. A good steady man could do well."

Joe Kehoe, a farmer who also ran a general store on Lot 15, Concession N, answered the call. He built a blacksmith shop on the same property and for a time the ringing of hammer on forge was a common sound.

Kehoe himself may have done some smithing initially, but within a few years he was renting the facilities to Robert Fletcher, a truly skilled craftsman capable of repairing or making nearly any metal object the local farmers could reasonably desire.

Fletcher took on an apprentice named Thomas Joslin to help him keep up with the demand for his skills. Around 1900, Fletcher moved his business to Washago and the by now fully trained Joslin took over the trade at Cooper's Falls.

Joslin, who invested considerable time and money in modernizing the facilities, was known for his interest in all things mechanical, from steam engines to newfangled automobiles. For example, a news clipping dated March 22, 1906, states, "Thomas Joslin, our enterprising blacksmith and machinist, has added a gasoline chopper to his many mechanical appliances, and farmers are not slow in taking advantage of the service."[11]

The interest in new technology couldn't save his business, however. In 1909, Joslin sold the failing shop and moved on, leaving Cooper's Falls without the services of a blacksmith. Another man was eventually found to fill his shoes, but within two years the shop was vacant once more, this time for good.

There's no sign of the blacksmith shop today, though some sources incorrectly claim otherwise. The cause of the confusion is the weathered, century-old building that stands across the road from the Cooper general store. To the uninitiated, it might look like a blacksmith shop, but it's actually anything but.

Many sources, including popular books, routinely misidentify this building as a blacksmith shop. In fact, it was a community hall, a place that hosted dances and meetings, and where Justice of the Peace Thomas Cooper held court.

The two-storey building was originally a multi-purpose community hall. It was used for socials, dances, Methodist services before the church was built, an exhibit hall for the fall fair, and even a courthouse where justice of the peace Thomas Cooper tried cases.

Later, it was used by the Coopers in conjunction with their store across the road. Bags of cattle feed and other large goods were kept within the building, while an attached implement shed was used for storing and assembling farm machinery. Customers shopping at the store could also feed and rest their horses in the drive-in shed. The garage-like structure on the western side of the building is just that, a garage built by Frank Cooper in the 1950s.

Sometimes, appearances can be deceiving, as the case of the misidentified hall at Cooper's Falls demonstrates. If ever one needs reminding of the vital importance of thorough research when presenting history, the case of this important building — its true purpose and heritage nearly erased by well-meaning but misinformed writers — should be brought forth.

Churches

Though only a small village, Cooper's Falls nonetheless boasted two churches, built side by side about two kilometres west of the community. Located along the main road to Cooper's Falls, the churches are the first buildings you see upon arrival and the last you see as the village recedes behind you. Whether intentional or not, this is only fitting, because the twin churches were — and to some degree remain today — central to the communal identity.

The first organized congregation in Cooper's Falls was Anglican. Thomas and Emma Cooper, and their children after them, were tireless supporters of the Church of England, and it was in no small part due to their religious enthusiasm that the Anglican faith developed deep roots in the community.

In 1874, local Anglicans began to meet in the nearby log schoolhouse (SS #4, Rama Township), but it was a less than ideal arrangement. Because it was primarily an educational facility, it lacked the architectural features central to organized Christian faith (such as a pulpit or altar), and there was no dedicated burial ground.

This situation lasted for ten years, until a real house of worship was built just west of town. Dedicated St. George's and officially opened on Sunday October 26, 1884, the new church was a handsome if modest building of frame construction.

"The neighbours drew the lumber and the timber for the foundation was kindly supplied by Mr. James Bailey," reported the *Orillia Packet*. "The window frames and sashes were made by Mr. Madden of Orillia. The contract for the erection of the church was taken by Mr. R. Densmore of Washago."[12]

The church measures 20 feet by 30 feet and comfortably seats eighty. Unfortunately, the congregation was never large enough to see the church filled, except perhaps on special occasions such as weddings.

Though St. George's Anglican Church is neither large nor grand, it holds two interesting distinctions. First, it is the most southerly church anywhere in Muskoka, beating out the neighbouring Free Methodist Church by no more than a few feet. In addition, it is the only Muskoka church in the Diocese of Toronto; all others are in the Diocese of Algoma.[13]

When Cooper's Falls began its slide into oblivion in the early twentieth century, and the village landmarks began to disappear, the troubled locals sought comfort in the church. St. George's was one of the few constants in Cooper's Falls, seemingly immune to the trends that worked against the community. Desperately clinging to something tangible of their past, something to retain their communal identity, residents fought to ensure their church's survival.

By the mid-1960s, however, a dwindling population necessitated an end to year-round services. Thereafter, St. George's opened only in July and August, when seasonal inhabitants swelled the congregation to a size worthy of attracting a travelling minister.

The church remains in use today, though it sees only occasional services during the summer. It has all the simple charm of a nineteenth-century church. When you enter you step into another time, as nothing of significance has changed since it was built more than a century ago. One of the highlights is a memorial window to William C. Cooper, son of village founder Thomas Cooper, the community's long-time storekeeper and tireless backer of the church.

St. George's neighbour, the Free Methodist Church, had a somewhat rocky beginning. It got its start in 1891, when area Methodists began to gather for services in a rented hall. For reasons that history doesn't record, the preacher and his flock were soon evicted form the hall and left homeless. Nineteenth-century Methodists were known for dedication that occasionally bordered on radicalism, so it's possible the congregation simply rubbed someone's nose the wrong way.

Shortly thereafter, the Methodist preacher began to hold sermons in the barroom of McNab's tavern, a local watering hole that served whiskey and beer to rough-and-tumble lumberjacks. A more unusual arrangement is hard to imagine. Methodists, on the one hand, were staunchly pro-temperance, but McNab would have earned most of his income from catering to bushmen. He had no incentive to promote temperance, and his clientele certainly would have had little time for individuals railing against the evils of alcohol.[14]

Yet, despite the seemingly incompatible nature of the two opposing views, the arrangement actually worked. In fact, McNab and his family were eventually converted to the faith, and they in turn convinced many others to accept Methodism.

In 1894, the congregation had grown large enough in size and wealth to be able to erect a true place of worship. A little frame church, the product of their pious efforts, was built on land donated by David Genno, another tavern keeper converted to the cause. Located almost adjacent to St. George's Anglican Church, it is in almost every respect of identical design.

The congregation was served by an itinerant preacher (known as a "circuit rider") who rode between Methodist churches in the region. From his parsonage in Housey's Rapids, the preacher would tend to the spiritual needs of Cooper's Falls, Severn Bridge, and Barkway. After the service, an adherent of the faith would provide the preacher with a meal and a warm bed in which to spend the night, allowing him to resume his circuit refreshed the next morning.

Cooper's Falls should probably have only ever had had one church. Even at its peak the population was not big enough to fill the pews of both, and expectations that the twin congregations would grow over time proved false. Unfortunately, Old World organizational disputes meant the two religions could not work together.

Taverns

Thomas Cooper was a leading advocate against "distilled damnation," as alcohol was then often called, and was morally opposed to the wanton drunkenness and transient, carousing lifestyle of the lumbermen who descended upon his peaceful community every spring and fall. Cooper went to great lengths to encourage others to abstain from the devil drink, and even though it was common practice at the time for stores to sell bottles of booze or "snorts" (or cups) of whiskey from an open barrel, he refused to do so. His conviction outweighed the lure of the dollar.

For a number of years, Cooper's Falls was the largest community in the area and boasted a large, well-attended annual agricultural fair. This authentic poster, which still hangs inside the Cooper General Store, advertises the 1887 festivities. With few exceptions, fall fairs are no longer a part of the Muskoka landscape.

But not everyone in town was as principled. Three taverns operated in town at various times, catering principally to the loggers who passed through Cooper's Falls in the autumn on the way to bush camps and in April, their pockets bulging with money, after a winter spent in the woods and upon the completion of the spring drive.

The first tavern to emerge in Cooper's Falls was owned and operated by David George Genno. Genno was a professional hotelier, having operated the Royal Hotel near Washago during the late 1870s and early 1880s.[15] This community was sustained by the lumber trade, but when logging companies advanced into Muskoka in the 1880s in search of fresh stands of timber, the village went through a severe economic depression. Many homes stood vacant, and businesses fled for greener pastures. Genno was among those who uprooted in search of new opportunities.

Searching for a new location to establish a tavern, Genno settled upon Cooper's Falls. Recognizing that the village was conveniently located near countless logging camps, and that lumbermen swarmed around town in droves thicker than blackflies in May, he decided that this was as ideal a choice as any to start anew. In 1884, he made the move and purchased a piece of land about one mile west of Cooper's Falls proper.[16]

Genno cleared the land, began farming, and opened a combined boardinghouse and tavern. The tavern wing was built of rough-hewn logs with a dirt floor, and was most likely a former settler's cabin that he simply outfitted with tables, chairs, and a bar. The attached boarding house was more hospitable, a three-storey frame building with modest but comfortable rooms. As was hoped, shantymen soon began to descend upon the tavern as a place to drink and cut loose.

The din of booze-fuelled raucousness that escaped from this establishment made Genno the target of local ire and the preaching of ministers. Genno ignored the masses for a decade or so, choosing profit over piety. But then, inexplicably, he suddenly began to hear the word of God. The tavern was closed around 1900, and as if in repentance Genno donated a parcel of land to the Methodist church.

The boarding house remained open long after the whiskey had stopped flowing in the tavern, providing the occasional traveller with a meal or a bed for the night. This business came to a sudden end when the entire building, including the now-silent tavern, burned to the ground in February 1917.

Another tavern that catered to the shanty toughs was that which belonged to Thomas McNab. This short-lived establishment, located about 365 metres west of the Cooper store, opened in the mid-1880s and closed about ten years later.[17] Unfortunately, there are few details about the McNab tavern, save that in its brief existence it played host to countless drunken celebrations, many of them ending in good-natured fisticuffs.

Finally, the King family ran a boarding house for the log drivers who shepherded timbers down the Black River each spring. It's likely that this establishment also had a barroom in which fatigued guests could chase away the exhaustion with a drink or three. The business outlasted the other taverns in town by a large margin, billeting soldiers during the First World War and later opening its doors to summer tourists who wanted to enjoy the solace of the rural region.

For a time, Thomas Cooper's dream of a peaceful community free of the influence of alcohol had been denied by the presence of taverns and the hard-drinking, hard-living lumbermen who patronized them. With these watering holes finally gone and the drunken boisterousness associated them a thing of the past, Cooper's Falls finally started to resemble the idyllic village its founder had always intended.

The Cooper's Falls General Store

As always when researching a ghost town, the most treasured things that we find are the relatives of the early settlers who gambled all to secure a new future for themselves and their offspring. The most endearing man was our portal into the past of Cooper's Falls, who greeted us with a smile and escorted us into the historical building that once served as the store and residence of town founder, Thomas Cooper. Our hospitable host was Frank Cooper, one of Thomas's nearly countless grandchildren.

Through Frank we had made a connection to Thomas and Emma Cooper, and to the community they helped build. He graciously walked us through the home, pointed out the pump organ that had been in the

Courtesy Richard Mount.

Three successive generations of the Cooper family ran the general store in Cooper's Falls. The original wooden store burned down in 1905. The replacement, built of brick and opened a year later, served until the 1960s and remains standing — and in the Cooper family — to this day. William Cooper, shown here, was proprietor from 1910 to 1923.

family for generations and Thomas and Emma's marriage certificate, lovingly hung on the wall alongside a photo of this devoted couple. He then led us into the store itself, preserved almost museum-like as it appeared when Frank closed the business forty years past.

Here, surrounded by shelves lined with stock and leaning on a century-old countertop, we learned the story of the Cooper's Falls store.

Shortly after Thomas Cooper arrived in Cooper's Falls, he opened a small store alongside his home. He recognized that he could make more money serving the settlers and countless lumber camps in the area than he ever could working the land, and with his background working in shops back in his native England a store seemed a natural fit. Cooper also petitioned for, and received, a post office licence.

It was around this business that the village of Cooper's Falls eventually developed. Everything a settler could reasonably expect to need could be purchased here. Everything from cloth and dry goods to nails, tools, and clothing items was stocked. Molasses and corn syrup, vital for cooking in those days, were stored in forty-five-gallon drums and sold to settlers in refillable five- or ten-pound jars. Kerosene lamp oil, the means of lighting until hydro was brought into the area in the 1940s, was sold by the gallon in metal cans.

Farm machinery, such as reapers and ploughs, was kept in the still-standing utensil shed across the road.

"There weren't that many people here at the time so my grandfather did most of his business supplying the lumber camps in Longford Township," relates Frank Cooper. "It took a whole day to reach a camp, so he would sleep over and return home the next day. Of course, since most logging was done in the wintertime, this was seasonal."

Thomas Cooper's establishment was the only store in a vast area, so as the years passed and the surrounding townships were settled farmers became an increasingly important source of revenue. People from as far away as Barkway and Lewisham frequented the store for their mail and supplies. Few of these customers could afford the luxury of paying in cash, so the barter system remained the principal method of exchange well into the twentieth century.

"During the winter months people would charge all their purchases to their account because there was no money then," explains Mr. Cooper. "In the summer they would pay much of their bill by trading blueberries, butter, and so forth. My parents and grandparents would buy potatoes from local farmers and store them in the basement for resale. As kids, we spent a lot of time in the basement pulling off sprouts."

By the early 1900s, William Cooper, Thomas's son, was taking an increasingly active role in the store to assist his aging father and was clearly being groomed to take over the operation.[18] William was an enterprising individual and was always looking for ways to increase the family holdings. Some of his ideas were ultimately failures (foremost among them a short-lived cheese factory), but the activeness of his mind and apparent ingenuity suggested William would eventually be a worthy successor.[19]

For a time, however, it seemed as though there may not be a store to inherit. In 1905, when the business was arguably at its peak, a fire destroyed the building and cost the Coopers all of their stock. It was a devastating setback, for both the family and the community of Cooper's Falls. At around the same time, a competitor, in the form of a store run by Joe Kehoe, emerged to threaten the Coopers' hard-won prosperity.[20]

But the Coopers were not dissuaded by a setback, as grievous at it may have appeared. Instead, they moved their retail operations across the street to the community hall while a new brick store was constructed on the soot-stained foundations of the original. A year later, it was open for service.

Business resumed as normal. By 1916, Kehoe had closed up shop, leaving the Cooper store as the only one in town once again. Thomas lived just long enough to see this happen, but with his passing the reins to the business went to William and his wife, Mary.

Frank Cooper and his siblings literally grew up in the store. His childhood was full of pleasurable times, and many of those times revolved around the general store that his mother ran almost single-handedly after the premature and tragic death of his father in a sawmill accident in 1923.

"We sold ice cream for a long time, the only place hereabouts to do that," he recalls. "I can remember my mother going down the steep steps to the cellar, taking the padded lid off the barrel, uncovering the can, careful not to get any ice or salt in the ice cream, filling a cone, repacking the barrel, and then climbing the steps. An ice cream cone sold for five cents. Hard to figure any profit in that."

"The store was a social place, and men would sit around for hours just talking," he continues. "I remember sitting on the box stove in the store listening to an old gent tell tales of the Boer War. It was pretty exciting for a kid."

That kid eventually grew up and took on the responsibility of assisting his mother in running the store.

Frank took over completely in 1948, but he didn't run it very long. By the 1950s, it was becoming almost impossible to compete with the prices or selection of larger stores in nearby urban centres, and with each passing year it became harder to justify keeping the store open. Finally, in 1960 Frank made the difficult decision to shut the doors and turn the sign to "Closed."

It's been more than four decades since, but Frank still hasn't brought himself to clear the store of its stock.

The walls are filled with mementoes of a time long past, and on the counter implements — a meat cutter, cheese cutter, and scales among them — await customers that will never arrive. Frank has a story for all of them. One hopes that one day all these treasures will end up in a museum or some such place where the ways of the past are not forgotten but rather shared with others.

That's Frank Cooper's ideal as well. He retains a passion for the store in which he was raised and is unwilling to completely let go of the past, lest it be forgotten. He still allows the odd visitor to tour the building and step into history, but while it was certainly a pleasure to see the general store, for us an even greater pleasure was meeting Frank Cooper and sharing in his memories.

9

LEWISHAM

The road is narrow and rutted, and the forest canopy grows overtop, shading out the sunlight to cast the area in perpetual gloom. You pass through mile after mile of forest, hoping desperately that the trail doesn't suddenly end and leave you with the unenviable task of retracing your steps. But the road doesn't stop. Instead, it continues. You inch your way through flooded stretches where swamps, filled with the skeletal remains of dead trees and beaver grass that stands taller than a man, break free of their natural confines and encroach upon the primitive roadway.

It's only after what seems like an eternity (but which is actually probably closer to twenty minutes) that you break free of the grim wilderness and emerge into the sunlight once again. Before you stretches a wide clearing, inhabited only by a weathered old schoolhouse and a pair of headstones standing forlorn in a nearby cemetery. Welcome to Lewisham.

Located in the depths of Ryde Township, Lewisham was never large, scarcely even a hamlet, in fact, and is today one of Muskoka's most obscure and isolated ghost towns. But though its story is brief, it's interesting nonetheless, full of merit, misery, and even murder.

The original survey of the area was conducted in 1861, and during that year timber licences were granted to Cook and Brothers from Midland. The following year, logging operations began, but settlement of the area would have to wait for another decade.

At the time, surveyor Robert T. Burns anticipated "early and easy success" for prospective settlers, this despite the rocky soil and preponderance of low, swampy areas. But in truth, and despite Burns's rosy predictions, success came neither early nor easy for the people of Lewisham.

Unaware of the harsh conditions, the first settlers entered the area in the 1870s. Among the first families to arrive, in 1876, were those headed

Courtesy Richard Mount.

The soil in Lewisham was too poor for reasonable farming, so most of the settlers sought work at area camps during the winter months. Without this supplemental income, farms in the area were not sustainable and Lewisham could never have developed.

by Noble Lawrence, John Brooks, Isaac Loshaw, Stephen Brundige, and John Fox.[1] Soon after, other prominent individuals arrived, including George Taylor and William Lowe. Eventually, there would be as many as twenty-five families in Lewisham.

Minnie (Johnson) Hepinstall, reciting her memories of the village at the age of seventy-six in 1970, paints a vivid picture of primitive lifestyle typical of Lewisham even more than twenty years after its founding: "Our house, like all the others in the neighbourhood, was made of logs … all the barns and other buildings were also of logs … there were no screen doors or windows. You could get mosquito netting at the store for five cents a yard and tack it on the windows. I think everyone had a smudge pot or two. They put chips in the pail, set it on fire, put grass on to make smoke, set it near the door to keep the insects out."[2]

Clearly, the people of Lewisham never enjoyed any real bounty from their bush farms. And yet, a small but thriving village developed. The heart of this community, "downtown" Lewisham as some modern people refer to it tongue firmly set in cheek, was at a crossroads where four trails met. One road (today known as Lewisham Road and the only one still passable) led north to Merkley Road and Barkway. Another disappeared into the forest in the east and linked up with a long-gone stretch of Barkway Road to the west. The final road, and the most important, led south to Cooper's Falls, a village that served as Lewisham's link to civilization. It was here that the settlers did much of their shopping, where men could find the closest tavern serving drinks, and where the stage originated. When residents of Lewisham said they were "going into town," they were referring to Cooper's Falls.

The crossroads was home to Lewisham's few noteworthy buildings. In 1882, John Taylor opened the first post office and store, later passing the reins of the business to long-time proprietor John Fox. The store carried all of the settlers' basic needs, but it was a far cry from the emporiums seen in larger centres, where an almost dizzying array of goods could be found lining the shelves. This store, as befitting the community it served, was of modest size and function.

John Fox was an enterprising individual who, in addition to running the store, also operated a steam-powered saw and shingle mill nearby. The mill produced for local needs only but was vital to the health of the community. Some people earned a few extra dollars working for Fox or by selling him logs cut on their properties. But the demand for cut lumber couldn't have been too high, since in the entire history of Lewisham only a single building was ever of frame construction.

In 1879, a log schoolhouse (SS #3) was built to serve the area youth. John Fox was contracted to erect the school and was paid $85 for his efforts. The first teacher was future storekeeper John Taylor. A few years later, Anthony Annis deeded an acre of land for All Saints Anglican Church. The little log structure was built later that year by Charlie Fenton and Isaac Loshaw, and rapidly became a focal point for the community.[3]

A short-lived tavern operated along the western road leading into Lewisham. William Frederick Hogue opened his log shanty to exhausted travellers, providing them with a place to refresh their horses and enjoy a simple meal. The hospitality was rustic but warm, and since it was the only such "public house" for many miles few road-weary people likely complained about the lack of refinement. Hogue gave the business up

From their home, Selina and Fred Hogue operated a short-lived and decidely rustic roadside inn on the outskirts of Lewisham. This hostelry — where weary travellers could find a bed and a warm meal — was one of very few businesses in town, joining a general store and sawmill.

Courtesy Carol Fraser.

after his wife, Selina, died during childbirth; there was no way he could manage the farm and play host to travellers simultaneously.[4]

The early 1890s was probably the heyday of the community. It was home to almost one hundred people, boasted a handful of community buildings that served as glue, binding the people together, and between logging and growing potatoes in their fields the settlers had enough to get by on. Stages ran twice weekly to Cooper's Falls.

But even while the town was prospering, a frightening event occurred that cast a dark pall over Lewisham, proving no community — no matter how tight-knit — was immune to violence and crime. Henry Edward was a hard-working and frugal man who almost literally saved every penny he earned. This money was kept hidden in a cashbox that was secreted in his home. No one outside the family knew of its existence. One morning, Edward was found dead in his home, a bullet blowing a hole the size of a silver dollar in the back of his head. The murderer had fired through a window from the shadows outside, presumably after watching Edward long enough to learn of the hidden stash's location. The $300 that had been painstakingly saved was never recovered, nor was the murderer ever identified.[5]

Though unrelated to the crime, decline began to set in around the same time, as the lumber was depleted and homesteaders grew frustrated with farms that were marginal at best. A general malaise set in, and gradually families began to move to less remote, more forgiving locations. By 1900, the population had plummeted to fifty, and the drop continued as the years passed.

The post office and store were closed by then-proprietor J.G. Taverner in 1927, and the school followed suit in 1949, leaving the final nine students to make their way the six kilometres to Barkway and back every day. A decade later Lewisham was completely deserted, a true ghost settlement.

Visiting the site today, some fifty years after the last resident abandoned his bush farm, reveals little of the community's past. The store and church were torn down long ago, and the sawmill was sold and moved to another location. A single home, built around 1915, lurks hidden behind a dense curtain of trees and is completely hidden from Lewisham Road.

The only readily visible building is the former schoolhouse, which remains in seasonal use as a hunt camp. Just off to the side is the cemetery, which marks where the church would have stood. Most of the markers sunk into the ground ages ago, leaving only a pair of markers of recent vintage and a commemorative stone plaque to remind visitors that this was once consecrated land and the final resting place of many hard-working pioneer settlers.

The Schoolhouse

As recently as sixty years ago the peal of children's laughter would have echoed across the forest clearing. When recess was over, the students would drag their heels while climbing the steps to the schoolhouse, reluctantly returning to their studies. Peering through the windows, you would have found a prim teacher standing before a chalkboard, juggling lessons for grades one through ten. The students' rambunctious antics have disappeared. They sit quietly at their desks, bent over notebooks, speaking only when spoken to. To misbehave was to court a date with the leather strap sitting menacingly on the teacher's desk.

Today, the clearing is eerily silent, a wake-like hush having descended upon it. The merriment of children playing has been replaced by an almost sombre atmosphere. Peering through the same window today, one would find all the structured organization of one-room schoolhouse education replaced by the chaos of a hunt camp frequented by men with no apparent interest in maintaining the building's heritage.

The former Lewisham School, once proud of its role in the community, has been reduced by nature and years of neglect to a sad and worn-out building that seems to wither away a little more with each passing year. Perhaps this unfortunate fate should come as no surprise, since SS #3 always endured a troubled and turbulent history.

By the year 1879, a decade or so after the first settlers had begun to arrive in Lewisham, there were enough children running around the wilderness village to require a schoolhouse. Education was important to our pioneer forebears, and it was also a matter of pride for any community to boast of a schoolhouse of their own.

School Section #3 was formed that year, a board of trustees appointed, and plans put in motion for the construction of a school. John Fox was contracted to perform the labour and was paid the sum of $85 for his time. The school was a rough-hewn log building, presided over in the first few years by schoolmaster John G. Taylor, an educated fellow who in a few years' time would become Lewisham's postmaster and storekeeper.[6]

The first hint of trouble emerged in 1886, when School Section #3 was split into two administrative sections and a second log schoolhouse, known as SS #7, was built south of Lewisham along the road to Cooper's Falls. This decision was made in order to shorten the trek many students endured while getting to school and back, especially important during the long harsh winter months. Despite the practical reasons for the move, it was unpopular among members of Ryde Township Council, who seemed to care little about the needs or desires of the residents and became fixated on reuniting the two school sections.

Sometime during the 1880s or early 1890s, a fire claimed SS #3 and it was replaced by a frame structure, once again built by John Fox.

In 1895, despite objections, Ryde Township forced the reunification of SS #3 and SS #7. The logical thing to do would have been to close one of the two schoolhouses. Instead, the township further antagonized everyone by keeping both schools open and forcing teachers to work half a year at

The Lewisham schoolhouse now serves as a hunt camp. This lonely building is all that remains standing in Lewisham. The store, the mill, the church, the farmhouses, and the barns are all long gone.

one school and the other half in the second. Some teachers flatly refused to alternate between the schools, and the local ratepayers threatened to withhold their taxes if the sections were not separated again.

The animosity continued for years, with everyone digging in to their respective positions. But the dwindling class sizes of the early 1900s (the result of families growing disenchanted with their meagre lots in

Lewisham) meant that far from having two full-time schools, the locals would actually have to lose one outright. As a result SS #7, the farthest afield and the less modern of the two, was closed in 1908.

While the amalgamation probably made sense to politicians in faraway council chambers, it was a harsh reality for many children in the area who would now have to make lengthy walks to and from school. Not merely inconvenient, such walks could be dangerous: "After the old log school near our first house closed, Bob and I walked to the new Lewisham School, which was three miles from our log house," recalled seventy-six-year-old Minnie (Johnson) Hepinstall in 1970. "One winter's day a high wind and snowstorm came up while we were in school. I nearly froze to death on the way home. Bob dragged and carried me and finally I got home. I was sick for a long time after that, and did not return to school until spring."[7]

Of course, none of this mattered to the township council, and SS #3 remained the only school in the vicinity.

Teachers were given a great deal of latitude when dealing with unruly students, up to and including the use of the strap. But they were not immune to controversy, as schoolmistress Kate Ruttan discovered.

Robert John Burnett, a large boy with a hair-trigger temper and a troublesome attitude, was always a handful for the hard-pressed teacher to control. Sometimes, to her dismay, she would have to resort to whipping to keep him in line. It eventually landed her before the judge, on charges of undue severity in applying the strap.

The hearing, held on June 11, 1892, was a local scandal. Ruttan had no time to hire a lawyer and was only too pleased to accept the services of William Lowe as her counsel. If found guilty, Ruttan could have been fined or dismissed, or perhaps even barred from teaching, and worse, her reputation would have been tarnished. Thankfully, Lowe put up an inspired defence.

Fourteen pupils and the school trustees came forward to testify that Robert John Burnett "when slightly whipped for malicious lying and obscene language, assaulted the teacher, nearly breaking her arm." It also came to light that the boy had previously also attacked his own mother with an axe and drawknife, revealing a pattern of unbalanced behaviour.

There was only one logical verdict: "The trustees, considering that the punishment afflicted on the boy was less than his offences merited, passed a resolution exonerating Mrs. Ruttan from all blame in the matter and expelled the said Robert John Burnett from school."[8]

For its size, the Lewisham School was unusually prone to controversy. And yet, the few lingering residents of Lewisham were sad to see it go when the decision was made in 1949 to close the school and divert the nine remaining students to Barkway.[9] They realized that with the closing of the school the community they had known for their entire lives, the community they had for so long denied was on its last legs, was finally well and truly dead. The realization was a painful blow to them.

"The school is still there, but I don't see it the way it is now," says eighty-six-year-old Jim Taverner, who received all of his education in the one-room school. "When I see it, I think back to the fun and games we had, the snowball fights, the young teachers, the faces of my classmates who are all dead and gone. I see the school the way it was, I guess."

The Store/Post Office

It took a while, but after the homesteaders had settled themselves into a routine a community began to develop. Each new stage in Lewisham's growth was cause for great pride: opening a school, building a church, cutting the first log at the sawmill. But the village never grew as large or as prosperous as the settlers had initially anticipated.

Its sole commercial enterprise was the general store and post office, an imposing structure that dominated the village crossroads and played a prominent role in the lives of area residents. Suitably, the various storekeepers and postmasters were without exception the wealthiest men in Lewisham.

John Taylor, a recent English immigrant, opened the combined store and post office at the crossroads of the fledgling hamlet in 1882.[10] It, combined with the church and school located almost directly opposite, emerged as the heart of the community, the few slender distinctions Lewisham ever had.

Courtesy Richard Mount.

Among the dozen or so families that comprised Lewisham were the Brunsons. Like their neighbours, they struggled to eke out a living from the thread-bare soil, and also like their neighbours they soon realized the futility of the effort and moved away.

Though Taylor served as postmaster and storekeeper only until 1888, he left a lasting legacy: it was he who named Lewisham in honour of his hometown in England. It's a safe bet that even in its prime Taylor's new home compared unfavourably to the pastoral beauty of the Lewisham that lay across the sea.

Succeeding Taylor was W.J. Tryon, who kept both positions only for two years before William Lowe bought him out. One of the early settlers, Lowe had settled in Lewisham in 1880 and, as one of the most successful farmers, was held in high regard. Becoming the storekeeper and postmaster only enhanced his standing and helped him get elected to various township offices, including that of reeve for many years. Lowe was so influential, so powerful in local matters, that he was called the "Emperor of Ryde Township" at the time.

In 1898, Lowe moved to Barkway and left the store in the capable hands of John Fox. Few storekeepers were as beloved as Fox, or as industrious. The man was always on the go; when he wasn't managing the store he was working the fields, and when he wasn't working the fields he was running his sawmill. But what he was best known for was his stature: John Fox stood a diminutive four feet tall.

After nine years in business, Fox sold to P.J. Brace, who in turn sold to J.G. Taverner in 1911. Taverner was the longest-serving storekeeper and postmaster, lasting sixteen years in total and overseeing the difficult final years of this village landmark.

Jim Taverner, a resident of Barkway and the grandson of J.G. Taverner, remembers the store well: "It was the largest building anywhere around these parts, with eight rooms upstairs and three downstairs, besides the store itself. It was a big frame house, the only one in Lewisham."

Given the desolate location and dwindling population at the time, J.G. Taverner's business was anything but a thriving success, but it made for a comfortable lifestyle for a while, at least. Finally, in 1927, by which time only a handful of people remained in Lewisham, Taverner made the torturous decision to close the store. The move was probably prompted by the government's decision to revoke the post office contract. Taverner held an auction to sell off the remainder of the stock, and then went into retirement.

Logs were dragged on skids from the forested interior to waterways by hard-working horses. Come the spring floods, the logs would be washed downstream to awaiting mills. This load, though it seems large, is actually only of moderate size.

What befell the once impressive store? According to Jim Taverner, it was torn down in 1945 or 1946, the valuable lumber needed elsewhere. Certainly there's no sign left of it in the forest clearing that was once Lewisham.

All Saints Anglican Church

To the hard-working, stoic people of Muskoka, religion was more of a consolation than an inspiration — a very necessary consolation when they had to bear so many tragedies in their lives. They required formal places of worship — churches — in which to find strength in others sharing similar hardships and to demonstrate to the Lord that their faith was unflappable despite all that life might throw their way. In the end, it was expected, or at least hoped, that their religious observance would be rewarded with thriving farms and a healthy community in the midst of the wilderness.

In many cases, and certainly in that of Lewisham, such hopes proved unfounded. The farms never proved bountiful and the hamlet struggled even in the best of years.

But that was for the future. When Lewisham was first settled the residents were full of enthusiasm and devotion to both their new homes and their God. All Saints Anglican Church was the expression of this strength of purpose.

For Lewisham's first decade, the drudgery of everyday existence and the scarcity of resources prevented the settlers from giving much time or thought to the erection of a church. It was simply not in the cards for a hamlet fighting to get off the ground, a luxury they simply couldn't afford. Instead, they worshipped in their homes.

Things began to change in the early 1880s. As the people became more established they could give more freely, and the vision of a church began to take shape. In 1884, Anthony Annis deeded an acre of land for the construction of All Saints Anglican Church, an all-log structure built by local farmers Charlie Fenton and Isaac Loshaw. The timber used was donated by homesteaders, and John Fox donated some cut lumber from his sawmill for interior work.

Upon completion, the church became the focus of the hamlet. Baptisms, weddings, and burials: all the stages of life were experienced and blessed within this humble house of worship. Family and friends witnessed these events together, sharing joys and sorrow as one, and it couldn't help but bring the community closer together.

All Saints watched as Lewisham reached its pinnacle around 1890 and slowly declined from that peak. With each passing year the pews were less full and the faith upon which the church had been built seemed to crumble. By the 1940s the village was almost empty and the church a hollow shell, all but devoid of spirit and passionate devotion. The hardships of living in the rugged isolation of Lewisham had simply worn people down.

All that remains today of the church, the only thing to remind us it had ever existed, is the cemetery, though it's barely recognizable as such today.

In the latter half of the twentieth century, after All Saints had closed, the cemetery was taken over by the Bracebridge Cemetery Board, which immediately closed it to further burials. Its one concession to those whose families lay within the hallowed grounds was to place a natural stone monument with a bronze plaque to memorialize the former community and its dead.

The decision to close the cemetery to interments made sense, but it didn't sit well with one family, and with one man in particular. Charles Loshaw, the grandson of early settler Isaac Loshaw, was devoted to his wife, Lisa Amelia, and was devastated when she passed away in 1943 at the age of thirty-six. He promised that one day they would be together again and wasn't about to let bureaucratic regulations get in the way of the solemn vow. In his golden years, Charles let it be known in no uncertain terms that his family was to bury him beside Lisa Amelia.

Charles passed away in 1974. His grieving family honoured his wishes, and without permission buried him with his long-dead wife. Legally speaking, it might have been wrong, but morally nothing could have been more right. Their stone is the only one in the cemetery today, the others having either sunk into the earth or, because many were likely wooden, simply rotted away over time.

The presence of a new, shiny headstone in the midst of an empty field in a deserted, mournful wilderness village is almost surreal. It reminds you on the one hand that Lewisham is dead but also that people remain who have strong emotional ties to the former community. You can't help but feel that as long as breath remains in these people, a part of Lewisham will always exist.

10
MONSELL

Monsell was one of those farming hamlets that emerged in the early years of Muskoka, when hopeful settlers flocked into the untapped region in large numbers, and that rapidly disappeared once the settlers realized the soil was all but useless for cultivation. Monsell clung tenaciously to life but has since vanished almost without a trace. Farms are overgrown, barns rotted away, and fields swallowed by regenerating forest.

Visiting the isolated site of Monsell today, a person is left incredulous that farms and a thriving village ever took root here. It's about as far from hospitable as Muskoka has to offer — the forests are thick and dark, the terrain hilly and dotted with marshlands. There's no place where even the most imaginative person could visualize fields of grain waving gently in the wind.

And yet, for a time in the late nineteenth century, that's exactly what one would have found here. The harsh reality of the land only makes Monsell's story that much more gripping.

Settlers began to arrive along the second and third concessions of Macaulay Township from late 1869 through the early 1870s, taking up hundred-acre plots of unbroken forest offered free to willing souls.[1] Few likely had any real concept of what they were getting into, as they wouldn't have seen the land prior to committing their names to the deeds and had already been seduced by the glowing reports being issued by immigration agents. The reality of Muskoka proved a disheartening surprise to many.

But despite what must have been initial shock and despair at the sight of the rugged wilderness that represented their futures, the early settlers of Monsell took to establishing their homesteads with enthusiasm and hope. These men and women hailed from Great Britain, where owning land was a privilege reserved for the wealthy. Driven by a desire to plant

Most references to Monsell suggest nothing remains of the tiny, short-lived hamlet. They're wrong. Numerous reminders of Monsell's past can be found among the regenerating forest, such as these stone posts flanking Blind Line, a secondary road leading past McCrae's Lake.

their feet on land they could call their own, a goal they never could have achieved back home, they fell upon the forest with axe and saw, carving islands of habitation out of the endless expanse of trees.

They were so successful, in spite of the odds, that within a few years a little community began to take shape, and with it the trappings of civilization. A frame school was built, a church followed, and in 1876 James Gregg opened a post office under the name Monsell.[2]

Monsell was never a large hamlet, and with its handful of homes and businesses strung out along the primitive roads, nor did it have a recognizable core. Nevertheless, while Monsell may not have been a community in form, it was most definitely one in spirit. Neighbours joined together to build and maintain the church and school, assisted one another in erecting barns and clearing stumps from the fields, and closed ranks to lend whatever feeble aid they could in times of need.

And there were many trying times in Monsell's short history to test the faith and fortitude of the settlers. The worst occurred while the village was still in its infancy, threatening to kill Monsell before it even had the chance to mature. The year 1879 saw nature at its worst. First came a destructive hailstorm in August that destroyed much of the grain crop. In its aftermath, farmers picked their ways through flattened fields, anguished at a healthy crop suddenly ruined. Hailstones the size of baseballs littered the ground, taunting the despairing farmers with their presence. This freak storm was followed by an early and killing frost that wiped out what little of the crop that had somehow survived. Everyone knew that desperate months lay ahead.

By early 1880, hundreds of families across the region were on the verge of starvation, among them many in Monsell. People were surviving on turnips or nothing at all. Neighbours, when they could spare a morsel, willingly and selflessly gave to those less fortunate. Weakened by poor diet, many people fell ill, and again communities came together to care for their own. The situation grew so dire — in all of Muskoka and Parry Sound District, not just Monsell — that the Colonization Roads Department had to step in with emergency aid to save lives.[3]

But from the fires of travesty was forged a stronger, more tightly knit community. Perhaps it was this unity of purpose and a collective resolve toughened by hardship that allowed Monsell not only to survive the disaster of 1879–80 but also to grow over the ensuing decades despite the fact that the soil tended to yield healthy crops of stones and little else.

At its peak around the turn of the century, Monsell boasted a population of about fifty, a brick school, a church, and probably a blacksmith, though no records of one have remained either on paper or in local recollection. The 1903 directory lists James Gregg as still the owner of the general store and James Clark as postmaster, presumably operating out of his own home.[4]

Slowly, however, one by one, the farms lining Monsell Road began to go fallow over the ensuing decades. For every settler who endured to make a go of their bush farm, there was another who conceded defeat and walked away. This was especially true of the second generation of homesteading families; few sons saw any future in Monsell and remained to succeed their aging fathers on the farm. Many fled for jobs in the city or joined the mass flight for the Prairies where arable farmland was still available.

The most spectacular find of an afternoon spent exploring Monsell's history is this stone foundation, all that remains of James Clark's barn. Looking at the dense woods and the rugged terrain, it's difficult for modern visitors to imagine any agriculture was possible here.

The village was living on borrowed time. If dejection didn't claim the original settler, death inevitably would, and as a result with each passing year it seemed another farm was left abandoned and the population of Monsell dwindled. A dark pall descended upon the once vibrant community, the reaper waiting to claim its next victim.

It didn't have long to wait. In 1925 the school closed, the general store having closed up shop some years prior, and four years later the post office was closed as well.[5] By then Monsell was little more than a name on a map.

Today it's not even that. Monsell is totally deserted and the forest has regrown, hinting at the sight that would have greeted the earliest inhabitants upon first arriving at their land grants. Monsell Road, which once would have been flanked by fields of wheat and echoed with the sound of horse teams struggling to pull wagons along its rutted surface, is now eerily silent as it winds over hills and through swamps. The road is barely maintained and all but impassible to anything but all-terrain vehicles during wet seasons.

This abandoned and rotting truck, found partly obscured by foliage in the woods, provides evidence that at least a few farms remained in operation into the 1940s.

But the jarring ride is well worth it. Along the road you'll find muted evidence of the community that once clung to life amidst the wilderness. There's a haunting barn foundation, imposing in its size, its stone walls cold and somehow eerie. Nearby is a rusting truck from the 1930s, left behind when the farmer turned his back on the failing farm. Across the road is a stone wall demarking the edge of a field. Elsewhere along Monsell Road, you can find stone gates, depressions where buildings once stood, and narrow trails that represent one-time farmers' lanes or side roads.

The Monsell Schoolhouse

In the early 1870s, only a few short years after the first settlers had arrived to put down roots along Monsell Road, a frame schoolhouse, SS #5, was built to accommodate the educational needs of the pioneer families.[6]

Building and afterwards maintaining a school was a true communal effort in those days, and residents had a very real say in how their children were educated. Townships were divided into school sections, with each section having an elected band of three trustees to oversee the schoolhouse and its operation. To these men went the responsibility of accounting for ratepayers' funds, acquiring a suitable site on which to erect the school, organizing the bee to raise the building, and hiring the schoolteacher on an annual basis.

The latter was oftentimes the most difficult chore, because the life of a pioneer schoolmaster or -mistress was a trying one. They were paid a mere pittance (often less than $20 per month), and in addition to teaching children they were expected to serve as caretakers of the school, arriving early to start the woodstove and leaving late to clean up after a long day. Worse, they were subjected to strict behavioural codes: they could not date or marry (it was considered unseemly for children to be exposed to someone in a romantic relationship); were forbidden from drinking or being seen in a public gathering spot, such as a tavern or fraternal hall; and must at all times remain proper and refined.

Gradually the pay increased and the invasive supervision of their lifestyles eased somewhat, but still the job was often too much for a teacher to long endure. Consequently, many left after a single season, some to find better employ, others — most particularly women — to marry. It's no wonder that the Monsell School went through a total of ten teachers during the period 1913 to 1925 alone![7]

Teacher turnover wasn't the only upheaval experienced by this small, isolated school. When originally built, the school was located on Lot 22, Concession 2, near the marsh-lined Beaver River and about a mile west of what would be — for a lack of better term — Monsell's core. At the time of building this location was considered central for the majority of students, but within a few years it became apparent that this belief had been misplaced and that, to serve the community better, the school would have to be moved.

There was some debate before the trustees finally determined that the ideal location for the schoolhouse would be nearer Gregg's store and Clark's post office, the two most important fixtures in the village around which most of the communal activity centred. To that end, a parcel of land was obtained from H.W. Haley (Lot 26, Concession 2), and during the winter of 1877 the building was raised off its foundations, placed on skids, and hauled to its new location by a team of horses. This new spot was far more ideal, and the Monsell School would remain here for the duration of its existence.

By 1903, the wood schoolhouse was falling into disrepair and the community had outgrown its meagre size. At considerable expense, especially in light of Monsell's lack of means, a new brick school was built on the same locale.

Records are sparse, but the school seems to have closed temporarily during the years 1914 and 1915. This might have been a result of low attendance, or perhaps because a schoolmaster couldn't be procured. It might be that both factors conspired to wipe out these school years. The First World War had started. Thousands of men across Ontario enlisted in the army in the name of King and Country, abandoning farms and jobs to perform their duty as they saw it. The sudden absence of so many men created a labour shortage, and the vacuum could only be filled by women and children.

In Monsell's particular case, this meant that wives and children would have been solely preoccupied with operating already struggling farms; education placed a distant second to providing for the family. The pool of students would have been small and the availability of a local teacher almost non-existent.

School doors opened once again in 1916 and remained open for another decade. One of the most popular postwar teachers was Nora Fraser, but her tenure was tragically brief. She taught the 1921 term, during which she became beloved by parents and students alike, and then during the summer hiatus went to Toronto for some reason no longer recalled. There, she was hit by a streetcar. The wounds were supposed to be superficial, but shortly after returning home her mind began to unravel. Nora was unable to teach for her 1922 contract, and in fact never returned to teaching, nor did she ever fully recover from her injuries. Her absence was dearly felt, both in the school and in the tight-knit community.[8]

There was only a flicker of life left in the schoolhouse by this point. Each year the number of students dwindled as, one by one, families abandoned their farms and moved away. By 1925, there was no longer any way to prolong the inevitable, and the Monsell School was closed. To teacher Irene Wiley went the sad duty of dismissing class for the final time.

No records remain as to when the schoolhouse was torn down, but no sign of it remains today. It's probable that the building was carefully dismantled so as to make use of the bricks once more.

James Clark and the Monsell Post Office

Because the road system was so poor and travel was such a difficult undertaking, settlers had to have all their necessities close at hand, certainly no more than a few miles away. Monsell is a product of that reality, one of those once common hamlets that existed only to serve the immediate needs of pioneer farmers.

Among these needs was that of a post office.

Modern readers may have a difficult time appreciating the importance of the post office to a community, especially those isolated in the northern wilds. Few settlers would ever venture further afield than the nearest town, and even into the 1920s phones were a rarity in rural Muskoka, so mail was quite often the only link with the outside world. Mail allowed settlers to remain in contact, tenuous and infrequent though it may have been, with family members elsewhere in Ontario or back in the old country, vitally important for keeping spirits up in the face of the adversity Muskoka would throw at those attempting to tame her.

There was another aspect to post offices that was equally important. If a community was graced by a post office it meant it had "grown up," officially recognized by the Canadian government. It was a matter of communal pride.

Monsell received its post office early, on May 1, 1876.[9] Because it was usually the first business in a new village, the Canadian government typically appointed the storekeeper as the local postmaster. This tradition initially held true in Monsell as well, where store proprietor George Gregg was awarded the prestigious position.

Though Gregg operated his store well into the 1900s, he was destined to hold onto the title of postmaster for only six short years. On June 1, 1882, farmer Richard Byers became the new postmaster, and henceforth, for the remainder of the Monsell post office's existence, it operated out of private homes.

Byers held onto the job of postmaster for even less time than had Gregg; in 1886 it passed to James Clark. Finally, under this redoubtable figure, the post office achieved some stability. In fact, Clark would operate the service for a remarkable tenure of forty-two years.

James Clark was a towering figure in Monsell's history. Born in County Tyrone, Ireland, in 1839, he immigrated to Canada to escape the crushing depression that gripped his homeland and inevitably found himself in Muskoka, the only place a man of few means could hope to acquire land of his own. He was one of the first settlers in Monsell, signing his name to Lots 26 and 27, Concession 1, on November 5, 1869.

Courtesy Gary Denniss.

Macaulay Township Council, 1890. James Clark is in the second row on the far right. Clark was a man with many roles — farmer, post master, Macaulay Township councillor, and school section trustee. When he died in 1929, a part of Monsell died with him.

As with the other farmers along Monsell Road, Clark devoted his first few years to clearing the land for crops, building a home in which to raise his family, and generally just trying to make ends meet.[10] He was more successful in these tasks than most, founding a farm that would last nearly to the middle of the twentieth century, and rapidly became among the wealthiest and most respected men in the vicinity.

In light of his local prominence, it should come as no surprise that Clark was put forward by his peers for public office. He was a school section trustee for the entire duration of the Monsell schoolhouse's existence and served as a councillor for Macaulay Township for a record term of thirty years. This was an era when the position of postmaster was a political appointment, oftentimes granted and taken away based solely upon patronage or the ebbs and tides of political fortunes. As a result, Clark's appointment as postmaster was a reflection of his role in township affairs and served to reinforce his status within the community.

Mail in those days was collected from Bracebridge and brought to the post office in large canvas sacks, where it was sorted and held for villagers. When people came to collect their mail, more often than not they loitered for a time, sharing news and discussing local events. Finding time for each and every patron was vitally important to Clark, both as postmaster and politician.

"Having charge of a rural post office was a task that involved more than just handling the mail and selling postage stamps," observed Bob Palmer in the *Huntsville Forester* in 1969. "Indeed, it was a position that, at times, required the wisdom of Solomon and the abundant patience of Job. It was to the local postmaster or postmistress that the troubled and weary unloaded their problems and gained a listening ear for their aches and pains. To each and every patron the guardian of the mail was expected to have just the right answer, a sympathetic comment or happy smile, as the case may warrant."[11]

James Clark was also well known for his religious convictions. An ardent Protestant, he was a leading member of the Loyal Orange Order, never missing a celebration of the Battle of the Boyne from the time he was accepted into the lodge at the age of seventeen until his death.[12]

Perhaps this religious fervour should come as no surprise, since he was born on the twelfth of July, the very day on which the battle was fought and commemorated. Clark also served as warden for the Purbrook Anglican Church for many years, and in fact it was his honour to lay the cornerstone when the church was built.

It's hard to say which was the greater blow to Monsell: the death of James Clark or the closing of the post office. The former came on June 7, 1932. His funeral was one of the largest ever seen in Muskoka, bringing together hundreds of Orangemen and some of the most prominent men from across the district.

The latter occurred a few years earlier, in 1929, when the population of Monsell was no longer deemed large enough to require a post office of its own. When the building closed, it was personal for the locals. The post office was part of the community, tied to the ebb and flow of life in this tiny village, central to its identity.

When it was gone, a large part of what remained of Monsell went with it.

The Primitive Methodist Church

There was only ever one church in Monsell, and it lasted perhaps only five or six years. Was this because, as one contemporary witness wrote, the residents were "half dead spiritually"? Would a church that had existed for such a short period of time have left any footprint to mark its passing, either physically or in communal lore? These were questions that plagued us as we began to explore Monsell's religious past.

We quickly learned that Monsell was in no way less faithful than other communities in Muskoka. To the contrary, it was home to some of the most religiously observant individuals we'd ever come across. It so happens, however, that most residents were Anglicans, and there was already an Anglican church in nearby Purbrook. In light of the small population of Monsell and the proximity to an existing church, there was thought to be no need — and probably no means — to build a new Anglican house of worship in the hamlet.

But that's not to say that other religious groups didn't see things differently. Among them were the Primitive Methodists, one of the smaller denominations in Muskoka.

A Primitive Methodist congregation was established at Monsell around 1870, though originally there were only seven or eight members who met in a private home. The faithful were served by a preacher who made the seven-mile trek from Bracebridge, a man of the cloth who was undeterred by even the foulest of weather. In the springtime, for example, much of the lowlands around Monsell would be flooded by winter melt-off and the preacher would be forced to wade knee-deep in chilled, murky water to reach the community and tend to his small flock. His boots would fill with water and his socks would freeze to his feet, but he never failed to provide a rousing sermon, despite his discomfort.[13]

Perhaps inspired by the selfless preacher and his moving services, others began to join the congregation so that by the late 1870s there were as many as nineteen Primitive Methodists in Monsell. There were now too many worshippers to continue meeting in someone's home, so it was decided that a church would be built.

In 1878, Sherman Baldwin sold one acre of land from his property (Lot 21, Concession 3) to the trustees of the Primitive Methodist Church for a token fee of one dollar. Later that year, a small frame church was erected on this site.

As fate would have it, the church was only used for five or six years. In 1884, the Primitive Methodist Church ceased to exist as a separate religious identity when it put aside dogmatic differences to unify with other Methodist groups. When this happened, there was naturally a consolidation and contraction of churches, and that at Monsell was one of those victimized. Its ultimate fate is unknown: some suggest it was demolished, others that it rotted away with age. More than likely, the building would have been dismantled so the wood could be salvaged and put to use elsewhere.

The church may be gone, but it's not entirely forgotten. Alongside Taylor Road there stands an unassuming wooden post, unmarked but clearly demarking something of past importance. It was a puzzle to us

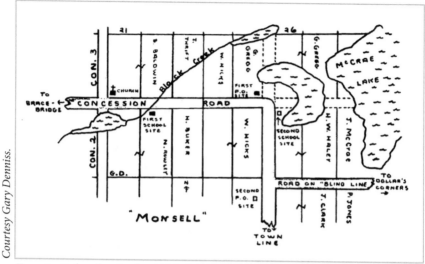

Even in its heyday in the 1890s Monsell was tiny, more a collection of farms strung along concession roads than a village with an identifiable core. It boasted a short-lived church, a store, a school, and little else.

Courtesy Gary Denniss.

at first, and theories flew back and forth between us. We eventually determined that this was the site of the short-lived Primitive Methodist Church and that someone had taken the liberty of marking it so we wouldn't forget that this section of bush was once, a long time ago, holy ground.

Murder in Monsell?

What could possibly drive a mother to kill her own child? That was the question being asked by residents of Monsell back in 1936 when a horrific act was committed in the midst of their peaceful hamlet.[14]

Orma Jones was like any other twenty-year-old of the era. She worked hard on the family farm but had dreams of one day meeting the love of her life and making a home for the two of them and the children that she and her husband would some day have together.

But until that time, Orma did all that her mother asked of her. Her father had died three years prior, leaving his wife with a large family to feed and a farm in desperate straits. With his absence, everyone had to work that much harder to survive, especially with the country in the midst of the Depression.

There were days when the chores never seemed to end, and Orma found herself working to the point of exhaustion.

The sun had just started to rise on August 20, 1936, the earth was beginning to warm, and the sky cleared for what promised to be a beautiful day when Mrs. Jones awoke for another busy day on the farm. There were the animals to feed, washing to do, fields to look after, and a host of other tasks. She was tired just thinking of her day ahead.

Mrs. Jones shouted for Orma to wake up and milk the cow so they could eat a small meal and then get started with their day. There was no answer. She called out time and time again, but got no reply. Mrs. Jones began to worry and decided to walk to the neighbouring farm of John Clark for help in finding her daughter.[15] The farm was about three kilometres away by road.

She arrived breathless at Clarks', pleading for assistance. She asked to use the phone, calling her daughter in Bracebridge and other relatives for help in finding Orma. A call was also placed to Fred Sander, the chief of police, who sent his son, Raymond, and a few other young men to assist in the search.

The Jones property was scoured thoroughly, but the girl was nowhere to be found. At wits' end, someone suggested that they search the home itself. Raymond opened the door slowly and stared aghast at a floor stained with blood.

He couldn't possibly have imagined what he would discover next.

Warily making his way around the blood, careful not to step in the crimson puddle, he went room to room searching for Orma, afraid of what he would find should he happen upon her.

Orma was discovered upstairs, lying face down on a bed. Her body was slumped over the covers, drenched in blood. Her hair was matted crimson, and as the young man drew nearer he could see that she had suffered several blows to the head. She appeared to be lifeless.

Orma was immediately rushed to the hospital, where doctors fought to save her life. She had six or seven deep wounds to the head, probably caused by an axe, which fractured her skull and pierced her brain. She had lost a considerable amount of blood.

Constable Hardwick went out to the Jones house to search for anything that could shed some light on this horrible crime that left a small community in shock. He found that Orma and her mother had been the only two staying at the house; the rest of the family were away.

Later an axe that had only recently been washed was discovered in the cellar. Was this the weapon that had been used on poor, helpless Orma, and if so, who had done the hateful crime? Suspicion began to fall on Mrs. Jones.

Inspector Ward, a seasoned detective from Toronto, was brought in to assist in the inquiry. Mrs. Jones was remanded in court and interrogated repeatedly about what had happened that morning. She apparently could not recall, leaving some to surmise that for reasons unknown Mrs. Jones had become temporarily insane, assaulted her daughter, and then suffered short-term amnesia.

The law, however, would have none of it. In the eyes of the police and prosecutors, Mrs. Jones had attempted cold-blooded murder and they fully intended to make her stand trial for her actions. The only thing that was uncertain was what crime she would be tried for, and that was to be determined by the outcome of Orma's desperate fight for life.

Incredibly, the young woman survived the vicious attack. In light of the gruesome extent of the wounds, her survival was considered nothing less than a miracle. But Orma's recovery in no way softened views towards her mother, and all of Muskoka watched with bated breath as she stood trial for attempted murder, praying that the cold woman would face her due justice.

This horrific drama shook the hamlet of Monsell to its very core. The residents attempted to bury it, to erase the blight upon their community's good name, and they seem to have largely succeeded, for the vicious attack and the scandalous trial — including its outcome — are all but forgotten today.

11
UFFINGTON

While not exactly a ghost town, the Uffington of today pales in comparison with its heyday of a century ago when it boasted a population of several hundred, the din of thriving commercial activity filled the air, and a steady stream of traffic passed along the busy Peterson Road.[1]

Uffington was a crossroads village like so many others across pioneer-era Ontario, owing much of its importance to its position astride a busy thoroughfare. But it's unique in one key respect: whereas most crossroads communities cluster around a single intersection, Uffington clustered around two. These twin crossroads — Hawn Road and Peterson Road in the west, Uffington Road and Peterson Road in the east — formed bookends, between which lay most of the village.

The community got its start in the 1860s, when a handful of resolute pioneers pushed into the oppressive tangles of Draper Township to settle homesteads.[2] These early settlers blazed the way for the wave of would-be homesteaders who flocked into the area during the following decade, facing down the worst that the wilderness could dish out and laying the vital foundation for the arrival of civilization.

It's difficult to imagine the hardships these first settlers stoically endured: harsh winters, fearless forest predators, maddening isolation, and an endless sea of trees that swamped the very land the settlers were depending upon to provide for their livelihood. "The wife guarded the home against wild beasts while the young husband wielded the axe against the mighty pine" — so read the obituary for Phoebe Bull Matthews, who arrived in 1862, but it might well have equally applied to any of the first arrivals.[3]

During the decade that followed, most of the land in the area was claimed by other eager homesteaders, and slowly a community began to emerge. Robert McMurray opened the first store, and George Spence opened another a mile or so to the east. And this was just the beginning; more than a dozen other businesses appeared soon after to transform this previously unnoteworthy stretch of road into the economic heart of Draper Township.

The Uffington that emerged was a rapidly growing and prosperous village, its fortunes tied to its strategic location astride the Peterson Colonization Road and two busy secondary roads. Every day, several stagecoaches and countless wagons would rattle through town, and invariably their passengers would want to stop at a hotel for liquid refreshment, a store for supplies, or at a smithy to have horses shod or wheels repaired. These passengers generated wealth for the many businesses that soon sprung up and prosperity for the community at large.

But Uffington was blessed in other ways as well. The land here is one of the few patches of decent farmland in Muskoka, meaning farmers were not fighting a life-and-death struggle for survival every day. This relative comfort allowed them to devote time and resources to communal functions (such as operating an agricultural society, hosting

Courtesy Christie Historical Committee.

Like so many communities across Muskoka, the people of Uffington relied upon the logging industry for much of its economic vitality. Money earned working winters at logging camps helped keep area farms afloat longer than the meagre gains yielded from the soil should have allowed.

seasonal fairs, and founding fraternal organizations), thereby enriching the village.

At the same time, there were also excellent timber resources in the vicinity. The benefits of a thriving lumbering industry were threefold: there were valuable winter jobs for farmers, a ready market for the farmers' goods, and numerous seasonal lumbermen who proved all too willing to spend some of their hard-earned money at local businesses.

Foremost among the businesses frequented by loggers were the two Uffington hotels, one sitting astride each crossroad.

In addition to the hotels, Uffington also boasted several blacksmith shops, two stores, three churches (Anglican, Presbyterian, and Methodist), a sawmill, an Orange Hall, a township hall, Richard Ketching's shoe shop, a school, and more than a dozen buildings. A stagecoach running between Uffington and Gravenhurst twice weekly was operated by John Coulson, and after him by George Foster. The population as of 1890, when Uffington was probably at its peak, stood at about two hundred, making it the largest rural community in Draper, Macaulay, Stephenson, or Ryde Townships.

The residents of Uffington were sure great things were in store for their village, that the prosperity would continue unabated. Almost to a man, they looked confidently towards the future.

Unfortunately, their confidence was misplaced. Within a few short decades, Uffington had lost its place as a major commercial centre and was devolving back into a sleepy village. Through a combination of events, the fortune that had for a time smiled on Uffington suddenly disappeared.

Trains struck the first blow against the town's fortunes. The railways passed the village by, electing to run their lines more westerly through communities such as Gravenhurst and Bracebridge. This decision was a devastating blow for Uffington. It reduced road travel to a mere trickle, depriving the community of its lifeblood. The once busy crossroads began to quiet appreciably, more so with each passing year.

Soon thereafter, the forests of the region having been played out and most of the worthwhile timber already culled, the timber industry moved further north in search of new forests to exploit. This had a profound effect on Uffington's economy, but nowhere was it felt greater than in the hotels that had subsisted almost entirely on the sale of alcoholic refreshment to the hard-working men employed in logging. Neither hotel survived long into the twentieth century.

Other businesses fared little better. Slowly, most of them moved elsewhere or closed up shop completely. At the same time, the village began to lose its mills. By 1920, only one general store and a blacksmith shop remained. The former closed in the early 1930s, and the latter in 1955. In the meantime, most of Uffington's buildings had been allowed to fall into ruin, their decaying forms casting the village in a ghostly shroud.

If the village wasn't dead, it was certainly mortally ill.

But fast-forward half a century and we find something of a rebirth in Uffington. Thanks to its proximity to Bracebridge and Highway 11, a number of modern homes have appeared on one-time pioneer lots, restoring a semblance of life to the once moribund community. It hasn't risen phoenix-like from the ashes, but one can at least detect a pulse once more.

That's not to say, however, that the shroud that once enveloped Uffington has entirely been lifted. It's still a sad, faded vestige of what it was a century prior. Farm fields have overgrown, barns have collapsed into piles of beams and timbers, and once prominent buildings stand in ruin.

The most notable of these decaying landmarks is St. Paul's Anglican Church. As recently as a decade ago it had a small but proud congregation. In 2005 it closed, its three regular attendees no longer able to maintain its upkeep. Today, it's weathered and vandalized, the sanctity of holy ground no ward against nature and troublesome youths.

A short distance away is the one-time Orange Hall. It fares somewhat better than St. Paul's but is badly weathered and seems humiliated by its new role as a storage shed.

Other buildings are more fortunate, having been given a new lease on life by caring owners. The schoolhouse and one of the former stores are well-tended private homes, and several pioneer-era homes still stand along the Peterson Road, now noticeably more tranquil than it would have been when these homes were originally built.

Uffington is but a faded vestige of its once vibrant self and will never get to relive those heady early days when it was the commercial core of the region. It's a blend of old and new, despair and optimism. For now, modern development is only slowly encroaching, and as a result the rich history of this village is never far away, always tantalizingly near at hand. It's in the historic homes and churches, several of which date back more than a century; it's in the cemeteries, where headstones of those who laboured to establish Uffington lean wearily with age; and, of course, it's in the Peterson Road that still forms the backbone of the community.

The Churches of Uffington

Lurking alongside the Peterson Road, the weathered and ruinous St. Paul's Anglican Church is a tragic landmark. It represents the last of Uffington's three churches, each of which were tied to the hopes and dreams of those settlers who came to this rugged land. In Muskoka, where life was difficult at the best of times, church and community often entwined in a relationship that was symbolic and symbiotic. People invested resources into building houses of worship out of a deep sense of faith and trusted that this faith would be rewarded by prosperity for themselves and their community.

That two of Uffington's three churches have long since disappeared, and the last remaining is now abandoned and derelict, demonstrates the depths to which the village's fortunes have plummeted in only a century.

When Sunday morning rolled around in the 1880s, when Uffington was at its peak, villagers had a choice of churches at which to worship. The Anglican church had the largest number of faithful, but there were also sizable Presbyterian and Methodist congregations who were equally proud.

Two of the churches, the Methodist and Presbyterian, watched one another from opposite sides of Uffington Road, just south of the Peterson Road. The former was located on the west side, the latter on the east.

The Presbyterian church was the shortest lived. Built around 1885, it didn't last long into the twentieth century, the victim of a congregation that was never large to begin with and a consolidation of churches across Ontario in the early 1900s with the aim of making fewer but healthier congregations.

Many times during the church's abbreviated existence, an ordained minister was not on hand for Sunday services. On such occasions, Albert Spring, a local farmer who used a natural eloquence to have himself elected reeve of Draper, would step up to the pulpit and provide a rousing sermon so as to not disappoint the entire congregation. When Spring moved to British Columbia around the turn of the century, it left a gaping void in the church that was never adequately filled.[4]

The Methodist church predated the Presbyterian one by more than a decade and endured long after it was gone. As early as 1863, circuit riders for the Primitive Methodist church claimed to be holding services in Uffington, providing religious succour for the few faithful souls that had taken up wilderness lots at this early date. Since there was no dedicated church in the area at this time, services would have been held in homes or barns, and would remain so for almost two decades. Nehemiah Matthews, a staunch Methodist, would frequently host these religious services, and his house, little more than a log shanty, became known as "the cradle of the Methodist Church."[5]

Uffington expanded rapidly during the 1870s, with homesteaders pouring into the region and on their heels businesses catering to their needs. As the community rose in population and wealth, the resident Methodists began to entertain the thought of a true church, one that reflected in its size and stature the depth of their faith.

In 1879, such dreams became reality. The Uffington Methodist Church was a large building — it had to be with a congregation numbering 142 — with a tall steeple that reached proudly up to the heavens. The attending minister at the time was James Woodsworth, the father of J.S. Woodsworth, the man largely responsible for establishing the Canadian Commonwealth Federation (CCF), the precursor to the modern New Democratic Party of Canada (NDP).

Sharing a circuit rider with other nearby communities was hardly ideal, especially for a community as large as Uffington had become. In order to attract a permanent minister, the locals built a fine manse in 1884. The gambit succeeded, and for decades a minister resided full-time in town, devoting his prayers and energies almost solely to the needs of Uffington's Methodists.

As the population of Uffington declined precipitously in the twentieth century, so too did the fortunes of the Methodist ministry. The congregation atrophied, the priest was withdrawn, and the church was forced to close. As late as the 1970s both the manse and the church remained standing. Today, however, both are gone and the village lacks any reminder of its Methodist heritage.

St. Paul's Anglican Church was the first church built in Uffington, a log predecessor to the current structure being erected in 1870 on land donated by William Kirkpatrick. For the first few years, at least, the village shared its reverend with other nearby communities: as late as 1876 the minister was holding Sunday morning services in Bracebridge and Sunday afternoon services alternately at Gravenhurst and Uffington.[6]

By 1889 the congregation had outgrown the primitive structure and it was decided that a new church should be built. That summer, the log church was torn down and a new frame church was raised on the same site. The consecration service was held in January 1890.

The size and wealth of the congregation was reflected in the stature and relative opulence of the church itself; it boasted a bell to announce Sunday service, numerous beautifully crafted stained glass windows, and enough room to comfortably seat one hundred people.

Its decline was painful and tragic. In 1900, the church would have been filled to overflowing with eager parishioners, forcing people to stand alongside the pews and at the back in order to hear sermons. A century later, there were fewer than five people routinely attending church, far too few to keep the parish intact and the building in shape. In 2005, the historic church experienced its final service. There was not a dry eye among them as the last remaining members of the 135-year-old congregation filed out and said their goodbyes to Uffington's last remaining house of God.

In the few short years since this sorrowful event, the church has weathered noticeably. It's clear that in all its glory the St. Paul's church must have been a point of pride for the community, but today this historic building is a sad site. The church bell is silent, for henceforth

St. Paul's Church has tended to the spiritual needs of Uffington for generations, but today its own spirits flag as services have been discontinued and the building falls into disrepair.

no parishioners will be attending service. We've come across a lot of neglected buildings in our search for the past, but it never fails to break our hearts, especially when the building in question was once a house of God. Shingles peel on the roof, stained glass windows lay shattered, and the front door hangs open and sways lazily in the wind. Inside, an organ stands tall at the back of the building, waiting to see if anyone will give it the honour of being played once more. Age and neglect has not diminished its majesty in any way. Beside it stands a 125-year-old baptismal basin, inscribed with the text, "presented by St. Paul's to the S. School — 1887 of Brantford, Ont." We question why no one has bothered to take it to safety. The rows of pews wait patiently for the feel of life to grace them.

Outside, the cemetery seems oddly bereft of headstones for such an old, large congregation. There are no more than half a dozen stark stones, all huddled in one corner, most dating from the late 1800s. Surely there should have been many more, especially in light of the tragic consequences of life in pioneer-era Muskoka.

In fact, it seems there were many burials in the cemetery, beginning with David Kirkpatrick, who died March 13, 1889, at the age of nineteen months. At one time, the churchyard would have been filled with silent stone markers, far too many of them bearing the names of children who'd fallen prey to illness and disease. With the passage of more than a century, however, most of these grim headstones have sunk into the ground or crumbled away. Walking the grounds, we unknowingly trod upon the graves of dozens of people whose names, sadly, are now forgotten. With no stones to mark their passing, it's almost as if these individuals never existed. It's hard to imagine anything more tragic.

St. Paul's Anglican Church was once a building that brought the community together in faith and devotion. Now it waits patiently to see if once again the people of Uffington will come together and restore the weathered but still magnificent building back to its splendour. All this church can do is wait, hope … and have faith.

The Uffington Schoolhouse

With the gradual rise of Uffington's population came the need for local schooling. The result was the one-room Uffington School House, School Section #3. There were actually three SS #3 schools in the village's history, the last incarnation of which is still used as a private residence.

Though there may have been improvised schooling within a private residence sometime earlier, the first organized school in Uffington emerged around 1868. Classes were held in a log building, quite probably a former settler's cabin, which was located on the northwest corner of the Peterson Road–Uffington Road crossroads. Cold and damp, the building was less than ideal, but it would have to do for the time being.

The chain of events that led to the second schoolhouse began 1872, when the members of the local Loyal Orange Lodge built a frame structure to house their meetings right next door to the log schoolhouse.[7] The deficiencies in the original school had by now become glaring, and so the trustees were desperately looking for a room to rent where classes could be held in greater comfort. Why not the new Orange Lodge right next door?

The trustees approached the Loyal Orange Order with their proposition, and they were only too glad to agree. After all, many of them had children and they couldn't have been pleased with the primitive conditions in the log cabin. The rent for six months of school was eight dollars.

About a decade passed, with the Orangemen and the village youth sharing use of the building. But then, in circumstances that are somewhat mysterious, it surfaced that the Loyal Orange Lodge didn't actually have a deed to the property and were therefore little more than squatters. Despite having built it with their own funds, they were evicted from the hall and watched with equal measures of anger and dismay as the building was turned over to the school trustees.

Hard feelings had barely subsided when the object of the controversy burned to the ground in 1877. Was it an accident or had a disgruntled Orangeman decided to take vengeance for the way his lodge had been treated? One will never know.

A new school, the third SS #3, emerged on the same lot in 1888. It was a handsome frame building, and large enough to accommodate the

Uffington went through three one-room schoolhouses in its history. The third and final, depicted here in its current incarnation as a private home, was built in 1888 and served until 1957.

children of a rapidly growing community.

Grades one through ten were taught here, with each grade designated by a separate row of desks. With a student population of around fifty packed into a single room, if not for the strict discipline of the Victorian era the schoolmaster's lessons would surely have been drowned out by the noise of rambunctious children.[8]

This school was in operation for sixty-nine years, finally closing in 1957 with the opening of the township's central school. The era of the one-room school house was at an end, replaced by more efficient centralized schooling.

While most schools had a similar archetype, thanks to new education legislation that created, for the first time, mandatory schooling requirements province-wide, each schoolhouse in fact had distinctive features. This uniqueness was because they were handcrafted and built at the direction of local school boards, not some far removed bureaucracy. As a result, they were the product of the values of their time and their communities, as well as an expression of the builder's skill.

That's why it's so heartwarming to see the old Uffington school-house still standing and in good repair as a private home. One hopes it will remain for many more years as a symbol of pioneer values and Uffington's history.

Post Offices and General Stores

In most cases, the village post office and general store were one and the same, and their stories were therefore inextricably intertwined. But Uffington is a different case altogether. For much of its history, the village post office and general store were separate entities, operated by different proprietors in different buildings. Except for a few short periods, and unlike residents of most villages, the people of Uffington didn't have the luxury of making a single stop to make their purchases and pick up the mail.[9]

Perhaps this unusual situation can be partly explained by the fact the post office predated the first store in town by almost a decade.

Throughout 1864, Andrew Thompson campaigned to have a post office serving Draper Township placed in Uffington, naturally with himself as postmaster. Located along the Peterson Colonization Road, one of Muskoka's main roadways, and centrally positioned in the township, Uffington was in fact an ideal choice. Thompson knew it, and the government agreed. On October 1, 1864, the Uffington post office officially came into existence, operating out of Thompson's home.[10]

Thompson left Uffington in June 1872, leaving the position of postmaster vacant. Into this void stepped Irish-born farmer John Doherty. At the time of his appointment Doherty was already a prominent man thereabouts, serving as treasurer of Draper Township and president of the Uffington Agricultural Fair. Being named postmaster only enhanced his standing.[11]

John Doherty handled the mail from 1872 until 1889, when he sold his eighty-four-acre farm (which was widely considered one of the best in the region) and moved out to Selkirk, Manitoba.

On May 2, 1889, the Uffington post office was moved from the Doherty home to the store of George Spence, marking one of the few times the fortunes of these two important institutions were linked. Spence, like Doherty before him, was an influential individual both in town and on the wider township stage. He was the reeve of Draper for thirteen years, during which time the township prospered and developed at an unprecedented pace, and he also served as the superintendent of the Methodist Sunday School and its recording steward. Spence's wife, Mary, ably supported him in his business and political endeavours, and was a leader in her own right, serving as president of the Ladies Aid of the Methodist Church.[12]

Spence had arrived in Muskoka from his native Ireland in the mid-1870s and initially settled down to farming. It was only years later, after he had cleared the fields and set the farm on the right footing, that he turned his thoughts towards opening a general store. Spence did not open the first mercantile in town — that honour goes to Robert McMurray, who was also the first reeve of Draper Township and a hotel operator in Uffington — but it was probably the most important, thanks in no small part to the presence of the post office.

Mail was delivered to Gravenhurst via train, where it was sorted by community and put into large sacks. In the early years, the postmaster was responsible for making the journey into Gravenhurst to pick up the mail, but that changed when a stagecoach began running between the two communities in the 1880s. The stage operated twice weekly, leaving Uffington at 10:00 a.m. and turning around at Gravenhurst at 2:30 p.m.

George Spence resigned from his position as postmaster in 1899, when he sold his store and moved to Tillsonburg in southern Ontario. Eventually, like so many people who gave up on Uffington, he ended up in the Prairies, where he boasted a prosperous farm.

Succeeding Spence as postmaster was elderly farmer David Cairns, who served from 1900 to 1908, and then Henry Buckler, a taxidermist and photo studio operator, who had the distinction of serving in the position longer than anyone, from 1908 to 1928.

After the Buckler era came to an end, the post office was finally reunited with the general store, now owned and operated by Samuel Hawn. In fact, Hawn would wear the title of postmaster twice, from 1928 to 1930, and from 1942 to 1956, in all cases operating out of what was by now the lone store in Uffington.[13]

The decline in Uffington's population, the improvement in roads and automobiles that allowed residents to take advantage of better shopping opportunities in Bracebridge, and the general malaise that affected the village ultimately doomed the Hawn store. The last of Uffington's businesses, it simply couldn't stand against the tides of modernity that were sweeping ever stronger over the country after the Second World War.

The building still stands as a home to people who remember with fondness a time when it served as a focal point for the community. As a result, we can confidently predict the former store will be well tended for years to come — just as a proud community landmark should be.

Loyal Orange Lodge Number 634

The Loyal Orange Order, a fraternal organization consisting of patriotic Protestants, played a prominent role in the political and social life of early Canada. Lodges typically boasted among their members some of the wealthiest and most important men in their respective communities, and as a result they wielded considerable influence. The secretive meetings held within these sanctuaries tended to have important repercussions for the community at large; members might join forces to promote an event, fund a public works, or campaign for or against a political appointee.

Uffington was one of only seven villages in Muskoka that could boast a Loyal Orange Lodge, and its people were particularly proud of this distinction. A glance at its membership roll is like reading a who's who of Uffington; everyone who was anyone was an Orangeman, or so it seems.

Orangeism was born in the late 1700s to combat widespread religious persecution against Protestants in Ireland, where violent attempts were being made to drive non-Catholics from the island. Forged in the fires of conflict, the Loyal Orange Order was vehemently patriotic, loyal to the British monarchy, protective of its secrets, deeply proud of its religion, opposed to any form of dissention, and generally anti-Catholic. These traits were brought with Orangemen to Canada, where the order took root in the early 1800s.

The first signs of Orangeism emerged during the War of 1812, and by 1822 annual parades were being held in Toronto. In 1830, the first Loyal Orange Lodge was founded in Brockville and in the decades that followed dozens emerged across the province, seven within Muskoka, the last being that at Uffington.

It was a proud moment for all involved when, on March 16, 1868, about a dozen men from Draper Township, most of whom hailed from the Uffington area, joined together to officially organize Loyal Orange Lodge Number 634 (L.O.L. 634). Warrant number 634 had originally been granted in 1855 to a lodge in Guelph in 1855, but this lodge went dormant after a few short years. L.O.L. 634 proved far more enduring in its second incarnation, becoming a presence in Uffington that remains to this day.[14]

Initially, Lodge members met in a rented room, but Timothy Patterson, a wealthy farmer and cattle breeder, took it upon himself to spearhead efforts to build a dedicated Orange Hall. Each member donated two dollars to the endeavour, but with only thirteen individuals on the roll it's likely that Patterson, who served as a moneylender in the community, provided additional funds to see the project through.

Lodge member James Smith offered a piece of land on the northwest corner of the Peterson Road–Uffington Road crossroads on which to build the hall, an offer that was eagerly accepted. This allowed work to begin in August 1871, when members gathered to cut logs for the building. Volunteers laboured tirelessly during their spare time throughout the autumn and winter to construct the hall, which measured 15 feet by 25 feet, so that by the spring of 1872 it was complete. L.O.L. 634 met for the first time in their new home on May 13, 1872.

To help provide for its upkeep, the Lodge agreed that for six dollars' annual rent the village school could move from the primitive log cabin it called home and hold classes within the Orange Hall. It was a situation that pleased all.

Almost all, at any rate. Around this time, and for reasons unknown, James Smith had a falling out with the Lodge. In rancour, he pointed out that the hall the Orangemen had worked so hard to build was sitting on private land. His land, to be precise. There had never been anything but a gentlemen's agreement between Smith and the Lodge for the use of the property, and consequently the Orangemen were evicted. The hall, henceforth, would serve solely as a school.

Homeless again, the Orangemen began searching for new land where they could start over. In July 1883, Matthew Patterson sold the Lodge part of the southeast corner of the crossroads (Lot 21, Concession 5) for one dollar. This is where the second and current hall was built. One can be certain that the trustees had learned from their previous mistake and this time had a proper deed drawn up and signed.

After some initial stumbles, L.O.L. 634 flourished. The twelfth of July celebrations that drew Orangemen from across Muskoka were often held in Uffington, and the Lodge reached a peak in membership in 1902, with forty-nine men on the roll. Among the notable members were Andrew Thompson, postmaster; Frederick Toye, township clerk for Draper; Charles Blackmore, a prominent local farmer and leader of the Methodist congregation; and James McCracken, a skilled carpenter who was responsible for many buildings in the area, not the least of which were the Methodist church and parsonage.

Though L.O.L. 634 was thriving at the turn of the twentieth century, as the decades rolled by it became increasingly difficult to find new members in the shrinking village to replace those who had died or moved away. And yet, while it withered, it refused to die. In fact, the hall was still in use into the 1990s, when the membership roll stood at three members.

"We didn't want it to end, but there weren't enough of us to keep it going either," remembers William Allen, one of the last of Uffington's Orangemen. "There has to be at least four members of a lodge, and when we didn't have that we were forced to close. It was a real shame."[15]

Today, the Orange Hall waits for members to once again grace this unique historical building, but waiting is all it can do. The Orange Order is dormant, men no longer meet behind closed doors, and their presence exists only in the minds of those few old-timers who are left in the community.

Despite being used as a storage shed, a function that insults its former role in the community, the hall still stands tall and proud. Mother Nature hasn't been kind at all, and the once very active building is forgotten and left in disrepair. But one can still visualize members coming and going, men who were respected by the rest of the community and who used their meetings to help chart the course of Uffington's development. When you look at this building now, all you might see is just a rundown piece of the past. But the souls resting in the cemetery across the road from hall see it as it once was: an important if somewhat mysterious aspect in the lives they once lived.

Blacksmiths

The village blacksmith was an integral part of any farming community. The items he shaped from white-hot metal weren't merely tools; they were the settlers' very lifeblood. He was called upon to make everything from nails and horseshoes to hinges, farm implements, and sleighs. That's why for more than half a century there was always at least one blacksmith, and occasionally as many as three, operating in Uffington.

Who exactly was the first blacksmith in Uffington is difficult to determine, because it seems both Adam Chamber and Lorenzo Johnson opened shops in 1882.

Adam Chamber came to Uffington in 1882, did some farming, and worked extensively in the lumbering business, where he spent months in the bush cutting trees during the winter. But he was an ambitious young man and wasn't satisfied with that life. He wanted to ply the trade of a blacksmith, and asked permission of local farmer James Kirkpatrick to erect a shop on an otherwise useless piece of marshland adjacent to the Peterson Road. Seeing nothing to lose, Kirkpatrick agreed.

Chamber built a large shop of logs, measuring 26 feet by 40 feet, and set himself up in business using only an ancient set of tools that had been passed down to him. He hammered away in the shop for about a decade, but the early 1890s saw him living in Port Carling.[16]

Like Chamber, Lorenzo Johnson also arrived in Uffington in 1882. Born in England but raised in the United States, Johnson came to Canada in the late 1870s and spent several years as a blacksmith in Grimsby. Newly wed, he headed for the wilds of Muskoka and the dream of a bright future.

The dream never quite came true. Johnson served his new community as a smith for a number of years, but he never really found the prosperity he had imagined. Worse, his body exhausted by a lifetime of arduous labour, Lorenzo Johnson died in 1913 at the age of seventy-three.[17]

John Pascall was the next blacksmith to enter the scene. Born in England in 1848, he came to Muskoka around 1881 with his wife, Elizabeth, and settled a two-hundred-acre farm. An industrious and tireless man, within a few years of settling down he had started a small sawmill and opened a smithy.

Pascall was an interesting character. "His mother had died in his early childhood," wrote Reverend Coburn in his journal. "His father having married again, John and the new mistress of the home could not 'hit it off'. So John ran away. As a result, he received no schooling. In fact, he could not read or write beyond signing his own name. Yet he was

Courtesy Luke Pascall.

Blacksmiths were vital but unheralded components in any pioneer community. Beyond shoeing horses, they were responsible for repairing wagon wheels and harnesses and for crafting all manner of metal goods. Uffington was lucky to have the services of skilled smiths John Pascall and his son, John Jr.

intelligent far beyond his neighbours. He took a daily paper and when the mail arrived someone in the house had to drop everything to read John the news. He was better posted on public affairs than many who had enjoyed superior advantages."[18]

Well-read, bright despite a lack of formal education, outspoken, and strong in his convictions, John Pascall became a leader in the church and a respected voice in the community. He and his wife were also known for their hospitality, often hosting dances for the townsfolk that would not wind up until daylight the next morning.

Business was apparently good for the blacksmith, because the *Bracebridge Herald-Gazette* noted that in 1897 Pascall was forced to build a larger shop, measuring 20 feet by 90 feet, to keep up with the increase in business.[19] In fact, business was so good that he came to dominate the local trade and drove out another short-lived blacksmith, James McKay, who vacated his business in 1903 and went to Purbrook to assist his brothers in operating a sawmill.

John's son, John Jr. (or Jack), was also a blacksmith. He worked with his father for a time, but instead of succeeding him moved to Utterson, where he opened his own shop.

Most blacksmiths, in addition to shoeing horses and crafting metal tools and household utensils, also served as wheelwrights and made repairs to wagons. We know for certain Pascall did — Reverend Coburn makes note of it in his journals — and it can also be assumed that most of Uffington's other smiths did likewise. It only makes sense: wear and tear on wagons and buggies bouncing along the rough Peterson Road would ensure a steady stream of customers from among the farmers, coachmen, and drovers who passed through, each one eager to have a wheel hurriedly repaired.

John Pascall, the longest-serving and most successful of Uffington's smiths, worked hammer and forge almost until the day he died, December 20, 1918.

The transition from horse to machine on the farm, in the lumber woods, and even along the rural roads was a gradual one and therefore the need for a blacksmith's services remained even at this late date. As a result, Jacob Matthias, from nearby Matthiasville, purchased Pascall's shop and succeeded him as village smith. He continued in that capacity until the 1930s.

Time marches on, however, and eventually the Matthias blacksmith shop was trampled underfoot by the full onslaught of the automobile era.

Today, their forges long since extinguished, all traces of the various smithies are gone. But neither the passage of years nor the evolution of technology can erase the contribution blacksmiths made to Uffington's development.

Uffington's Hotels

As it was in any crossroads community, a hotel was among the first commercial buildings to appear in Uffington, built to cater to the traffic struggling along the Peterson Colonization Road. Travelling along early Muskoka roads — riddled with stumps, rocks, and ruts — would have been time-consuming and exhausting. Frequent stops were required to rest weary passengers and horses.

Since Uffington had two crossroads, it perhaps only made sense that it would also have two hotels.

Robert McMurray was an ambitious man. Shortly after arriving in Uffington, he opened a general store and then used his wealth and prominence in local affairs to get himself elected as the first reeve of Draper Township. That wasn't enough, however. McMurray saw the potential for a hotel in town, one that offered home-cooked meals, warm beds, and above all, the greatest profit maker, cheap booze. McMurray's hotel was built adjacent to his store, at the west end of Uffington, and proved successful from the start.

Unfortunately, much of the clientele consisted of boisterous shantymen employed in area logging camps, rugged men who had a tendency to drink too much and acknowledge the niceties of civilized behaviour too little. This tended to sully the hotel's reputation among the more respectable elements. The people of Uffington had good reason to be leery of the lumberjacks. One episode that occurred during the annual Uffington Fall Fair in the 1880s demonstrates why.

Exhibits for the fair were displayed in the upper rooms of McMurray's inn, predominantly preservatives, baked goods, and women's handicrafts. This meant that the women and children who frequented such exhibits had to pass through the barroom and run the gauntlet of drunken louts, something they were understandably reluctant to do. Generally, despite their misgivings, they could get by without incident. But there were exceptions.

This particular evening, the hotel was full of watery-eyed, slurred-speaking men whose manners — assuming they had any — had been drowned by whiskey. These brutes intimidated women and children in the exhibition halls upstairs, their crude behaviour essentially holding them prisoner. Mrs. McMurray, the hostess, asked the men to make way and allow the women and their children to leave, but her pleadings were ignored. Her second request, more forceful this time, was met by obscenities.

Entering the picture at this point was knight in shining armour and local farmer Mat Watson. He didn't ask the drunkards to make way; he *told* them to, and backed up his demand with his fists. This led to a fierce brawl between Watson and five glassy-eyed louts. Incredibly, when the tempers had cooled and the punches had stopped, it was Watson who was still standing. The gentleman then escorted the women and children to the exit, cementing a reputation for himself as the toughest and most chivalrous man in Draper Township.[20]

Similar acts of drunken violence and misbehaviour plagued Uffington's other hotel. Located at the eastern end of town, at the intersection of Uffington Road and the Peterson Road, the hotel was built sometime before 1879. In December of that year, William Briggs took over ownership of the establishment.

He had hardly settled into the role when the ugly nature of hotel proprietorship during the nineteenth century revealed itself.

It was a blustery winter night, and a small gathering of patrons huddled near the fireplace to ward off the bone-gnawing chill. At one table, three untamed shantymen found that whiskey was equally effective at chasing away the cold, and in the pursuit of warmth drained several bottles. Judgment clouded by drunkenness, they became rowdy and began abusing the other patrons. Briggs refused to serve them any further drinks and urged them to go outside to clear their heads. The shantymen seemed ready to cause trouble but backed down when the other patrons stood solidly behind the innkeeper. Tails between their legs, the drunks fled into the night.

But they didn't go far. Instead, they lurked in the shadows, waiting for everyone to depart and the inn to close for the night. A burning desire for vengeance at the perceived slight warded off the biting wind. They watched as the last of the guests filed out and disappeared from sight. Only then did they reveal themselves by throwing curses at Briggs and a rock through the barroom window.

Briggs rushed outside to drive them off, but one of the ruffians, a troublemaker named John Dougherty, confronted the innkeeper with a knife and stabbed him three times in the chest. Briggs collapsed, his blood staining the snow crimson, and yet Dougherty continued his ruthless assault, stabbing the helpless victim three more times in the back. Incredibly, Briggs survived, but only because of the heavy coat and thick woollen garments he wore.[21]

The hotels of Uffington were caught in a quandary. The loggers undeniably were good for business, helping to make the proprietors wealthy men, but they also brought with them lawlessness, uncouth behaviour, and violence. On the one hand, hoteliers might frown upon the antics of the shantymen, but on the other they realized that as soon as the logging camps disappeared they would lose a good portion of their clientele.

As it turned out, the worst fears of the hoteliers were realized. When the timber was depleted in the 1890s, the lumber interests pulled up stakes and went further north in search of untapped tracts of trees. Naturally, the loggers went with them. The absence of these hard-drinking sorts, combined with decreasing traffic along the Peterson Road and the rise of the Temperance movement calling for enforced abstinence of drinking, meant that the hotels experienced a death spiral in their fortunes.

Neither hotel remained open long into the twentieth century (certainly, both were closed by the mid-1920s) and neither exists today, one having met a fiery demise while the other was demolished due to decay.[22]

Village Tragedies

For such a small community, the village of Uffington had more than its share of horrific tragedies. From drownings to unfortunate accidents, in pioneer days the struggle to survive was difficult and all-consuming. It seemed one must never let down one's guard; the minute one did, tragedy saw its opportunity and swooped in for the kill.

After we stumbled upon the first story and were moved by its circumstances, we felt it important to share several such tragedies, if only to show how truly trying living was in those harsh, unforgiving days.

Frederick Nowell Toye was the township clerk for Draper and kept all the town records in his home in Uffington. He was a careful and painstaking man, devoted to both his family and his duties. It was his misfortune to play a central role in one of the worst tragedies to happen to the little hamlet.

Rain fell in heavy and continuous sheets during the day of May 28, 1888. The villagers complained that the rain never seemed to end, but when it finally did that night the mosquitoes came out of the woods in black clouds to plague the sleeping populace.

The Toye family were all tucked in their beds and asleep, all save for seventeen-year-old Mary Bella, who was studying to be a teacher. Just outside the porch door on a tin dish a smouldering smudge mixture was placed to ward off the mosquitoes. It was standard procedure for the smudge to be moved away from the door for safety at bedtime, lest a stray ember catch the house on fire. On this day, her mind perhaps cloudy from fatigue, Mary Bella didn't think things through and placed the smudge in the shed adjoining the house.

An hour later, she looked on in horror as she saw flames creeping along the wall adjoining shed and home. The house had caught fire, and the flames were spreading rapidly. She called out to her parents to alert them to the danger, and then ran to the neighbours' for help. But when help finally arrived their worst fears were confirmed. There was no sign of life in the house.

It appeared that Toye, awoken by his daughter's cries, had tried to put out the fire. When he realized it was too far gone he tried to go to his office to retrieve the township books. Toye's body was found just outside the office door, still on his hands and knees.

While this was going on, Mrs. Toye went for her babies. She managed to get to their rooms where they lay peacefully sleeping, completely unaware anything untoward was happening. Unfortunately, Mrs. Toye was trapped by flames and couldn't escape. She was discovered with a child under each arm, a grim symbol of pioneer motherhood.[23]

Uffington was shocked and saddened by the tragedy. One can only imagine the scars Mary Bella bore for the duration of her life.

But the Toye family wasn't the only one to suffer loss. Albert Spring had his share of misfortune as well.

One bright Sunday morning on his way to church, Spring came face to face with a bear. The bear grunted and flared his nostrils menacingly and refused to back down despite the noises that Mr. Spring made in an attempt to intimidate him. He was sure he was living out the last terror-filled moments of his life, that momentarily he would be mauled and eaten by the hulking black bear. But he refused to die without a fight and instead reached for a log that lay on the roadside. Bellowing defiance, Spring charged the bear and literally battered in the beast's skull.

Mr. Spring was lucky that day — he had averted tragedy — but it seemed his children didn't have the same luck. One of Spring's sons was killed in a logging bee and another drowned at the Tretheway Falls. He probably questioned himself daily why Lady Luck had smiled upon him and allowed him to survive but snubbed his sons and cut short their promising lives.[24]

In pioneer days, tragedies seemed to occur almost daily. Drownings happened frequently, partly because swimming was not a universal skill as it is today and partly because of the dangerous activities that pioneers engaged in on water (foremost among them the annual logging drives). But even though they happened with such frequency, the stories are still heartbreaking.

One of the most horribly moving was the tale of Will Kinsett's death. After finishing his daily chores, the young lad hitched up the cart to take his mother for a drive. While waiting for his mom to finish dressing appropriately for the outing, Will and his little brother went down to the river to quench his horse's thirst.

While at the river, the horse somehow lost his footing and both it and the buggy slid into the water. Dragged down by the weight of the buggy, the horse began to drown. Will, who loved the animal, jumped in to try to unhitch the horse while his brother raced for help. Will managed to get the horse free, but he got caught in the harness.

By the time his brother returned with help there was no sign of either Will or the horse he had heroically tried to save. Will had loved the animal so deeply that he willingly put his own life in jeopardy in an attempt to rescue it.[25]

These three tragic stories represent just a sampling of the many that occurred in Uffington, and they are mirrored by similar dramas that took place in all pioneer-era Muskoka villages. It's hard for modern readers to imagine just how tenuous life was in those days. One false step, one poor decision, one twist of fate and your life could be snuffed out. Existence in the wilderness of Muskoka wasn't just one of hardship, but also one of heartache.

For the families and friends who lost loved ones in those difficult days, for those who faced unimaginable tribulations on an almost daily basis while laying the foundations for the Muskoka we all know and love, our thoughts and prayers are with you.

12

SELDOM SEEN AND
OTHER GHOST TOWNS

Muskoka has far too many vanished hamlets, lost settlements, and villages that are but a "ghost" of their previous selves to comfortably fit into one book. In fact, we've identified several dozen in total, each with a fascinating story to tell. This final chapter provides capsule entries for half a dozen more villages that are wrapped in a deathly shroud, providing a preview for *More Ghost Towns of Muskoka*, the sequel to this first volume.

Seldom Seen

Could there be a more appropriate or atmospheric name for a ghost town than Seldom Seen? If so, we've yet to run across it. And in this particular case the name truly applies, for Seldom Seen was a tiny and short-lived community, located in an obscure and isolated corner of Muskoka, more a rural settlement of loosely strung farms than a true hamlet.

But, though Seldom Seen lacked both legs and size, it was a community all the same, and a tight-knit one at that.

Settlers began arriving in the northwest corner of Macaulay Township in the mid-1870s, concentrating their efforts on homesteading in the area south of Deer Lake. Though they struggled mightily to transform the grim landscape into a bountiful granary, suffering at the hands of both the elements and the terrain, the settlers never lost their sense of humour; they good-naturedly named their corner of the township Seldom Seen because of the isolation in which they lived.

Two individuals stood head and shoulders above the other settlers. One was Alfred Lee, farmer, schoolteacher, and assessor. The other was William C. Denniss, a school board member, township councillor, and township treasurer.

In addition to farmsteads, Seldom Seen included a general store that operated out of a private home and a small sawmill, but the only public building ever erected was a schoolhouse located near Gibb Lake. This school had a colourful history and was the subject of much controversy, and it was around this building that the community seemed to gel.

In 1875, a log schoolhouse (SS #7) was erected to see to the educational needs of the area youth, with Alfred Lee as the first schoolmaster. In 1886, however, this school was closed and a new one was built miles to the southwest, too far away to be of any use to the children of Seldom Seen.

The residents were up in arms over the slight and, led by Alfred Lee and William Denniss, they formed a new school section and built a new schoolhouse (SS #8), known locally as Gibb Lake School. Once again, Alfred Lee served as the first teacher. The township council was strongly opposed to the formation of this school section and made several attempts to close it down, but the ratepayers of Seldom Seen would not back down and were able to retain their school autonomy for a time. The influence wielded by both Lee and Denniss in municipal matters clearly played a decisive role in winning the bureaucratic war.

Gibb Lake School closed in 1912, the last school in Macaulay Township to open and the first to close. A few years later, it was consumed by a mysterious fire. By this point, the store and sawmill had both closed, and many of the homesteaders had been defeated by the harsh, unarable landscape. Seldom Seen, a community that one had to strain to see even in its heyday, had disappeared.

Perhaps appropriately, the last remnant of Seldom Seen was the homestead of Alfred Lee, a man who had dedicated his life to the settlement and in many ways defined it. His two-storey home, an island of refinement and culture in a sea of desperation, stood until well into the twentieth century before it too was abandoned and succumbed to the ravages of time.

The small community was — as its name implies — seldom seen in its time, and isn't even that today, having completely disappeared from the landscape.

Beatty's Siding

For a fleeting moment, Beatty's Siding was a hive of activity. More than two dozen trains passed through every day, sometimes stopping to take on water or timber. Teams of horses ploughed fields, cutting straight furrows in sandy soil. The ringing of axes echoed through the woods, interrupted intermittently by the thunder of trees crashing to the ground.

You wouldn't know it today, though. This spot, three kilometres west of Swords on the Seguin Trail (formerly the Ottawa, Arnprior and Parry Sound Railway), is deathly silent now, and to the untrained eye nothing remains to indicate there was ever any human habitation here.

Beatty's Siding was born in 1894 when John Rudolphus Booth launched his railway empire by building the Ottawa, Arnprior and Parry Sound Railway, intending to link his eastern Canada rail lines with Georgian Bay. His route cut across central Ontario, from the nation's capital in the east to Depot Harbour, near Parry Sound, in the west.

Three kilometres west of Swords (then known as Maple Lake Station), the railway built a passing siding and a water tower to serve its trains. A pump house on nearby Spectacle Lake ensured the water tower was topped off, and a "shim shack" was erected where men who were employed by the railway stayed while working in the area. This collection of buildings became known as Beatty's Siding.

Charged with looking after the railway's interests here was Fred Mullen. In addition to maintaining the facilities, he did a little farming, operated a small shingle mill on Spectacle Lake, and even spent time digging in a feldspar mine he began on the south end of the lake.

But Mullen wasn't the only person living here. Several other families called Beatty's Siding home as well, including the Bathens, Graingers, Mays, and Turcotts. They did some farming, but mostly they worked for the Ludgate Lumber Company, which had a large mill on Spectacle Lake and hauled logs from the watersheds around Clendenning's Lake, Horseshoe Lake, Whalen's Lake, Swords Lake, and Long Lake.

This little community had close ties with neighbouring Swords. The families were interconnected through marriage and blood, the children of Beatty's Siding attended school at SS #1 alongside youngsters from

Swords, and the Swords general store was the only place where folks from Beatty's Siding could make purchases and pick up their mail. In fact, the two communities were so tightly bound that many people mistakenly assumed they were one and the same.

Unfortunately, Beatty's Siding suffered the same fate as Swords. First, the Ludgate Lumber Company moved out when it had exhausted the timber in the area. Most of the families, dependent on lumbering for their livelihood, pulled up stakes shortly thereafter, and by 1910 there were no more than one or two inhabited homes left.

One of those who refused to leave was Fred Mullen, who remained behind, faithfully tending to the railroad facilities. Gradually, train traffic began to dwindle, and it stopped altogether in 1945, but Mullen wasn't there to see the end: he died a decade earlier, in 1935. His widow turned her back on the little frame house they had called home for half a century, and when she left the curtain was finally closed for good on Beatty's Siding.

Today, virtually nothing remains of the once busy rail siding, nothing to evoke its lost legacy. The sole exception is the concrete footings of the pump house at Spectacle Lake, which can still be seen if you know where to look.

Jerusalem

The remains of this settlement are lost within the regenerated forest between High Falls Road on the south, Highway 11 on the east, and Falkenburg Road to the west. Little remains of it today, but to be honest there was little enough to begin with.

And therein lies the dilemma that historians struggle with: was Jerusalem a small hamlet or just a really large homestead? Was it a community of friends and neighbours, or was it inhabited solely by an extended family? No one knows for sure. The community lasted for such a short period that it had no chance to weave itself into the fabric of Muskoka's history. As a result, little accurate information on Jerusalem exists today, forcing us to rely upon loose strands made up of rumour and second-hand stories.

We do know that Jerusalem was founded in 1866, that Thomas Peacock was the first settler, and that it was nestled in a deep valley surrounded by heavily forested hills. Within a few years, the hills had been denuded of trees, the forest replaced by fields where hardy crops and hay for livestock were grown. The soil was threadbare and able to provide only for the settlers' barest of needs.

Despite hardships, after a couple of years had passed the lone Peacock cabin had grown into an eight-building settlement. Since several of the buildings remained standing and in fair order into the middle of the twentieth century, we know that at the very least two or three were homes. But what of the remainder? Were they barns and outbuildings, or were they in fact other dwellings? Knowing the function of the various buildings would go a long way to determining whether Jerusalem was actually a hamlet.

Another question surrounds where the name of the settlement originated. The Peacocks were religious folk and probably named it after Psalm 125 in the Bible: "The hills stand about Jerusalem; so does the Lord stand round his people, from this time evermore." In this scenario, the name reflected hope and faith.

However, some believe — falsely in our opinion — that Jerusalem was named because the hills were soon stripped of trees, making it similar to its biblical counterpart, a barren infertile region unable to support its population.

Regardless of whether the infertility of the land had a role to play in the naming of the community, the reality was that the soil was incapable of supporting people beyond subsistence levels, leading to despair and hopelessness. The promised land Jerusalem was not.

The residents moved away, abandoning cabins that have since slowly been devoured by time. Jerusalem, hamlet or homestead, has now been reduced to a few rotting timbers in a forgotten valley. Where the whinny of horses pulling ploughs once floated upon the breeze, and the echoing of axes biting into trees rarely stopped, there remains only the howl of the wind through dark woods.

Bear Lake

Norway is a land of extremes. On the surface, the sparkling seas, the verdant green woods, and the panoramic grandeur of the mountains are glorious to behold. But Norway's mountains, glaciers, dense forests, bogs, and chilly lakes are bleak, foreboding, and dangerous. Half of the country is buried under snow for more than six months of the year.

Lack of land and resources had caused Norwegians to venture afar for centuries, and in the 1800s thousands came to Canada. Some settled in Muskoka, establishing the hamlet of Bear Lake.

These desperate families, several dozen in number, arrived in the 1880s and congregated upon the shores of Bear Lake in Muskoka. They had been lured there by the promise of jobs offered by local lumber concerns. In exchange for cutting trees and working at the mills, every man would be granted 160 acres of land to farm. To the land-starved Scandinavians, it seemed like a deal too good to be true.

It probably was, but for a while this cruel reality was masked by the excitement that came with establishing new homes and a new community, which they called Jarlsberg after a town in Norway. In addition to the mill, there would have been a school, store, post office, and blacksmith to provide all the bare essentials to the residents. At one time, three sawmills operated along the shores of the lake.

Sadly for the people of Jarlsberg, within a decade or so the harvestable lumber had been culled and the lumber companies had moved away. The villagers were left in a bind: do they stay and hope to scratch a feeble living from their rocky farms, or do they follow the jobs and leave their little community behind? Some of the settlers chose the latter, following the sawmills to new homes further north, but some others elected to remain in Jarlsberg. These stalwarts survived largely by cutting cordwood and logs for pulpwood.

Inevitably, over time, the Norwegian character of the community was diluted. Names were Anglicized (Johan Nilson became John Nelson, for example) to better fit into Canadian culture, marriages with non-Norwegians became increasingly common, and in 1893 the village's name was changed to Bear Lake when a railway station of the same name was built nearby.

As the twentieth century dawned, it revealed Bear Lake in a steady and unrecoverable decline. One can't survive on hope and determination alone; when that realization sank in, the few remaining residents resigned themselves to their fates and moved away.

Yet, one reminder of their community and culture remained, and still remains today: St. Olaf's Church, proud house of worship named for Norway's patron saint, serving as beacon of Scandinavian heritage and Bear Lake's history to this day.

Hoodstown

Scenic Lake Vernon is today ringed by cottages and homes, some of them occupying the site of the spectral community of Hoodstown, which fell victim not to economic hardship or resource depletion but rather to plans gone horribly awry.

Following the opening of Muskoka for settlement, railways began to extend their reach into the dense forests, leading to heady optimism and a rush in land speculation. Everyone knew that trackside property was extremely valuable and that communities served by the railways were destined to boom. As a result, people tried to guess where the tracks would head and then snatch up any available land along the way. Guess right, and a fortune would be yours. Guess wrong, and your land would be all but worthless.

Unfortunately for them, Charles and Janet Hood guessed wrong.

Charles Hood was a mechanical engineer who resided with his family in Toronto and owned a steamship that plied Lake Ontario. When he learned of the land boom starting in Muskoka, he saw an opportunity to make a quick buck and sold his ship to finance his plan. With his knowledge of engineering, he attempted to ascertain the route the Northern Railway would take as it plunged through Muskoka on its way to points farther north, and the route the Ottawa, Arnprior and Parry Sound Railway would follow as it crossed the breadth of Ontario.

After careful consideration, Hood became convinced that one, if not actually both, would wind its way past a point on the northwestern shores of Lake Vernon. As a result, he and his wife bought extensive tracts of land in the area and built a sawmill on a set of rapids, grandiosely called Hoods Falls, in the river connecting Fox Lake and Lake Vernon. They figured the community that would develop here would need lumber for construction, and who better to provide it than they?

Initially, things went as planned, and a village named Port Vernon did indeed begin to develop here. A post office was opened in 1877, and other businesses and services soon followed. Things were looking promising, so in 1889 the Hoods registered a town plan of forty acres, intending to sell the subdivided village lots for a tidy profit. Many of the lots were indeed purchased within a few years, and in time Port Vernon gave way to Hoodstown.

Hoodstown had 276 lots on nine streets, and by the middle of the 1880s boasted three general stores, three churches, the Hood mill, a rather notorious hotel frequented by rough-and-ready lumbermen, a blacksmith, one or two other artisans, and a dozen or so homes.

Hoodstown's heyday was short-lived. In 1886, the Northern Railway took an unexpected detour to the east and passed through Huntsville instead of Hoodstown. The OA&PSR, meanwhile, came no closer than sixteen kilometres to the north. The Hoods' dream lay shattered, and Hoodstown began to atrophy.

By 1892 the post office had closed, most of the businesses had transferred to Huntsville, and many of the lots lay empty. The community that had aspired to greatness was soon enveloped by the forests, a humiliating end to the Hoods' grand vision.

Today, a few modern homes and cottages exist where Hoodstown once stood, but the area is positively languid and it's almost impossible to envision the bustling community of yesteryear.

Emberson

Emberson is among the most obscure and least known of Muskoka's ghost towns. The village is almost a rumour, something old-timers talk about while relating their tall tales of yesteryear, leaving many to question whether it ever truly existed at all. But exist it did, and for a surprisingly long time considering how quickly it was erased from our collective memory.

A community of bush farmers and loggers, Emberson was settled in 1876 by a handful of hopeful and perhaps naive people who thought they could tame this distant corner of Brunel Township. The concession road leading to Emberson was narrow and rutted, winding over rock and through swamp, heightening the sense of isolation the homesteaders felt. Largely cut off from the outside world, they drew into themselves, seeking comfort in one another and creating tight bonds that saw the burgeoning community through tough times.

In April 1876, Emberson gained a post office under the management of Henry Jarvis. There may also have been a short-lived sawmill and church in the hamlet, but details are sketchy and if they existed at all they certainly left no legacy to speak of. Beyond these meagre gains, Emberson had little of which to boast. Children had to go east into Franklin Township in order to get an education (SS #2 at The Portage, to be precise), and all purchases had to be made even further afield. It was community bound together by spirit rather than man-made structures.

Despite the glaring lack of civilization's trappings, Emberson continued to grow. By 1900, there were about sixty people here, every one of them toiling almost endlessly just to eke out an existence. When they weren't working on their bush farms, an endeavour that more often than not was largely fruitless, they were labouring with logging companies to earn some hard-to-come-by cash.

The reality — and everyone knew it — was that eventually the timber would run out. It might be a decade in coming, it might be longer, but none of the settlers had any illusion that their good fortune could outlast the supply of trees. When the logging companies left, Emberson would be put on life support.

That dreaded day came around 1910. The logging camps gone, the soil too harsh to cultivate, most families moved away. It wasn't a sudden, panicked mass exodus, however. The post office didn't close until 1924, indicating that the people of Emberson only slowly drifted away as their faith, their bodies, their determination, and their land finally gave out.

Today, the crop fields have reverted to forest, the homes and barns collapsed, the roads overgrown and all but indistinguishable. Emberson doesn't even exist on maps; it lies in deep woods, about two kilometres north of Muskoka Road 11 and the same distance east of Muskoka Road 7. Though difficult to get to, once there those with a particularly keen eye and patience to spare, and who know where to look, may make out the occasional foundation or fragment of a stone wall amid the trees.

These meagre vestiges serve as grim headstones to a community long dead.

Muskoka Mills

Muskoka Mills was conceived by the promise of wealth. During the early 1850s, the newly formed Muskoka Milling and Lumber Co. began looking for a site from which it could harness the resources of Muskoka timber rights. Eventually, surveyors selected a location at the mouth of the Musquash River. Here, the planned mills would be easily accessible by steamers off Georgian Bay and yet still be in a sheltered cove where logs could be collected after being driven down from the interiors.

From this decision was born Muskoka Mills, Muskoka's largest deserted lumber town.

At the heart of the community was the massive steam-powered mill. Employing two hundred men full-time, and as many as four hundred during peak periods, the mill routinely churned out 20 million board feet of lumber per year.

Cut lumber was towed away by horse-drawn wagons along a network of tramways and then stacked to dry for a year in piles that extended all along the shoreline. All summer long, an endless parade of steamers and schooners arrived in Muskoka Mills to carry lumber to ports all over the Great Lakes.

Muskoka Mills soon became home to as many as five hundred people, and perhaps double that seasonally. Mill hands lived in humble company-owned homes and boarding houses that ringed the shores of the bay and shopped at a company store. Within a few years, the community boasted a hotel, school, church, and blacksmith.

Despite its size, Muskoka Mills remained isolated from civilization. The only practical link to the outside world was by steamer, and this link was obviously severed come wintertime. As a result, the community maintained a frontier mentality throughout its brief existence.

The Muskoka Milling and Lumber Co. was at the centre of what must surely rank as one of the first environmental legal actions in Canada when the federal government accused the company of allowing excessive sawdust to fall into the water, thereby damaging the fish spawning grounds. It was their belief that mills such as this were responsible for the declining commercial fish industry on Georgian Bay. In the end, the government's case fell apart and legal action was dropped.

By this point, it no longer really mattered. The mill and the town it supported were sinking faster than a ship floundering in a Lake Huron storm. The reason for the decline was twofold. First, when the interior of Muskoka was settled in the 1860s, most of the land from which the company had culled timber became private homesteads and the trees on them no longer free for the taking. Worse, competition from mills across newly settled Muskoka, particularly the seventeen at Gravenhurst, proved even more damaging.

The operations at Muskoka Mills began to dwindle, and as profits plummeted it became clear that the day was soon approaching when Muskoka Milling and Lumber Co. would close up operations. The company cared nothing for the future of the community; it was in business for maintaining profits, not towns. In the cold-hearted reality of the lumber industry, Muskoka Mills was an expedience that, when its usefulness had expired, would be cast aside.

That day came in the 1890s. Most everyone followed, abandoning homes that no longer held any value or dreams. Muskoka Mills disappeared virtually overnight.

One hundred years on, the foundations of the mills can still be seen around the mouth of the Musquash River, but in general nature has long since reclaimed the one-time mill village of Muskoka Mills.

AUTHORS' NOTE

Anyone with information on any of the communities appearing in this book is encouraged to contact the authors by mail c/o Dundurn Press, 3 Church Street, Suite 500, Toronto, ON, M5E 1M2, or by email at muskokaghosttowns@hotmail.com.

NOTES

Chapter 1: Swords

1. John Rudolphus Booth emerged from humble stock to become arguably Canada's most powerful industrialist of his day. He was born in 1827, near Waterloo, Quebec, the child of Irish immigrants. He began his climb in the business world with a small, Ottawa-area sawmill around 1854. By 1892, he had become the largest lumber producer in the world, and provided the pine used in all of the Cunard ocean liners, including the ill-fated *Titanic*.

   He also operated a railway that ran from the eastern seaboard to Lake Huron, a fleet of steamships plying the Great Lakes, a cement company, and a pulp and paper mill. He died in 1925 and was still running his business empire to the very end.

2. The school was located on Lot 21, Concession 5.

3. Much of the information regarding the school comes from an October 2005 interview with Shirley Jordan, a member of the Christie Historical Committee, as well as *Meanderings and Memories* (Christie Township: Christie Historical Committee, 1994), 10–13.

4. Post office dates and names provided by Muskoka postal historian Larry Matthews.

5. This tale, as well as a great deal of information regarding the Swords general store is related in *Meandering and Memories*, 27–29. Jim McRoberts never again ventured into retail. He was a farmer first and foremost (Lot 21, Concession 4), but also worked in the lumber camps alongside other men from the community. His home still stands today.

6. The train derailment was related by Jack Sword, a descendant of the pioneering family who was born in the village in 1917 and raised there.

7. No one in the community has any idea of the station's fate, though all agree it was literally there one day and gone the next. Jack Sword remembers it thusly in a June 2004 interview: "It was a small building, measuring 20 by 20, and was located in the 'V' on the southeast corner of the road-railway intersection. Inside was a pot-bellied stove fed by coal, and a freight shed was attached."

8. The John Sword homestead was located on Lot 21, Concession 6.

9. The land John Sword purchased, the land upon which the Maple Lake Hotel sat, was Lot 20, Concession 6.

10. Much of the information regarding the hotel was courtesy of Jack Sword, the son of Percy Sword. He was born and raised in the hotel and retained several souvenirs and photos. We interviewed Mr. Sword in 2005 and found that, despite the passage of years, he retained vivid memories of the building:

> The bar had a separate entrance so that people wouldn't have to enter through the hotel. You wouldn't want dirty mill hands trekking through the foyer, after all. The bar was a large room, with large mirrors hanging over the bar like you see in westerns. Copper funnels were used in those days to pipe alcohol from barrels to bottles. The entire building was lit with carbite gas. Not many buildings had carbite gas because it was expensive and dangerous. Gas would be piped by copper tubing from a storage tank to all rooms, creating open flames in wall-mounted lamps. Fires and even explosions could occur, but never here.

11. This tale is related in *Meanderings and Memories*, 22.

12. There's much confusion about the *Buffalo Flyers*. Some writers mistakenly link the name to the tourists themselves, as if it were

a title of sorts for an unofficial club consisting of Americans who made the trip to Maple Lake each year. Some writers even call these tourists American Flyers, again in error.

13. The Ludgate timber rights were mostly on Lot 20, Concession 6. The Ludgate Lumber Company was once a mid-size logging and milling concern. The owner and founder was James Ludgate (born 1868 near Peterborough), who established himself as a respected "walking boss" for lumber companies in the Parry Sound District before striking out on his own in 1894. He would eventually operate sawmills and work timber rights all over the district, most notably at Key Inlet and Ardbeg. Ludgate was financially devastated by the Depression and was forced to absolve his lumber company.

14. This story, related by Guy Smith himself, appears in *Lots More ... Parry Sound Stories* (Parry Sound: The Hay Press, 2005), 268. Smith shares his memories about logging and Swords in several other books penned by John Macfie, including *Tales from Another Time* (Parry Sound: The Hay Press, 2000) and *Parry Sound Logging Days* (Toronto: Boston Mills Press, 1987).

Chapter 2: Rosseau Falls

1. The Snider Furniture Company operated several mills throughout Muskoka and other parts of Ontario, all devoted to the sole aim of providing the lumber needed for the manufacture of furnishings. The mill in Gravenhurst was just one of seventeen that operated there at the time.

2. Dates and names of postmasters were provided by Muskoka postal historian Larry Matthews. The Rosseau Falls postmasters and their dates of service were as follows: William Snider (December 1, 1880, to November 18, 1899), Herman Mutchenbacker (February 2, 1900, to February 9, 1906), S.F. Golton (June 1, 1906, to November 7, 1906), E. Whitmore (March 1, 1907, to October 21, 1909), John Fry (February 1, 1910, to March 20, 1924), and A.A. Fry (February 12, 1925, to November 29, 1928).

3. These figures provided by Doreen Nowak, a member of the Rosseau Historical Society whose father was born at Rosseau Falls in 1892 and whose grandfather sold logs culled from his property to the mill. Doreen's father kept a diary and makes mention of the mill several times, including the following, dated May 13, 1923: "This afternoon we drove to Rosseau Falls. They were driving logs all day on a Sunday. It is a slow game — water level very low."

It was unusual for a mill to operate on a Sunday, and especially unusual for logs still to be driven downriver in late May. What's important to note is how frenzied the activity at the mill apparently was, even at this late date in the 1920s.

4. During an October 2005 interview with the authors, Doreen Nowak fondly remembers the mill site from her youth: "The steam boiler was on the opposite side of the river from the mill. Overhead pipes brought the steam to the mill. As a young girl in the 1940s I remember crossing the river on these pipes. There was also a log chute down the falls, parts of which were still evident in the 1940s."

5. Specifications for the *Rosseau* come from Richard Tatley's *The Steamboat Era in the Muskokas, Volume I: To the Golden Years* (Toronto: Boston Mills Press, 1983), 92. Her ultimate demise is revealed in Tatley's *The Steamboat Era in the Muskokas, Volume II: The Golden Years to the Present* (Toronto: Boston Mills Press, 1983), 49.

6. Much of the information on the *Theresa* comes from Tatley's *The Steamboat Era in the Muskokas, Volume II*, 121–123.

7. This story was passed on by Diane Rotz, Peter Mutchenbacker's great-granddaughter through his son, Herman. Herman made a succinct reference to the tragedy in his diary on July 9, 1900. It reads simply: "When I lost Clarence Groh off the steamboat."

8. Most of the information related directly to the Mutchenbackers comes from the files of Diane Rotz, a granddaughter of Herman Mutchenbacker, and Herman's journals.

9. Asa was born March 24, 1867, and died in 1950; Herman was born January 11, 1871, and died November 20, 1946; Maria was born April 16, 1861, and died May 6, 1928; Clara was born July 1, 1879, and died May 13, 1913; Lizzie was born in 1863 and died July 7, 1922 (all dates courtesy of Diane Rotz).

10. The familial problems are never fully explained, though Herman hints at the rift in his diary. For example, an entry in July 1901 reads: "Trouble with my father in the business." The last logs cut by the Mutchenbackers at Rosseau Falls occurred on August 22, 1901.

11. Forest fires weren't the only dangers the Mutchenbackers faced during their time in Mafeking, as this excerpt from Herman's obituary in the *Toronto Star*, November 21, 1946, indicates: "Before the railway came, he traveled into the Hudson Bay country by dog team. He had no fear of the Ontario brush wolf, but the Manitoba timber wolf was a bolder breed. On one winter journey a hungry, growling pack chased his dog team. As they closed in, Mr. Baker jettisoned at intervals his grub, frozen caribou, salt pork and oatmeal. Since the pack paused to fight over these morsels, he was able to shake them off."

12. Herman purchased Bigwood on May 8, 1919. Bigwood is located on the French River, in Parry Sound District.

Chapter 3: Falkenburg Junction

1. Falkenburg Station is located on Muskoka Road 4, just north of Bracebridge. It's a far cry from the busy self it was one hundred years ago, but it does still boast St. George's Church and a large sawmill. The old Hays General Store, a landmark for many years, is a feature exhibit at Muskoka Heritage Place in Huntsville.

2. Matthias Moore Family Reunion booklet, 1993.

3. Thomas George died in Parry Sound in 1912 at the age of eighty-two.

4. *Orillia Packet*, March 12, 1875.

5. Robert J. Boyer, *A Good Town Grew Here: The Story of Bracebridge* (Bracebridge: Oxbow Press, 1975), 49.

6. Excerpt as appears in the Matthias Moore Family Reunion booklet, 1993.

7. Details of the strife after Susan's death as provided by Patricia Evans, a descendant of the Falkenburg Moores.

8. George Bernard Moore moved his mill to Lot 20, Concession 1, of Monck Township. Later, in 1830–31 he moved the mill again to Lots 17 and 18 of Concession 1, Monck. With the purchase of these lots also came the Hays General Store (now preserved in Huntsville's Muskoka Heritage Place). To supplement the sawmill, a planing mill was built in 1932. Fire destroyed this operation in 1960, drawing to a close the Moore lumber business after eighty-eight years and three generations.

9. Excerpt from Matthias Moore's diary, as it appeared in the Matthias Moore Family Reunion booklet, 1993.

10. St. George's has been a central part of Falkenburg Station since the move, and it has been lovingly tended to throughout. In 1890 the present chancel and vestry were built using material from a log church at Bardsville. In 1904, the interior walls were lined with ash boards. Electricity was installed in 1946, and a basement was put under the church in 1966.

11. The aged barn and home that are today located at the north end of Falkenburg Junction are said to sit on the same foundations occupied by the former hotel and the hall.

12. We do know it was built on Lot 4, Concession 11, about half a mile north of the Junction.

13. Excerpt school board notes, as quoted in a Moore Family Tree essay provided by Patricia Evans.

14. *Ibid.*

15. Much of the information on the post office was provided by Larry Matthews, Muskoka postal historian. Falkenburg postmasters and their dates of service are as follows: William Holditch (August 1, 1863, to 1865), Robert George (May 1, 1865, to September 25, 1871), Matthias Moore (April 1, 1872, to 1893), and Susan Moore (September 1, 1893, to October 6, 1894).

    It's interesting to note that post offices existed at both Falkenburg Junction and Falkenburg Station at the same time for almost three years (the latter opening on November 1, 1893).

16. Information courtesy of Larry Matthews.

17. *Ibid.*

18. The story of this honourific appears in the Matthias Moore Family Reunion booklet, 1993.

19. Matthias married twenty-four-year-old Susan Fielder on January 1, 1849. They had ten children together: Francis (1851–1913), George M. (1853–1940), Fanny (1855–1934), Harold (1857–1890), Emma (1858–1938), Arthur (1860–1936), Alice (1862–1924), Helen Maude (1863–1936), Saxon Lloyd (1865–1948), and Gilbert (1871–1909).

20. Moore Family Tree essay provided by Patricia Evans.

21. In 1871, Matthias had forty acres under cultivation and two as orchard. He produced 400 pounds of butter, 80 bushels of oats, 60 bushels of rye, 14 bushels of peas, 250 bushels of potatoes, 600 bushels of turnips, 5 bushels of fruit, and 26 acres of hay.

22. As quoted in Matthias Moore Family Reunion booklet, 1993.

23. As quoted by Diane Rimstead in "Matthias Moore: His Muskoka Legacy," appearing in the *Muskoka Sun*, July 8, 1999.

Chapter 4: Dee Bank

1. *The Gazeteer and Directory of the County of Simcoe, including the District of Muskoka for 1872–73* (Toronto: Presbyterian Printing House, 1972), 145.

2. Very little information exists about the Dee Bank Hotel, though it is clearly marked on the Watt Township map found in the *Guide Book and Atlas of Muskoka and Parry Sound Districts 1879* (Toronto: H.R. Page, 1879), 60. Beyond that, only scattered references remain.

3. *The Gazeteer and Directory of the County of Simcoe*, 145.

4. *Ibid.*

5. Post office notes from Larry Matthews, Muskoka postal historian.

6. Gary Denniss, *A Brief History of the Schools in Muskoka* (Bracebridge: Herald-Gazette Press, 1972), 54.

7. Dee Bank teachers since 1911 included the following: Vida Lougheed (1911–13), Kathleen Reading and Olive Dickinson (1914), E.C. Bogart and Edna Hough (1915–16), M. Jenkins and Edna Hough (1917), Selena Ottaway and Edna Hough (1918), Mrs. G. Wilson and Edna Hough (1919), Mrs. Ballingall and Florence Beals (1920), Mrs. Ballingall and Clara Vanderlip (1921), Florence Beals and Anna Perkins (1922), Florence Beals and T.C. Bradford (1923), T.C. Thomas (1924), Orma Snider (1925), Annie McCulley (1926–29), Myrtle White (1930–31), Hazel Jackson (1932), John Kaine (1934–36), Isabel Macarthur (1937), Penelope Cameron (1958), Peggy Crozier (1959), Betty Yeoman (1960), Ethel Boyce (1961–62), Mrs. J. Barnard (1963), and Ruth Loxton (1964).

8. Interview with Aubrey Bogart, October 2005. Bogart notes that the school had no electricity until 1932.

9. Seymour Penson, "Seymour Penson and his Muskoka Neighbours,

Part I," *East Georgian Bay Historical Journal,* Vol. III (Meaford, Ontario: East Georgian Bay Historical Foundation, 1983).

10. The only other gristmill in the vicinity at this time was Alexander Bailey's gristmill in Bracebridge, completed in 1865.

11. William Albert Shea, *History of the Sheas and the Birth of a Township* (Peterborough: College Press, 1966), 65–68.

12. *Ibid.*

13. Interview with Aubrey Bogart, October 2005. According to Bogart, the rumour of the day was that the fire was purposefully set to cash in on insurance money. Bogart remembers as a small boy in the 1920s playing near the remains of the mill, which including foundations and burnt lumber.

14. James Barber's land consisted of Lots 24 and 25, Concession 9.

15. The Dee Bank post office opened on January 10, 1874, under A.B. Shannon. He operated it until April 3, 1877, and was then succeeded by I.M. Sheppard (1877–78), John Fraser (1878–79), and then John Barber. Post office notes from Larry Matthews, Muskoka postal historian.

Chapter 5: Germania

1. Denniss, *A Brief History of the Schools in Muskoka,* 131.

2. Teachers since 1911 included the following: Julia Wise (1911–15), Ida Weis (1916–19), Florence Speicher (1920), Ellen Draycott (1921–23), Mary Regan (1924–25), Jessie Grant (1926), Findlay Shackleton (1927–28), Hilda Clarke (1929–30), Nellie Nash (1931–35), Eunice White (1936–37), Isabel McQuay (1938), Sarah Lazzara (1939–41), Barbara Eaton (1942), Frances Armstrong (1943–44), Willa Goheen (1945), Margaret Vogt (1946), Jean Bruce (1947), Beverley Witherstone (1948), Eldon Matches (1949–50), Rebecca Boyd (1951), Mrs. Cross (1952–53), Charles Wood (1954–55), Margaret Fraser (1956–58),

Barbara Tingey (1959), and Michael Kennedy (1960).

3. It was located on Lot 11, Concession 5.

4. Denniss, *A Brief History of the Schools in Muskoka*, 132.

5. Interview with Mary Fitzmaurice, February 2005.

6. Interview with Velda Gilbert, February 2005.

7. When Nick Weis left Germania, he moved to Toronto and became a house builder. He even built his sister Julia's home in Detroit after she left the community.

8. Much of the information on the Weissmuller family and their mill came via Ellen Murray, the great-great-granddaughter of Herman Weissmuller.

9. After the Speicher sawmill burned down, Mary Fitzmaurice's father purchased the gutted engine and repaired it. "My father was an engineer, so although he did not use it as a mill he had a heyday using it to do other things," she recalls. "Just to give him an excuse to use his engine."

10. The Weissmuller family moved to Bala around 1897 and built a new, larger mill there. The mill is still there today and still operated by the Weissmuller family.

11. Much of the church information comes courtesy of Godfrey Cook, unofficial historian of the church. His mother's family has been involved with the church since the 1800s.

12. Much of the post office information comes courtesy of Larry Matthews, Muskoka postal historian. The list of postmasters and their terms of service are as follows: John Weissmuller (September 1, 1884, to July 1, 1885), William Stamp (November 1, 1885, to April 15, 1906), Julius E. Rusker (July 11, 1906, to March 4, 1909), Willis Conke (October 27, 1909, to October 1, 1919), Mrs. Mary Conke

(October 27, 1919, to April 7, 1923), James Kirkhouse (June 28, 1923, to May 31, 1938), Mrs. Elizabeth Carleton (May 31, 1938, to August 1938), James Joseph Henry (August 11, 1938, to July 21, 1942), William Cecil Kirkhouse (September 11, 1942, to April 15, 1943), Delia Mary Goldner (July 13, 1943, to December 26, 1947), Beatrice Elizabeth Flynn (April 3, 1948, to November 30, 1957).

13. Interview with Mary Fitzmaurice, February 2005. Velda Gilbert points out that after the village store closed, and despite the services of the peddler referenced by Mary Fitzmaurice, most of the shopping was done in Gravenhurst on a semi-weekly basis.

14. Much of the Weis family history comes courtesy of Mary Fitzmaurice, unless otherwise noted.

15. Interview with Evelyn Weis Lawrie, December 2004.

16. Information regarding the Gilbert family comes, in large part, via a March 2005 interview with Velda Gilbert, a ninety-plus-year-old lifetime resident of Germania.

Chapter 6: Ashdown Corners

1. Account written by Charles K. Beley, January 1949, provided by Rosseau Historical Society.

2. Kelly Collard, *Rosseau: The Early Years* (Rosseau: Rosseau Historical Society, 1999), 9. Mrs. Alfred Clubbe also points out the primitive conditions in which they initially lived in Ashdown Corners: "The neighbours made a 'bee' and built us a house. The cracks between logs were chinked with moss. There was a bough roof and mud floor for two years. The cold was dreadful as we had only one small stove. A pail of water would freeze solid during the night and so would bread. There was one small store, but the storekeeper never got in enough flour in the fall to do until spring breakup, so we had to live on potatoes and salt pork for six weeks."

3. Many of the early records for SS #1 Humphrey, as the Ashdown School was known, no longer exist. However, the teachers from 1909 until its 1947 closing include the following: Margaret Hall, Mary Nicolson, Teresa Drury, Gladys Clement, Jessie Warde, Christabel Ditchburn, Bessie Turnbull, Louise Homuth, Florence Hall, Effie MacMillan, Jane McCans, Malcolm MacLennan, Grace Cameron, Glen Wright, Marguerite Armstrong, Gladys V.J. Elder, Grace Moyer, Isabelle Hammel, Ruthe Moreman, and S. Amy Beley.

4. Rosseau House was officially opened in 1871, though Pratt built the sprawling three-storey hotel in 1870 and took a few guests that summer. Pratt was a jovial host who was beloved by guests and villagers alike. The hotel was never rebuilt after it burned down in 1883, but Pratt never seemed embittered. "Well, Ditchburn," he said to his friend, William Ditchburn, as they surveyed the cooling ashes, "it was a good fire while it lasted. I'm sorry that sawhorse of yours was burned; it should have been returned."

5. *Parry Sound North Star*, June 11, 1896.

6. The cemetery is located on part of Lot 79, Concession 2.

7. Numerous hamlets sprung up along the Nipissing Road, but almost all are now ghost towns like Ashdown Corners. These include Seguin Falls, Dufferin Bridge, North Seguin, Rye, and Spence (the former Spence Hotel survives today, restored as if new, at Muskoka Heritage Place in Huntsville).

8. Much of the information on Hugh McCans comes courtesy of Sarah McCans (September 2006 interview), a descendant.

9. From the files of the Rosseau Historical Society.

10. *Orillia Packet*, June 15, 1871.

11. Dufferin Bridge, located north of Seguin Falls, boasted a sawmill, store, and hotel in 1879. Later, it added a blacksmith, shoemaker,

and carpenter. The soil here is pitiful, so the community largely survived by catering to stagecoach traffic along the Nipissing Road and through the thriving lumber trade.

12. At the time, Spence was a thriving little community, home to two stores, a blacksmith shop, two sawmills, a church, a school, about a dozen log homes. Most of the fifty inhabitants were farmers, but the soil was too threadbare to provide for anything beyond subsistence-level agriculture. They, and the village they founded, were sustained by logging and serving the needs of travellers.

13. Much of the information on Benjamin Beley comes courtesy of Mary Beley of Rosseau during August 2006 exchanges with the authors.

14. Benjamin Beley's diary, courtesy of Mary Beley, dated June 10, 1867.

Chapter 7: Millar Hill

1. L.W. Hiscoke, "The Story of Millar Hill," *Huntsville Forester*, June 20, 1963, 10. This article and a wealth of information came from area resident and former history teacher Ben Boivin during a June 2007 interview with the authors.

2. Post office notes from Larry Matthews, Muskoka postal historian.

3. Notes from Martin Lasseter and Bob Constable, September 17, 1972. Robert Burns was born September 22, 1886, in Toronto and died in 1970.

4. Hiscoke, "The Story of Millar Hill." Dr. Reazin's career as a medical missionary took him to the Northwest Territories and the Yukon, where he also prospected and traded in furs. Eventually, he returned to Ontario and, after a graduate course in medicine, entered into private practice in Toronto. Later, he was appointed medical officer of the Transportation Commission. Upon his retirement, he accepted a position from Limberlost Lodge as resident physician and lived there — in the converted Millar Hill Schoolhouse — until his death at ninety-four in 1963.

5. Denniss, *A Brief History of the Schools in Muskoka*, 197.

6. The information for the Lasseter family comes from two primary sources: an article in the *Huntsville Forester* in 1963 by Joe Cookson, entitled "The Lasseters of Franklin," and notes written by Martin Lasseter (Walter Lasseter's son) and Bob Constable, September 17, 1972.

7. William Henry Lasseter was born in England in 1849 and immigrated to the United States as a young man with his wife, Hannah Smale, born in 1845. Hannah died in 1901.

8. Walter James Lasseter was born in 1873 and died in 1946. Samuel Valentine was born in 1876, dying at the age of forty-two in 1918.

9. The two children born at Miller Hill were Spence Matthew (born in 1878) and Harry (born in 1881, only a few short months before Henry's tragic death).

10. The stone home was built in 1899, according to notes left by Martin Lasseter.

11. Thomas Quinn's first daughter, Mary Jane, was born 1874. We have been unable to determine the name of his first wife.

12. Thomas Quinn was wed on March 16, 1877. His first two children with Caroline, both born in Cartright Township, were Thomas and Mary Elizabeth.

13. Albert (or Bertie), twin sister Beatrice, Thomas, and Mabel Florence all died 1894. In fact, according to descendent Pearl Drinkwater, all four bodies were carried out at the same time.

14. Faint vestiges of the mill remain in Dwight, as well as a cabin that once housed the family of mill workers.

15. Most of the information regarding the Millar family comes via Robert Constable, the grandson of David Millar through his daughter May,

who has spent a great many hours researching his family history and compiling data on Millar's Hill (October 2007 interview).

16. The children of David and Susan Millar were: John (1877–1892), Lillian Jane (Lily) (1878–1902, died in childbirth), Malcolm Franklin (or Frank) (1880–1960), May (1883–1971), Robert (1885–1916, died in the First World War), Kate (1887–1964), Jessie (1889–1894, died of diphtheria), Bessie (1891–1894, died of diphtheria), Joey (1893–1894, died of diphtheria), and Ernest Victor (1885–1965).

17. There is some debate about whether it was Susan Millar or David's mother, Margaret, who tended the ailing Quinn children. Dates of death are confusing and inconclusive, but since Margaret Millar was born in 1794 and would have been 102 at the time, we're confident Susan was the unfortunate woman.

18. *Huntsville Forester*, June 20, 1963.

Chapter 8: Cooper's Falls

1. *Orillia Northern Light*, October 15, 1869. The Dodge Lumber Company, of New York, was one of several large logging interests operating in Washago and Orillia and culling logs from the Severn and Black River watersheds. Cut lumber would be sent to southern markets via train.

2. *Orillia Times*, November 4, 1887: "For several months there have been men prospecting for minerals in the neighbourhood, and for some time mysterious heavy parcels have been taken out by a strong buckboard. It is now reported that Mr. Kehoe has been offered $6,000 for part of his farm on the Black River. On Monday there were several covered buggies and democrat wagons passed here en route to the diggings."

3. Born in 1922 and the grandson of village founder Thomas Cooper, Frank Cooper has carried on the family tradition of being the leading citizen of the community. He was the last proprietor of the general store, runs a construction company out of the former mercantile,

owns extensive tracts of land in the area, and serves as unofficial village patriarch with a wealth of knowledge and stories. Much of the information for Chapter 8 was culled from his memory during a May 2007 interview with the authors.

4. The misidentification of the blacksmith shop is so widespread and seeped its way into so many accounts that it threatens to be intractable. Ron Brown's *Ghost Towns of Ontario 2* and *Ghost Towns of Ontario* are probably the most high profile perpetrators of this myth, but it has also appeared in numerous newspaper accounts and on websites.

5. Much of the information on Thomas and Emma comes from *Recollections: A Cooper Family History 1734–1996*, written by William Cooper. This book is an invaluable reference for Cooper genealogy.

6. Some published sources mistakenly report that Thomas and Emma's third child, Albert Lawrence Hunt Cooper, was born during this voyage. These references, as well as family tradition, say that Albert received his middle name because he was born while the steamer was passing through the St. Lawrence River. In fact, Albert was born on March 20, before the family set sail, and was likely named for a family member in England.

7. The information for SS #4 comes largely from Gabrielle Lotimer, *Recollections of the Past: The Story of Rama Township* (Washago: Township of Rama, 1989).

8. The *Orillia Packet* for September 28, 1877, praises the excellence of Cooper's Falls as a mill site: "There is a good mill privilege with plenty of timber at Cooper's Falls, presenting an excellent opening for saw, shingle and grist mills." As it worked out, only a gristmill never appeared in town.

9. *Recollections of the Past.*

10. Frank Cooper notes that his father purchased the mill for $1,000 in Southwood. As indication of how much cutting was done in the few

short years that his father ran the sawmill, he says the following: "I remember a big hill of sawdust as a child which has now rotted away, leaving a deep gulley about twenty feet deep. So you get an idea of how much logs would need to have been cut to create a pile that size."

11. *Orillia Packet*, March 22, 1906.

12. *Orillia Packet*, October 1884.

13. St. George's was originally a part of the Diocese of Algoma, alongside all other Muskoka churches. However, on July 9, 1962, ownership was transferred to the Diocese of Toronto. Information regarding the church came from a June 2007 interview with Robyn Haus, Secretary of St. Luke's House, Parish of Washago, and a May 2007 interview with Len Glowa, Warden of St. George's Anglican Church.

14. The details of this story largely come from *Recollections of the Past: The History of Rama Township*.

15. Larry D. Cotton, *Whiskey and Wickedness, Volume 3: Muskoka and Parry Sound Districts* (Barrie: Larry Cotton and Associates, 2004), 14. Washago at the time was known as the "San Francisco of the North," an exciting boomtown alive with vice and flowing in riches. It was propped up by the lumber trade and was home to numerous watering holes where loggers and mill hands could indulge in alcohol. Hoteliers, like Genno, quickly became familiar with drunken brawls and even Old West–style gunplay.

16. Genno settled on the north half of Lot 12, Concession N.

17. McNab's Tavern was located on Lot 13, Concession N.

18. Thomas Cooper would die on December 30, 1918, his beloved wife, Emma, joining him on January 26, 1923. William Cooper didn't long operate the store on his own; he died on May 9, 1924. Mary Jackson Cooper, his widow, continued to run the store — with the help of son, Frank — until she died in 1960.

19. The Coopers had a large cattle herd, and so in 1900 William Cooper attended the Agricultural College in Guelph with the intent of opening a cheese factory. Some blame the venture's lack of success on the primitive refrigeration methods of the day, which made it difficult to transport the product to markets or to store it for sale in the store. Others point out that there was likely too much competition, both from farmers who manufactured their own cheese and from larger cheese manufacturers. In any event, the cheese factory never took off and did not materially benefit the store as intended.

20. Joe Kehoe's store, which probably started around 1900, was located on the northeast corner of Lot 15, Concession N. Contemporary photos show it to be well stocked and modern looking, a real threat to the Cooper stranglehold on retailing in Cooper's Falls.

Chapter 9: Lewisham

1. John Brooks, born in Kent, England, and his wife, Rebecca Readman, arrived 1876. Rebecca was actually John's third wife, the previous two — sisters, incidentally — having died in Nobleton, Ontario. The family was known for growing hops, used in brewing beer and in leaven for bread. John died in Lewisham on June 21, 1898, at the age of seventy-eight.

2. Excerpt from memories appearing in Murial Johnson Hall's *As the River Bends, Volume 2* (self-published, 1970). Minnie was the daughter of John Johnson, who came to Lewisham as a seventeen-year-old with his widowed mother and two brothers. This manuscript, as well as additional information on Lewisham, came courtesy of Richard Mount during an October 2007 exchange with the authors.

3. Denniss, *A Brief History of the Schools in Muskoka*, 144–45.

4. Notes courtesy of Carol Fraser. The primitive tavern run by William Frederick Hogue was located near Riley Lake. Selina's gravesite is unknown, but it's presumed she was buried on the property, probably nearby the tavern. Hogue took his four kids to Saskatchewan around 1900.

5. Notes courtesy of Carol Fraser.

6. J.G. Taylor lasted only a few short years as Lewisham's schoolteacher, and in his wake were many others. Records prior to 1911 have been lost, but those since then include Nellie Carew (1911), H. Baldson (1912), Lucy Mather (1913), Mary Bayne (1914–15), Cora Stein (1916), Mary Bayne (1917), Greeta Polmateer (1918), Margaret Still (1919), May McPhee (1921), Jessie Coombs (1922), Mary Thompson (1923), Ruth Lawson (1924), J. Blanchard (1925), E. Newberry (1926), L. Faulkner (1927), Miza Jenner (1932), Greta Day (1934), Ken Harnden (1935), Fred Noble (1936), G. McKeown (1937–38), Doris Dickson (1939), Ed Hooten (1940), Annie Watson (1941), Hazel Pilger (1942–43), Joyce Clarke (1944), and Lucy Boden (1947–48).

7. Hall, *As the River Bends, Volume 2*.

8. *Muskoka Herald-Gazette*, July 28, 1892.

9. Eighty-six-year-old Jim Taverner remembers the closing of the school vividly: "The school closed when I was sixteen. I had just bought an old Model-T Ford and so I was in charge of taking the nine students the six miles to Barkway for school. In the wintertime I used a covered sleigh I had made up. God it got cold; it was minus 40 degrees some days!" (Interview with the authors, October 2007.)

10. Postal information courtesy of Larry Matthews, Muskoka postal historian. The Lewisham postmasters and their dates of service are J.G. Taylor (1882–88), W.J. Tryon (1889–90), William Lowe (1890–98), John Fox (1898–1907), Sarah Brace (1907–08), P.J. Brace (1908–11), and J.G. Taverner (1911–27).

Chapter 10: Monsell

1. The first three settlers in what would be Monsell were George Gregg, James Clark, and John McRae. Gregg received Lots 25 and 26, Concession 3, on October 26, 1869. John McRae, who lent his name to nearby McRae Lake, received Lot 30, Concession 1, and Lots

28 through 30, Concession 2, on November 5, 1869. James Clark received Lots 26 and 27, Concession 1, also on November 5, 1869.

2. Post office notes from Larry Matthews, Muskoka postal historian.

3. Elizabeth Hunt, from Sinclair Township, wrote Crown Lands Commissioner J.B. Pardee in March 1880. Her letter (*Colonization Roads Papers*, Public Archives of Ontario; RG 52, I-A) is indicative of the anguish and privation experienced by many Muskoka settlers of the time:

> Having heard that the Government are helping some of the settlers who lost their crops last year by the Frost, I venture to write to you as a last resource, not knowing in what other direction to appeal. We have been here two years and have 12 acres cleared. We should have come through very well had it not been for the frost but everything as taken but potatoes and turnips which has been the only food we have had this winter and now they are exhausted. We have seven children all young to keep and my husband can get no work as no one around here is well enough to give employment. If you could put us in the way of within the scope of your official capacity you will be doing a kindness for which we would tender our most heartfelt thanks, ours are not fancies wants — we only ask for bread which we have been without for over six months this winter.

More information on the famine of 1880 can be found in the *East Georgian Bay Historical Journal Vol. III* (Meaford, Ontario: East Georgian Bay Historical Foundation, 1983), 1–11.

4. 1903 Directory.

5. The Monsell post office closed June 30, 1929.

6. Much of the information on the Monsell school comes from Gary

Denniss's *A Brief History of the Schools in Muskoka*, 119.

7. Records of teachers prior to 1913 have been lost. Those teachers employed at Monsell schoolhouse onward include Mona McQueen (1913), Gladys Cronyn (1916), Beatrice Hillman (1917), Gertrude Crozier (1918), Edna McMurray (1919–20), Nora Fraser (1921), Mrs. M. Fraser (1922), Dalton Kirk (1923), Bernice Ellis (1924), and Irene Wiley (1925).

8. Information provided by Carol Fraser, whose husband, Peter, was Nora Fraser's nephew. Nora died in 1980, having spent much of her tragic life in a series of psychiatric hospitals.

9. Post office notes from Larry Matthews, Muskoka postal historian.

10. James Clark was married to Sarah Clark, who was born in either 1846 or 1859 (the dates vary depending upon the census). Together, they had three children: George (born 1878), Jane (born 1880), and John (born 1883). John carried on the family farm after James's death, operating it well into the 1940s.

11. Article excerpted in Gary Denniss's *A Titch of Muskoka* (Bracebridge: self-published, 2005).

12. James Clark was a prominent Orangeman. Information on the Loyal Orange Order can be found at http://www.orangelodge.com.

13. This anecdote comes from Gary Denniss's *Macaulay Township in Days Gone By* (Bracebridge: Herald-Gazette Press, 1970), 61.

14. Much of the details of this story came from the August 26, 1936, edition of the *Bracebridge Herald-Gazette*, as well as periodic follow-ups as events unfolded.

15. John Clark was the son of James Clark, Monsell's former postmaster and the long-time councillor for Macaulay Township.

Chapter 11: Uffington

1. The Peterson Colonization Road was the longest of the colonization roads, running 180 kilometres from the Opeongo Road in the east to the Muskoka Road in the west. It was built from 1858 to 1863 at a cost of $39,000 and was named for surveyor Joseph S. Peterson. Poor soil disappointed hopes of large-scale settlement along the road, and by the 1870s sections were overgrown. Portions remain in use today, most notably Highway 62 between Maynooth and Combermere, which largely shadows the original route.

2. Among the earliest settlers in Uffington were James Blackmore, Thomas Buckler, William Chattle, Michael Cook, John Doherty, George Foster, William Kirkpatrick, Nehemiah Matthews, Robert McMurray, James Smith, George Spence, and Frederick Toye.

3. Gary Denniss, *Muskoka Scrapbook, Vol. 1* (Bracebridge: GarDen Press, 2002), 41. Phoebe Matthews was born on December 19, 1829. She and her husband, Nehemiah Matthews (born 1830) came to Muskoka in 1862 and settled on Lot 15, Concession 6, of Draper Township. Phoebe died in 1913, while Nehemiah died twenty years later in 1923.

4. Albert Spring owned a number of lots on Concession 8. He was heavily involved in logging and farming, in addition to local politics.

5. Notes courtesy of Carol Fraser.

6. *Ibid.*

7. Gary Denniss, *The Spirit of the Twelfth* (Bracebridge: self-published, 1982), 80–81. This invaluable book relates the story of the Loyal Orange Order in Muskoka in great detail, and spends considerable time focusing on individual lodges.

8. Records of Uffington's teachers prior to 1911 have been lost, but those who served since that year include Robert Ferguson (1911), Adina Gordon (1912), Grace Farmer (1913–14), M. Bowie (1915), Jean

Crozier (1916–17), Mrs. Broad (1918), Ella Adamson (1919), Mary McCracken (1920), Mary McPherson (1921), G. Moulding (1922), Ruby McNeice (1923–26), Clara Goltz (1927–28), Myrtle Carr (1929), J. Somerset (1930), Dalton Kirk (1931), D. Skinner (1932), J. Reid (1934–35), Gertrude Hawn (1936–38), Gordon McKeown (1939–41), Evelyn Howell (1942–43), Mrs. Sam Hawn (1944–46), Charlotte Wilford (1947), Evelyn Whitton (1948–50), Alberta Black (1951), Mrs. A. McCallum (1952), Mrs. Hawn (1953), Pat Miller (1954), J. Anderson (1955), Ruth O'Brien (1956), George Hermer (1958), and Peter Johnson (1959).

9. Post office information courtesy of Muskoka postal historian Larry Matthews.

10. Andrew Thompson was appointed on October 1, 1864. Other postmasters in Uffington's history include Jacob Spence (date of appointment unknown to December 27, 1870), Andrew Thompson again (1871 to 1872), John Doherty (July 1, 1872, to March 27, 1889), George Spence (May 1, 1889, to February 2, 1899), David Cairns (April 1, 1900, to September 9, 1908), Henry Buckler (October 8, 1908, to August 29, 1928), Samuel Hawn (September 5, 1928, to October 21, 1930), Alexander Murray (November 17, 1930, to May 11, 1933), Thomas Edward Weaver (July 26, 1933, to May 18, 1942), Samuel Hawn (August 13, 1942, to July 10, 1956), Walter Allen (August 24, 1942, to June 5, 1957), and finally Mrs. Minnie Roberts (acting postmaster from July 17, 1957, through the end of the year).

11. John Doherty was born in Ireland in 1834 and married Elizabeth Wright (born 1845). In 1889, he sold his farm to Thomas Fielding of Barkway for the sizable sum of $1,800 and moved to Manitoba. The auction of his farm equipment was said to be the largest of its kind in Muskoka to that date.

12. Notes courtesy of Carol Fraser.

13. Interview with Mrs. Walter Allen, September 2007.

14. Much of the information on the Loyal Orange Lodge comes from Gary Denniss's book *The Spirit of the Twelfth*, 78–84.

15. Interview with William Allen, September 2007.

16. Notes courtesy of Carol Fraser.

17. Lorenzo Johnson was born December 31, 1846, in England and married Flora Hill (born 1852 in Grimsby, Ontario) in 1880. A respected member of the Loyal Orange Order, he died on December 26, 1913, of cancer, and his funeral was well attended by Orangemen from across Muskoka.

18. Scanned excerpts of Reverend Coburn's book, *A Country Parson*, appear on the Pascal family website, http://862.homestead.com/greatgrandfather.html. The focus of the website is the Uffington Pascals, and it contains a host of well-researched material.

19. *Bracebridge Herald-Gazette*, September 9, 1897.

20. L.R. Fraser, *The History of Muskoka* (The Thomas Company, 1942), 103. Mat Watson, who settled on land along the 7th Concession and married Mary Jane Corrigan, was a simple farmer. The brawl in the hotel was not the first time he had a brush with lumbermen; he similarly engaged the notorious Gravenhurst Press Gang, a band of roughnecks who terrorized Gravenhurst for years, and won.

21. Cotton, *Whiskey and Wickedness*, 45–46.

22. Interview with William Allen, September 2007.

23. Notes courtesy of Carol Fraser.

24. *Ibid.*

25. *Bracebridge Herald-Gazette*, July 23, 1914.

BIBLIOGRAPHY

Boyer, Robert J. *A Good Town Grew Here: The Story of Bracebridge.* Bracebridge, Ont.: Oxbow Press, 1975.

Christie Historical Society. *Meanderings and Memories.* Christie Township, Ont.: Christie Historical Society, 1994.

Collard, Kelly (project coordinator). *Rosseau: The Early Years.* Rosseau, Ont.: Rosseau Historical Society, 1999.

Collard, Kelly (project coordinator). *Rosseau: Then and Now.* Rosseau, Ont.: Rosseau Historical Society, 2004.

"Community Notices." *Bracebridge Herald-Gazette,* 9 September 1897.

Cookson, Joe. "The Lasseters of Franklin." *Huntsville Forester,* 1963.

Coombe, Geraldine. *Muskoka Past and Present.* Toronto, Ont.: McGraw-Ryerson, 1976.

Cooper, William C. *Recollections: A Cooper Family History, 1734–1996.* Australia: self-published, 1996.

Cotton, Larry D. *Whiskey and Wickedness, Volume 3: Muskoka and Parry Sound Districts.* Barrie, Ont.: Larry Cotton and Associates, 2004.

Coupland, Heather. "Germania Church has mouse-proof organ." *The Muskokan,* 5 August 1999.

Currie, Ted. "Falkenburg: The Old Station." *The Muskoka Sun,* 7 September 1989.

Dennis, Gary. *A Brief History of the Churches of Muskoka.* Bracebridge, Ont.: self-published, 2002.

Denniss, Gary. *A Brief History of the Schools in Muskoka.* Bracebridge, Ont.: Herald-Gazette Press, 1972.

Denniss, Gary. *A Titch of Muskoka.* Bracebridge, Ont.: self-published, 2005.

Denniss, Gary. *Macaulay Township in Days Gone By.* Bracebridge, Ont.: Herald-Gazette Press, 1970.

Denniss, Gary. *Muskoka Scrapbook, Vol. 1* Bracebridge, Ont.: GarDen Press, 2002.

Denniss, Gary. *The Spirit of the Twelfth.* Bracebridge, Ont.: self-published, 1982.

"Drowned at Uffington." *Bracebridge Herald-Gazette,* 23 July 1914.

Fraser, L.R. *The History of Muskoka.* The Thomas Company, 1942.

"Girl Found in Farmhouse with Severe Head Wounds." *Bracebridge Herald-Gazette,* 20 August, 1936.

Guide Book and Atlas of Muskoka and Parry Sound Districts 1879. Toronto, Ont.: H.R. Page, 1879.

Hiscoke, L.W. "The Story of Millar Hill." *Hunstville Forester,* 20 June 1963.

Irwin, H.W. *The Gazeteer and Directory of the County of Simcoe, including the District of Muskoka for 1872–73*. Toronto, Ont.: Presbyterian Printing House, 1972.

Johnson Hall, Muriel. *As the River Bends, Volume 2*. n.p.: self-published, 1970.

LePine, John. "The Famine of 1880." *East Georgian Bay Historical Journal, Vol III*. Meaford, Ont.: East Georgian Bay Historical Foundation, 1983.

Lotimer, Gabrielle. *Reflections of the Past: The Story of Rama Township*. Washago, Ont.: Township of Rama, 1989.

Macfie, John. *Lots More … Parry Sound Stories*. Parry Sound, Ont.: The Hay Press, 2005.

Macfie, John. *Parry Sound Logging Days*. Toronto, Ont.: Boston Mills Press, 1987.

Macfie, John. *Tales from Another Time*. Parry Sound, Ont.: The Hay Press, 2000.

Moore Family Tree essay, provided by Patricia Evans.

Orillia Packet, 15 June 1871.

Parry Sound North Star, 11 June 1896.

Penson, Seymour. "Seymour Penson and his Muskoka Neighbours." *East Georgian Bay Historical Journal, Vol II*. Meaford, Ont.: East Georgian Bay Historical Foundation, 1981.

Rimstead, Diane. "Mathias Moore: His Muskoka Legacy." *The Muskoka Sun*, 8 July 1999.

Shea, William Albert. *History of the Sheas and the Birth of a Township*. Peterborough, Ont.: College Press, 1966.

Tatley, Richard. *The Steamboat Era in the Muskokas, Volume II: The Golden Years to the Present*. Toronto, Ont.: Boston Mills Press, 1983.

Tatley, Richard. *The Steamboat Era in the Muskokas, Volume I: To the Golden Years*. Toronto, Ont.: Boston Mills Press, 1983.

INDEX

Abbey, David, 43

Agar, Albert Alexander, 44

Annis, Anthony, 177, 187

Ashdown
James, 111, 112, 124, 127–30
Valettia, 124
William, 129–30

Bailey
Caroline, 143
James, 165

Baldwin, Sherman, 200

Barber
James, 73–75, 82–85
John, 73, 74, 82, 83
Phineas, 82

Bardsville (Ont.), 67

Barkway (Ont.), 94, 97, 167, 172, 177, 179, 183, 185

Bear Lake, 234

Beardmore Tannery, 43

Beaver River, 194

Beley
Benjamin Sowden, 111, 117, 129, 131–33
Charles, 122
George, 131
Lucy, 131–33

Beley Point, 133

Bigwood (Ont.), 47, 48

Black River, 152, 154, 158, 161, 162, 170

Blackmore, Charles, 218

Bogart
Aubrey, 77, 84–86
James Cyrus, 85, 86
Eleanor (Cook), 85

Booth, John Rudolphus, 16, 23

Brace, P.J., 185

Bracebridge (Ont.), 16, 43, 52, 54, 55, 57, 61, 64, 72, 75, 83, 85, 91, 94, 140, 198, 200, 202, 206, 210, 216

Briese, Albert, 83

Briggs, William, 224, 225

Brooks, John, 176

Brown, James, 130

Brundige, Stephen, 176

Bryers, Richard, 197

Boyne River, 136

Buckler, Henry, 216

Burnett, Robert John, 182, 183

Burns
Robert, 136, 175
Sarah, 136
Thomas, 136

Cairns, David, 216

Carleton
Elizabeth May, 105
Patrick, 105

Chamber, Adam, 220

Cheap Cash Store, 111, 129

Chermola, Pasquale, 71

Cleghorn, Alexander, 70

Clark, Elizabeth Jane, 71

Clark
James, 191, 194, 197–99
John, 202

Clendenning's Lake, 231

Clubbe, Alfred, 112

Cockburn, A.P., 43, 133

Colonization Roads Department, 191

Cooper
    Emma, 152, 156–58, 165, 170, 171
    Frank, 154, 155, 161, 162, 164, 170,
       173–74
    Mary, 173
    Thomas, 152–67, 170–73
    William, 153, 162, 166, 172, 173
Cornish, Walter, 22
Couke
    Mary, 104
    Willis, 104
Coulson, John, 206

Dawson, Thomas, 11
Dee River, 72, 78, 81, 82
Deer Lake, 99
Denniss, William C., 229
Densmore, R., 165
Dodge Lumber Company, 152
Doherty, John, 215
Dufferin Bridge (Ont.), 124
Dwight (Ont.), 137, 139, 145

Edgington (Ont.), 19, 20
Edward, Henry, 178
Emberson, Lucy, 139

Fairy Lake, 150
Fenton, George, 187
Fletcher, Robert, 163
Foster, George, 206
Fox, Gertrude, 139
Fox, John, 176, 177, 180, 185, 187
Fox Lake, 103
Fraser, Nora, 195
Fry
    Albert, 35, 39
    John, 35

Galloway, David, 50
Genno, David, 169
George, Thomas, 49, 50, 53, 54, 56, 66
Gibb Lake, 230
Gilbert

    George, 89, 90, 100, 108, 109
    Henry, 109, 110
    Katherine, 90, 108
    Margaret, 108
    Rachel, 109
    Velda, 91, 92, 97, 109
    William, 89, 108, 109
Gordon, F., 39
Gouldie, James, 161
Grassmere (Ont.), 146
Gravenhurst (Ont.), 39, 41, 42, 43, 45, 52,
    89, 103, 105, 201, 210, 216
Gregg, James, 190, 191, 194, 197
Groh
    Clarence, 44
    John, 45
    Maria, 45

Haley, H.W., 195
Hawn, Samuel, 216
Hekkla (Ont.), 115, 116, 121
Henry, James Joseph, 105
Henshaw, William, 43
Hillside (Ont.), 147
Hogue
    Selina, 178
    William Frederick, 177, 178
Holditch, William, 49, 66, 67
Holt Timber Company, 47
Hood
    Charles, 235, 236
    Janet, 235
Horseshoe Lake, 231
Housey's Rapids (Ont.), 105, 167
Howard, Robert, 54, 55
Hueber, Annie, 61
Humphrey House, 122, 123, 129
Huntsville (Ont.), 146
Huntsville and Lake of Bays Navigation
    Company, 146
Huntsville Forester, 198

Irwin
    Dick, 111

William, 123, 124

Jackson, John, 50
Jarvis, Henry, 237
Jennett, James, 71
Johnson, Emma Margaret, 82
Johnson, Lorenzo, 220
Jones, Orma, 201, 202, 203
Joslin, Thomas, 163
Junction Hotel (Ashdown Corners), 122, 124, 130
Junction Hotel (Falkenburg), 49, 53, 55

Kaine, John, 77
Kaufman Furniture Company, 35, 29, 41
Kaufman, Milton, 47
Keal, Jessie, 71
Kehoe, Joe, 153, 163, 173
Ketching, Richard, 206
Kinsett, Will, 227
Kirkhouse, James, 105
Kirkpatrick
    David, 212
    James, 220
    William, 210

Lake of Bays, 143, 150
Lake Rosseau, 33, 34, 36, 37, 39, 42, 111, 112, 118, 121, 125, 127, 133
Lake Solitaire, 139
Lake Vernon, 235, 236
Lamont, D., 93
Langmeade, Joseph, 135–37, 145–47
Lasseter
    Hannah, 140–42
    Henry, 140, 141
    Samuel Valentine, 140, 142
    Walter, 140, 142
Lawrence, Noble, 176
Lawson, Cyrus, 112, 121
Lawson
    Harriet, 22
    John, 22
    Wilson, 22

Lee, Alfred, 229, 230
Long Lake, 231
Loshaw
    Charles, 188
    Lisa Amelia, 188
    Isaac, 176, 187, 188
Lowe, William, 176, 182, 185
Loyal Orange Order, 62, 63, 198, 199, 212, 213, 216–19
Ludgate Lumber Company, 17, 22, 28, 29, 30, 231, 232

Magnetewan Hardwood Company, 44
Magnetewan River and Lakes Steamboat Line, 44
Mainprize, John, 120
Maple Lake Hotel, 17, 18, 25, 27, 28, 31, 32
Marr, Susanna, 82
Martin, Charles, 112
Matthews, Nehemiah, 209
Matthias, Jacob, 222
Matthiasville (Ont.), 222
McBrien, Australia B., 160
McCans
    Elizabeth Ann, 120
    Elizabeth Jane, 126
    Henry, 120
    Henry Hugh, 112, 119–21
    John, 120
    Robert, 120, 125
    Sarah, 120
McCracken, James, 218
McMurray, Robert, 204, 215, 223, 224
McNab, James, 70
McNab, Thomas, 166, 167, 170
McPeak
    Adam, 45
    Clara, 17
McRoberts, Jim, 22
Millar
    David, 134, 135, 146, 147, 148, 150
    Susan, 148–50
Mills, Maude, 71

Moore
Ada Louise, 61, 70
Alice, 71
Arthur, 52, 57, 58, 61, 64
Chad, 57, 71
Emma, 70
Fanny, 70
Frank, 70
George, 71
George Bernard, 52, 53, 57–59, 70, 71
Harold, 61, 71
Matthias, 50, 51, 56, 57, 60–71
Nellie, 71
Saxon, 57, 71
Susan, 57, 61, 67, 69
Mullen, Fred, 231, 232
Muskoka Colonization Road, 49, 50, 53, 151
Muskoka Milling and Lumber Company, 238, 239
Musquash River, 238, 239
Mutchenbacker
Asa, 33–35, 37, 39, 43, 45
Clara, 45
Herman, 35, 39, 44–48
Lizzie, 45
Maria, 45
Peter, 33, 34, 35, 37, 39, 43, 45
Theresa, 35, 43, 45

Nelson, Jane, 119
Newel, Frank, 80
Nipissing Colonization Road, 11, 16, 111, 116, 117, 118, 119, 122, 123, 124, 127, 128, 132
Nipissing House, 122, 124

Ochs, Edna, 139
Orillia (Ont.), 81, 152, 157, 165
Orrville (Ont.), 20, 22
Ottawa, Arnprior and Parry Sound Railway (OA&PSR), 17, 18, 23, 24, 25, 28, 231, 235, 236

Palmer, Bob, 198
Parks, Matthew, 159
Parry Sound Colonization Road, 11, 49, 53, 72, 111, 119, 123, 127, 128, 132
Pascal
John, 220–22
John Jr., 222
Patterson
Matthew, 218
Timothy, 217
Peacock, Thomas, 233
Pearson, Lida, 139
Percival, Charles, 50, 54, 62
Peterson Colonization Road, 204, 207, 208, 212, 215, 218, 220, 223, 224
Philips, Joseph, 125
Port Carling (Ont.), 220
Port Cockburn (Ont.), 27
Pratt, William H., 113
Purbrook (Ont.), 199

Quinn, Thomas, 136, 143–45

Reazin, Henry, 138, 139
Redfern, Arthur, 125
Rickard, Georgina, 125
Roscoe House, 55
Roscoe, J., 55
Roscoe, Marion, 70
Ross, Benjamin, 124
Rosseau (Ont.), 11, 27, 34, 38, 43, 112, 113, 120, 124, 125, 130, 133
Rosseau (steamship), 34, 43
Rosseau House, 113
Rosseau River, 33, 35, 36
Rossgar, Julius, 104
Rossmoyne Inn, 133
Royal Hotel, 169
Ruttan, Kate, 182, 183

Samway, Jane, 61, 70
Sander
Fred, 202
Raymond, 202

Scott, Thomas, 112
Severn Bridge (Ont.), 167
Shadow River, 35, 43, 121, 122, 133
Shannon, John, 72, 76, 78, 80, 81, 86
Sirett
   Ebenezer, 111, 126, 127, 128
   Alfred Tom, 114, 117, 127
   Eliza Marsh, 114, 128
   Harry, 125
   William, 128
Smith, Guy, 32
Smith, James, 218
Snider Lumber Company, 33–35, 43
Snider, William, 39
Spectacle Lake, 231
Speicher, Charlie, 100, 102
Spence (Ont.), 129, 130
Spence
   George, 204, 215, 216
   Mary, 215
Spring, Albert, 209, 227
Stamp, William, 103, 104
Stoneman, W.C., 19, 126
Sword
   Annie, 26, 27
   David, 16, 31
   Ella, 32
   John, 16, 25–28, 31
   Katherine, 27, 32
   Lyde, 22, 31
   Margaret, 31
   Percy, 27, 32
   Thomas, 15, 22, 31, 32
Swords Lake, 231

Tally-Ho Coach Line, 27
Taverner
   Jim, 183, 185
   J. G., 185
Taylor, Archibald, 78
Taylor
   George, 176
   John, 177, 180, 183, 185
Thompson, Andrew, 215, 218

Thomson's Corners (Ont.), 93, 103
Theresa (steamship), 35, 43, 45
Three Mile Lake, 72, 78, 81
Toye
   Frederick, 218, 226
   Mary Bella, 226
Tretheway Falls, 227
Tryon, W.J., 185

Ullswater (Ont.), 71
Utterson (Ont.), 104, 105

Walton, George, 22
Washago (Ont.), 11, 151, 156, 162, 165, 169
Watson, Mat, 224
Waugh, Margaret, 19
Wellington Hotel, 50, 54, 55, 62
Weis
   Caroline, 94, 106, 107
   John, 94, 106, 107
   Julia, 38 94
   Nick, 89, 95, 96, 97
Weissmuller
   Herman, 89, 90, 98, 100, 103, 108
   John, 103
   Maria Dorothea, 98, 109
Weissmuller Lake, 89, 92, 98, 99, 104
Weissmuller Lumber Company, 89, 95, 98–100
Wettlaufer, Nikolaus, 100
Whalen's Lake, 231
Whitmore, E., 39
Wiley, Irene, 196
Windermere (Ont.), 74
Woodsworth
   James, 209
   J.S., 209

ABOUT
THE AUTHORS

Andrew Hind and Maria Da Silva are freelance writers who live in Bradford, Ontario. They specialize in history and travel, particularly that of Muskoka, a region they've come to intimately know and love over the years. Together, they contribute regular features to *Muskoka Magazine*.

Andrew's articles have appeared in magazines and newspapers across Canada, in the United States, and in England. Locally, his work can be seen in the *Muskokan*, *Beyond the City*, and *Muskoka-Almaguin Sideroads*. Andrew developed a passion for history early on, especially for unusual and obscure events and people that are typically overlooked or quickly forgotten. He hopes, through his writing, to bring these fascinating stories to light for a modern audience.

Maria writes feature articles for the *Muskoka Sun*. She's always had a passion for history, but despite coming from a country — Portugal — with a rich past, she never dreamed that her future would lead her into writing about ghost towns.

Ghost Towns of Muskoka represents Andrew and Maria's third book. They previously wrote *Strange Events of Ontario* (Altitude Publishing, June 2006), a book examining the mysterious and mythical side of Ontario lore, and contributed four stories to *Holiday Misadventures* (Altitude Publishing, November 2006), a book that tells of Christmas stories that are anything but merry and joyous.